COSMIC ASTROLOGY:
THE BOOK OF ANSWERS

Cosmic Astrology:

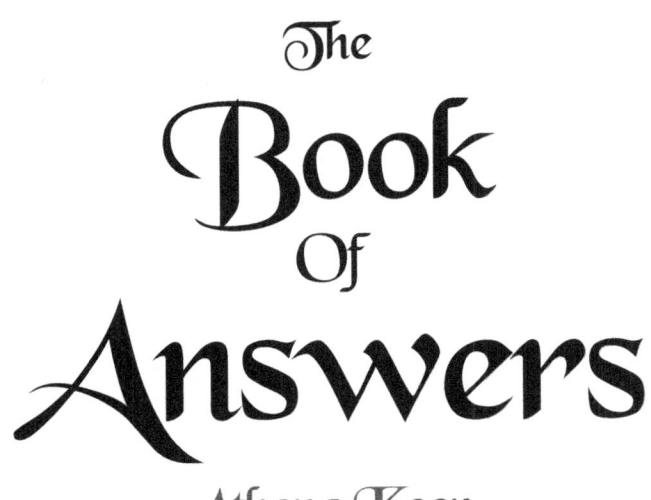
The Book Of Answers
Athena Keen

.: ILLUSTRATIONS :.

Anastasiya Drake
Amir Mansour
Steen
Sam Gorrin
The Cosmic Joker

THE ORACLE'S LIBRARY

Cosmic Astrology: The Book of Answers

by Athena Keen

theoracleslibrary.com

Copyright © 2014 The Oracle's Library

Cover Art Copyright © 2014 Anastasiya Drake

This book, cover art and all contents
contained within must not be reproduced in any form
without written permission from the publisher.
Illustrations are the property of the artist
and may not be reproduced without
prior written consent.
All rights reserved.

ISBN 978-0-578-14863-2

"Platonic Space" & "The Encirclopedia"
thecosmicjoker.com

Copyright © 2014 The Cosmic Joker

The Oracle's Library

The Oracle's Library is an independent publisher of
Philosophy and things of a Metaphysical nature.

"Explore the cosmos, where above meets below."

theoracleslibrary.com

Acknowledgements

I would like to express my gratitude to the Cosmic Joker for kindly allowing his works "Platonic Space" and "The Encirclopedia" to be displayed within the Book of Answers. More designs by the Cosmic Joker can be found at his website:

thecosmicjoker.com

"The Art of Affecting Consciousness through Synchronicity, Sacred Geometry and Symbolism"

About the Illustrators

Anastasiya Drake is an illustrator, designer, and developer who lives and works in The Bay Area in California. Her work can be found on anastasiyadrake.com.

Steen draws from a studio in Queens, NY.
Her work can be found at steendraws.com.

Sam Gorrin scrawls in perpetual hermitudity atop his monolith in Eugene, Oregon. His works are located at facebook.com/synchronousink

With additional illustrations by concept artist Amir Mansour.

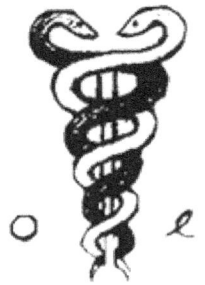

These words were written as an antidote —
to cure the loneliest Robot.

Table of Contents

I.	Introduction to Astrology	13
II.	Natal Chart Basics	27
III.	The Significance of Angles & Aspects	41
IV.	The History of Astrology	63
V.	Celestial Folklore	75
VI.	Astrological Symbols of Ancient Civilization	85
VII.	The Stars — Nature's Calendar	99
VIII.	Equinox & Solstice	119
IX.	Zodiac Archetypes	133
X.	The Limiting & the Limitless	159
XI.	Evolution & Extinction Cycles	183
XII.	Cosmic Astrology	209
XIII.	Encyclopedia of Astrology	219
	References	271

I. Introduction to Astrology

What is **astrology**?

Astrology is the ancient practice that seeks to interpret the relationship between the cosmos and life on Earth. At a glance, the planets and stars seem such arbitrary objects that shift like clockwork in the sky. In the present day, the stars have faded into the background — dimmed as the backdrop behind the glare of city lights, so that we neglect to look up at their beauty in awestruck wonder. And so, we have not yet come to the realization that there are forces that exist outside this world much greater than the sheltered surface upon which we live.

It seems more common in this day and age that we struggle to find significance in memorizing star patterns or simply pointing out the constellations in the night sky. We neglect the practice altogether, and throw it off as some form of over indulgence for amateur astronomers and crazed astrologers elated with lunacy. But with a closer observation of the planets and stars, the patterns of existence and interactions between take the shape of a divine melody, and with these patterns, we begin to unlock the beat of the drum in which chaos parades about the universe.

So what does astrology mean for us humans?

From horoscopes to natal charts, astrologers have tried to make use of the zodiac signs and planetary information they collect from the sky. Each interpretation varies from one astrologer to the next, but the key idea resounds just the same. **Our lives are very much intertwined with the motion of celestial bodies.**

This idea was once appreciated to the point that it resembled worship among the peoples of ancient civilization. Ancestors of the past were so keen to understand and interpret the night sky that they crafted legends into the stars and crowned the planets deities. Though the reasoning appears lost through the ages, those very names remain the same ones we use to name the planets and stars, even today.

How does it all work in theory?

Much of astrology brings us back to one freeze frame in time, the moment of birth. In astrology, the position of the stars and aspects between planets play a vital role in the formation of character and determine our initial essence as a human being. These **astrological aspects** are found by measuring the relationship of angles between celestial bodies on the backdrop of constellations that paint the stars of the zodiac belt. In order to calculate the natal chart, the exact birth time and place are needed. With this data, the individual's birth chart or natal chart is formed.

Natal charts are used to detect configurations, aspects and planetary transits that predict future trends or conditions for the individual. **Transits** can refer to the revisiting of planets, such as Saturn's return that is said to wreak havoc on one's natal chart with a transit every thirty years. When it comes to relationships, natal charts interpret the nature of the energy exchange between two people. It can feel quite heavy with the weight of multiple conjunctions or connect us with the invisible strings of grand trines.

On a wider scale **mundane astrology** interprets the

influences of the motion of the Sun, Moon, and planets in orbit for the whole of humanity. The Sun's orbit is marked with a zodiac sign for every month, while the Moon circles through every sign in just under a month. Perhaps it's the planets that entice the most curiosity, when they stop dead in the sky and begin to float backwards through the zodiac in retrograde motion.

The Moon, Planets and Sun

What are the individual characteristics of the celestial bodies?

Sun

Sol or the Sun is the most powerful force in the immediate sky once worshipped by the ancients as the giver of life. This brilliant star graces the shadows with light and emits fiery energies of vitality, generosity, and reason. The Sun sign in astrology embodies the character of our outward expression and represents the totality of the ego. It can distinguish the nature of our pursuits in life and describe the essence of our individuality and conscious thoughts. We cannot hide it, as much as we try. It is the mask we always wear — the surface appearance we show without any realization. Others absorb it upon meeting us and take it with them as a first impression.

Moon

The Moon is the ruler in the realm of instincts. It connects us with forms of higher emotion such as empathy and illuminates intuition and extra-sensory thought. The Moon encompasses all feminine aspects, as it cycles through the zodiac every twenty-eight days. In astrology, the Moon sign indicates the nature of our emotional reactions. We look to the Moon to find the external representation of our emotion. The Moon is the connection to our shadow self.

Mercury

Mercury is the dexterous planet of mental processes. It rules the mind and expresses conscious thought in the form of logic and reason. Mercury holds the key to an individual's memory and intelligence. The gift of eloquence in lecture or literature is indicated by the Mercury sign. Messages are often associated with Mercury as well as all types of communication.

Venus

The gleaming planet Venus symbolizes genuine beauty and love. Venus rules our personal magnetism and describes the people and situations we most often attract into our world. The Venus sign in astrology indicates the relationships that we seek in the arena of friends and romantic partners. This sign shapes our aesthetic interests in art, literature, and music. Venus appeals to the senses and embodies the things in which provide the most comfort and pleasure.

Mars

The blunt force of Mars calls us into action. Mars does not hesitate but jumps on the fight. Its aura of power, passion, and determination fuel the urge to battle, and with this courage, we persevere. In astrology, the Mars sign marks our own individual realm of desire. It links us to our passions and the things we hold in high value for which we would be willing to put our life on the line.

Jupiter

Jupiter is best viewed as the jovial father of the planets with benevolent demeanor and infinite wisdom. From Jupiter, we are graced with an air of creative expansion and growth that can quickly turn into abundance or even excess. Jupiter grants us knowledge through travel and communication. The Jupiter sign in astrology is tied to our own broad vision of the world. It indicates our personal philosophy of life and represents the nature of our own individual intellect.

Saturn

Saturn is burdened with the weight of restriction and sorrow. Saturn lifts the veil between wishful thinking in abstract thought and the external truth in reality. It provokes the most painful but necessary lessons that can only be learned by overcoming adversity. Saturn focuses on what is practical and conservative. The seriousness of Saturn gives it a cold presence, yet we find stability in its wake. The Saturn sign in astrology can signify the nature of our affliction in life. We must seek isolation to find inspiration and inner wisdom in order to conquer Saturn's trials.

Uranus

Uranus is the most spontaneous force in the solar system with the power to unleash sudden catastrophe. It is linked to chaotic disturbances as the product of restricted liberties. Uranus acts on impulse — rotating on its own eccentric axis perpendicular to the status quo — and embodies all things bohemian and sarcastic. Uranus holds an inventive attitude and creates a new, original way of doing things. The Uranus sign can disrupt the present with sudden 'eureka' moments of discovery and rapid change.

Neptune

Neptune is the distant trickster and ruler of mystery in the solar system. This outer planet slips on the rose-tinted glasses and allows us to live within the bounds of our own fantasy. Neptune is a theatrical character that puts on a play — dragging us into the depths of our imagination and desire through grand illusions. In astrology, the Neptune sign is where we conquer our own phantoms and develop the highest forms of human empathy. Neptune is also linked to the aether that manifests dreams and visions and is used to indicate forms of extrasensory perception.

Pluto

Pluto skirts the edge of our world, where the largest ideas are born to captivate the whole of society. It circles through the zodiac once every quarter millennium. Pluto holds an element of destruction and death — though the outcome is not always negative, as its presence also indicates a rebirth. The Pluto sign in astrology is a generational marker that moves slowly through each zodiac sign. As it does, it shifts the core values of the entire population and improves upon these ideas with the steady waves of influence into society over time. With Pluto, we rise from the ashes and replace the past through restoration and new forms of progression.

The Galactic Center

The Galactic Center is a fixed point in the sky where the galactic bulge is found at the heart of our Milky Way Galaxy. At this location, it is thought that there exists a super-massive black hole around which our Sun and all the stars in the galaxy revolve. The Galactic Center is found by following the narrow glow of the Milky Way to the point where it crosses the zodiac belt on the cusp of Ophiuchus and Sagittarius. This seemingly minute zone in the sky is extremely loud and emits the most concentrated source of starlight in the galaxy.

The Galactic Center is the mother of our solar system, and from it we draw divine wisdom and healing vibrations. We observe the Sun pass this center each year just before the winter solstice and celebrate its passing with the lengthening day.

> "There is a way on high, conspicuous in the clean heavens, called the Milky Way, brilliant with its own brightness. By the gods go to dwelling of the great Thunderer and his royal abode… Here the famous and mighty inhabitants of the heaven have their homes. This is the region which I might make bold to call the Palatine [Way] of the Great Sky."
>
> —Ovid, *Metamorphoses*

Signs of the Zodiac

What is the significance of the **zodiac belt**?

The **zodiac belt** is the narrow strip of constellations in the sky, where the celestial bodies of our solar system are spotted in orbit around the Sun. The planets appear to circle the Earth in the plane of this belt. The planets, Moon, and Sun can be found within one of the zodiac constellations at all times of the year. Astrology interprets these orbits by framing each planet through the lens of each individual zodiac sign, so that the celestial bodies are enriched by the characteristics of each constellation they pass through on the journey.

Aries

The first sign of the zodiac, **Aries** grants us a running start. Aries symbolized by the ram is a forceful and adventurous spirit that initiates life into action. Though like the ram, the sign Aries can become temperamental and even violent under pressure. Aries empowers us to confront challenges with courage and manifest our will into reality. Those under Aries are hardworking individuals and often approach life's obstacles with energetic enthusiasm.

Taurus

Taurus, the second sign of the zodiac is quick to offer a smile. The bull is a beautiful, fun-loving creature with steadfast determination and head held high. Taurus is susceptible to self-indulgence and seeks out the sensual pleasures in life. Taurus is among the best companions to keep, since this gentle soul is the most patient and loyal friend. Those under Taurus are romantics at heart and often succeed in the domestic realm.

Gemini

The third sign of the zodiac, **Gemini** is symbolized by the dualistic nature of the twins. Geminis are entertaining conversationalists — the perfect company to pass the time. The curious and analytical nature of Gemini fuels self-expression and invention in those under this sign. Geminis often wear two masks on the surface and can appear superficial when both are exposed. If overwhelmed, a Gemini must avoid patterns of excessive worry to keep from losing sight of focus.

Cancer

Cancer the crab is the fourth sign of the zodiac with a tough shell and a tender heart. Cancers are naturally reserved and take a more cautious approach to life. The crab may come across as quiet and shy — then surprise everyone with a sudden outburst, when it is least expected. Those under Cancer are imaginative and dreamy with an intuition that seems almost uncanny. Cancers are self-sacrificing individuals when it comes to family and protect their own at all costs. When in distress a Cancer becomes restless and easily discouraged.

Leo

Leo throws us into the heat of the fire, when we enter this fifth sign of the zodiac. This powerful lion holds the creative energy and ambition of a great leader. Though like a great leader, such impulses of the heart must also carry a measure of dignity. Thus, Leos often come across as vain and arrogant when pursuing material pleasures unrestrained. Leo is one of the most affectionate and loving signs that holds to be the most faithful and true.

Virgo

Virgo the sixth sign is the maiden of the zodiac. The maiden is kind and takes pleasure in serving others before self. Virgos are neat and organized individuals that offer the most helpful practical advice. The ingenious and introspective thoughts of a modest Virgo very rarely grace the presence of reality in conversation. Virgos are meticulous by nature and often get caught up in the minute details. Those under Virgo are the skeptics of the zodiac and have a tendency to become over-critical.

Libra

The scales of **Libra** the seventh zodiac sign strive to bring balance back to reality. Libras are sweet and kind individuals that act with tact and hold the power of persuasion. The sign Libra draws equilibrium back into the world through cooperation and justice. Those under Libra are often artistic and thrive best in a social environment full of uplifting relationships. When the scales become tipped, Libra is left undecided and emotionally unbalanced.

Scorpio

The eighth sign of the zodiac **Scorpio** is known for its sting. The scorpion captivates admirers with personal success and alluring magnetism. Scorpios are intense and passionate individuals governed by the will of inner desire. Those under the sign Scorpio have an extraordinary imagination and shape the world with creative visions. Scorpios are full of secrets. If threatened, this sign has a tendency to become self-absorbed and suspicious of others.

Ophiuchus

The forgotten sign **Ophiuchus** the serpent-bearer grants us strength to heal the world. Ophiuchus is an open-minded and refreshing soul, unconditioned to the rules of reality and often misunderstood. Many are confused by the ambitions of Ophiuchus, the seeker of higher knowledge and universal wisdom. Ophiuchus feels lost in the material world and navigates through life on intuition. When in the presence of Ophiuchus, we often lose track of time and converse over the most unusual subjects. This sign can become easily frustrated, when others do not care to listen.

Sagittarius

Sagittarius the ninth zodiac sign lends us the aspiration of the archer. Sagittarius symbolized by half man, half beast presents the internal struggle between the instinct of conquest and the rational mind. Sagittarius rises to the challenge and overcomes adversity with effort and sincere enthusiasm. The freedom-loving spirit of the archer inspires us all to share in this optimism. Those under Sagittarius are idealistic and extremely ambitious with an anxious inability to wait.

Capricorn

Capricorn the goat and tenth sign of the zodiac invites us to restore cosmic order. Capricorns are organized and economical individuals that initiate the practical construction of reality. Those under Capricorn are highly focused and detailed thinkers that often allow the head to rule the heart. While Capricorns are the most trustworthy friends, they also make the worst enemies. A Capricorn will manipulate entire situations to secure the desired outcome.

Aquarius

The eleventh sign of **Aquarius** inspires our altruistic outlook for humanity. Aquarius depicts parallel waves of vibration or electricity that influence the world with the spirit of invention. Aquarius is a tolerant and rational sign graced with a kind and gentle disposition. Those under Aquarius are guided by reason and weigh each outcome under sound or unsound. Aquarians often let emotions get the best of them and combat these moods with unconventional and rebellious expression.

Pisces

The twelfth sign of **Pisces** embodies the struggle of the soul trapped in the material body. The restrained fishes of this sign present the weight of captivity and inhibitions in our present life. Pisces are known as the silent mystics of the zodiac. This sign practices self-denial and withdraws like the hermit to find clarity. Pisces are highly intuitive and vivid imaginers that craft themselves into schemes of higher thought. In such cases, Pisces become imprisoned inside the realm of the abstract with impractical and fatalistic attitudes toward life.

Introduction to Astrology

II. Natal Chart Basics

What is a natal chart?

A **natal chart** also known as a birth chart is used to map the celestial bodies in their corresponding zodiac at the time of birth. This is where we find not just the Sun sign used in modern day horoscopes, but the Moon, Venus and all other locations of each of the planets. The nativity in astrology is a useful tool in presenting a person's individual aura or personality characteristics. To create a natal chart, the native's exact birth date, time and place are needed to map a precise depiction of the cosmic conditions upon entering this world.

With this information, each of the planets are placed into a wheel diagram of the zodiac at the exact locations they existed in time — the natal chart. This data is then used to measure the angles between the planets, Moon, and Sun to draw up **astrological aspects**.

Astrological Aspects & Transits

What do **astrological aspects** tell us about a chart?

Astrological aspects illustrated by chart patterns such as conjunctions, oppositions, trines, sextiles, and squares refer to specific angles between the celestial bodies. Each of these aspects gives the native insight into individual strengths or everyday challenges. These initial aspects of nativity are also used to calculate personal **transits** that occur when a specific occupied spot is revisited later in life. Last, astrological aspects are used to predict compatibility in relationship astrology or synastry.

Conjunction

A **conjunction** is an astrological aspect in which two or more celestial bodies can be found at the same point on a natal chart within an **8 degree orb of 360 degrees** — a circle. These aspects often find the two planets in the same sign. Conjunctions are considered constructive in nature and call for the planets involved to work in cooperation with one another. However, all aspects should be read on an individual basis. Because of this, a conjunction is derived from the characteristics of those planets involved. Strong and stable, slow-moving outer planets may find it more difficult to harmonize with the quick impulses of the fast inner planets.

Conjunctions can cause tension or ease, since these require the participating planets to function as one individual entity. It is important to measure the impact of a conjunction along with all other aspects by the degree of separation, also known as the **orb**.

Opposition

An **opposition** is an aspect in which two or more celestial bodies can be found at opposing points in a natal chart within an **8 degree orb of 180 degrees** — a semicircle. These aspects find two or more planets in opposing signs of the zodiac. Oppositions are all about balance. It becomes a conscious effort to maintain balance between these opposing forces. There is an ever-flowing exchange of energy, like a tug on the negative and positive polarity between opposite planets. With this abundance, the result is quite overwhelming with the ability to inspire greatness or unleash destruction — and with passion. These intense influences can be measured by the nature of the planets involved. The Moon and Sun are considered opposite, just as the influences of Mars and Venus. With these complimentary types of oppositions, the energy is raised to a higher caliber and affects the native in a deep way.

Oppositions weigh heavy on a chart and have the potential to create imbalances that are expressed in the external reality. These challenging aspects can either be highly rewarding or personally devastating.

Trine

A **trine** is an aspect in which two or more celestial bodies are separated at thirds along the natal chart within an **8 degree orb of 120 degrees** — a triangle. These aspects become highly complementary when the occupying planets are found in the same elemental sign. Regardless, the trine is a favorable position that requires no effort on the native's part. These points often suggest a natural ability to combine the influences of participating planets in a creative way. The trine points to a place of ease — a supportive and perpetually balanced force. The trine is an excellent aspect for relief from the weight of heavy astrological influences.

With such easy flowing energy, the trine is also a source of laziness. Trines lack the challenge of maintaining balance between planetary influences and require less attention; thus the trine sustains rather than changes.

Square

A **square** is an aspect in which two or more celestial bodies occupy separate quadrants of the natal chart within an **8 degree orb of 90 degrees** — a square. In this way, the signs are often of the same functioning type in traditional astrology cardinal, fixed, and mutable. The planets involved naturally gravitate toward contradicting purposes. The square aspect points to disagreement between the participating planets that requires conscious adjustment. Squares initiate growth through change, which can either be uplifting or disassembling. The outcome depends on the nature of the planets involved or the ability of the particular sign to adjust. Fixed signs, as indicated, find it more difficult to make adjustments.

These aspects are better expressed in stressful circumstances. Squares challenge the native to overthrow old habit patterns. Through reflection and self-denial, the square helps to accomplish ambitions.

Sextile

A sextile is an aspect in which two or more celestial bodies are separated by one zodiac sign in the natal chart within a **6 degree orb of 60 degrees** — a hexagon. These aspects are often between two signs of the same polarity, both with a compatible manner of expression — male or female. In such cases, the signs either male or female promote the positive or negative perspective, where positive describes the assertive nature of masculine and negative, the receptivity of the feminine. The sextile combines these like energies to assist in the manifestation of favorable outcomes. These aspects often prove more compelling and constructive than the gentle and harmonious nature of the trine.

The sextile encourages adjustment and promotes balance through

Natal Chart Basics

change. Because of this, the sextile requires less effort. Sextiles present opportunities that prompt external revision with ease.

How do **transits** weigh in on an individual's natal chart?

Transits refer to daily astrological aspects observed, when a celestial body revisits a point of significance on the individual's natal chart. As a transiting planet passes one of these sensitive areas, the nature of the original aspect of nativity is activated. Except, the transiting planet now grants its influence to the initial aspect and provides a fleeting moment of fortune or catastrophe. This is all dependent upon the nature of those planets or aspects involved.

Outer planetary transits provide insight into the cycles of nature. Often the planet Saturn is considered a dreaded transit that revisits its original location once about every thirty years. Because of this, when we reach the age thirty, sixty, or even ninety, Saturn prompts an important lesson that will greatly impact the way in which we carry on in the future down our own individual life path.

Jupiter is another transiting planet that provides us with a more uplifting effect. When Jupiter transits its initial position of nativity, it bestows the gifts of wisdom and life experience on the native. Jupiter transits through the zodiac belt once every twelve years. Slow moving Saturn and Jupiter transits have longer lasting effects that unfold over the course of a year.

How do planetary **transits** affect the wider world?

Outer planets point to lasting effects on the external reality. Transits connected to Uranus often provoke catastrophic consequences. However, they can also point to a spontaneous breath of excitement — a fortunate happenstance or new way of branching out from the norm. Uranus rotates in the opposite direction of the remaining planets. Because of this, Uranus transits throw us for a loop. Both Uranus and Neptune are linked to civil unrest and describe the passing of world affairs — beyond what's presented on the surface. Neptune is the ruler of widespread illusion and the ideology of the collective. Its influences have the greatest effect on the invisible realm.

In these cycles, Uranus transits in half the time as Neptune. It takes Neptune 165 years to circle the zodiac and Uranus, just 84 years. The transits of these two outer planets work hand in hand. Uranus transits break down the current reality to make way for Neptune's latest grand illusions.

Moon transits are often linked to the feminine cycle. The Moon travels through the zodiac in just 28 days — making it the fastest transiting object used in astrology. Mercury and Venus never stray far from the Sun and play an endless game of 'hurry up, and then wait' with each passing. This apparent observation of the Mercury and Venus is caused by the phenomenon **retrograde,** when a planet slows and stops dead in the sky to reverse its motion backwards through the zodiac. In retrograde, these close inner planets constantly communicate information with the Sun to prompt new changes in our outward expression.

What is significant about a **retrograde** period?

Retrograde

The Moon and Sun never retrograde. The motion of retrograde is caused by the position of Earth overtaking that of another planet on its orbital path around the Sun. This illusion is caused by each planet's path of orbit. Mercury is the most sporadic planet that retrogrades each time it gets ahead of the Sun in the zodiac belt. But the retrograde period of any planet marks an important moment in time. This point of slowing just before the planet turns to reverse marks the moment in which the retrograding planet is the closest possible distance to the Earth.

Retrogrades in astrology can be read as a reconditioning for the planet involved. While the planet retraces its path in time backwards through the signs, the planetary influence is internalized and reconsidered to suit the current reality. It is a moment of re-evaluation. When this task is done, the planet returns once again along its path forward through the zodiac; thus the change of direction is set into motion.

Relationship Astrology — Synastry

How does relationship astrology or **synastry** work?

> "The meeting of two personalities is like the contact of two chemical substances: if there is any reaction, both are transformed."
>
> —Carl Jung,
> *Modern Man in Search of a Soul*

In relationship astrology, **synastry aspects** are drawn to compare the natal charts of two people in order to reveal the nature of their meeting. Synastry is also used to illustrate the energy exchange that resonates between family, friends, or lovers. Those relationships that impact us the most are often drawn up with invisible ties in synastry. In such cases, the line between coincidence and fate can become blurred.

One's personal aspects can provide a favorable influence over the deficient area of another person's natal chart. Likewise, difficult aspects can be drawn between two charts that either provoke tension or prompt change and growth as a lasting effect of the relationship. Balanced synastry aspects provide a harmonious arena for expression between two people. Synastry aspects are derived by comparing two natal charts in the same fashion as described for interpreting an individual's chart aspects.

Traditional Astrology Explained

What is significant about the moment of birth?

The initial conditions and environment of one's own development have been thought to weigh heavy on a person throughout life. Humans are conditioned from a young age to adapt to their environment. School children are introduced to the social norms of society and taught to adopt the most current moral values in trend. Those who succeed are praised, those who fail, disciplined. Some would argue that the nature of early development holds key importance in how an individual will adapt later in life. In fact, many people thrive in the conditions that were presented to them in early development. They are naturally more inclined to mimic familiar settings or repeat old habit patterns for better or worse.

In this same way, a person's natal chart can be considered the initial environment of cosmic conditions presented at birth. The nativity exhibits the purest form of our existence, before any conditioning has occurred. We enter this paradigm at one significant moment in time, resonate with it and accept this pattern written in the sky as our own personal signature as time goes on.

In astrology, timing is everything, and if nothing else, the most important aspect when entering a plane of existence. With a closer look at the hours that unfold with the zodiac after the moment of birth, the very nature of our life path is narrated in the twelve **astrological houses.**

The Houses & Invisible Aspects

What is the purpose of the **astrological houses**?

The **astrological houses** represent external affairs. House astrology is a psychologically retrospective process that invites the native to define the influences of the signs and planets as these aspects shape life's events in the external reality. The houses represent our personal approach to life. In this way, the celestial bodies describe activities, while the zodiac signs represent the nature of these activities. Through house astrology, the native is given a stage to observe their life path with an objective point of view. The houses start with the ascendant and divide the sky up into 12 slots of 30 degrees to complete 360 degrees around the zodiac belt.

What types of points create **invisible aspects**?

Ascendant

The **ascendant (ASC)** or rising sign is the zodiac sign rising above the eastern horizon at the moment of birth. With the ascendant, we draw the line of self-awareness with our entrance into this life. The ascendant is found on the cusp of the first house on a natal chart — or at the point of zero degrees. From the zero degree line marking the ascendant, the houses begin to unfold as the zodiac belt reveals itself in time over the eastern horizon. The ascendant describes the pronounced aspects of our aura and appearance — those traits in which the world uses to estimate the measure of our own personal aptitudes and abilities.

Midheaven

The **midheaven (MC)** marks the cross of the meridian and the ecliptic, opposite the Imum coeli (IC). It is situated halfway between the ascendant and descendant. The midheaven is found on the cusp of the tenth house in a natal chart. It describes our impulses toward ambitions and the direction of intellectual and physical capabilities.

Descendant

The **descendant (DSC)** can be found opposite the ascendant and marks the point of declination. At this position, the Sun recedes beneath the visible horizon indicated by the sunset. The descendant is found on the cusp of the seventh house on a natal chart. It describes the manner in which we relate to the world and indicates relations that complement our ascendant.

What do the **astrological houses** indicate in a natal chart?

I.   The **first house** describes our early childhood and the manner in which our lives develop. It governs what distinguishes us as individuals — both our unique contributions and quirks. The first house describes our outward presentation and those idiosyncrasies that define our human quality.

II.   The **second house** describes our personal resources and desires for gain. It indicates the nature of those special qualities and strengths we possess — to do with what we will. The second house displays our individual gifts that we utilize and share with the world.

III.   The **third house** describes our environmental experiences and manner of knowing. It represents social lessons and relationships with siblings or the community. The third house indicates our perceptive and adaptive abilities that guide us to learn from and cooperate with others.

IV.   The **fourth house** describes our early residence and emotional foundations. It rules the home and shapes our own personal sense of domestic security. The fourth house indicates gifts of our parents, heritage, and inherited adaptations in which we express in family or domestic life.

V.   The **fifth house** describes our creative urges and offspring. It represents all forms of self-replication through emotional expression or reproduction. The fifth house defines our personal legacy and things that are actualized as a product of our existence.

VI. The **sixth house** describes our personal responsibilities and daily routine. It represents our service to others and the nature of our own personal approach to work. The sixth house displays our adaptability to everyday crises and the health of the physical body.

VII. The **seventh house** describes our relationships and public image. It indicates partnerships of every type that require a combined effort toward a common goal. The seventh house depicts the give and take in life and the ways in which we see parts of ourselves reflected in others.

VIII. The **eighth house** describes our personal sacrifices and the evolution of self. It signifies the death of the obsolete and release from limitations. The eighth house indicates regeneration through change and invites us to abandon the desires of the ego.

IX. The **ninth house** describes our personal philosophy and standards in ethics. It represents our wisdom, intuition, and dealings with the abstract mind. In the ninth house we meet experiences that promote higher learning and opportunities to expand beyond our personal viewpoint.

X. The **tenth house** describes our professional life and public influence. It indicates our position in society as the product of our occupational role. The tenth house prompts happenings in our career development and represents the nature in which our aspirations manifest in reality.

XI. The **eleventh house** describes our future goals and ideals with respect to humanity. It displays our associations that contribute to the external manifestation of personal ambitions. The eleventh house grants us with the awareness of potential possibilities for progress.

XII. The **twelfth house** describes our unconscious experience and karmic obligations. It indicates trials of faith or activities of cause and effect. The twelfth house provokes situations in which we must confront unconscious motives and atone for past-doings.

True Borders

What would an astronomer have to say about astrology?

For anyone who has taken the time out of their day to study the sky, it quickly becomes apparent that the widely accepted twelve constellations of the zodiac do not match up with reality. In truth, the signs of the zodiac belt hardly fit within the neat 30 degree slots of space assigned to each constellation in traditional astrology. In fact, when we take this into account, Virgo and Pisces stretch far beyond their borders at opposite ends of the zodiac, while Aries is cut short with a fitting description as an abrupt fire sign.

Unfortunately, the signs **Ophiuchus** and **Orion** are completely absent from the traditional twelve zodiac, and for this reason, we must question, why? When we take a closer look at the constellations at night, both of these signs still hold a place among the stars. Simply not stating them in astrology will not erase them from the sky.

It is more likely we have yet to notice the significance of these signs. As they exist, Ophiuchus and Orion stand at pivotal areas in the zodiac. These zodiac signs hold the intersection where the plane of the zodiac belt and the Milky Way Galaxy cross paths with Ophiuchus to mark **the Galactic Center** and Orion, the furthest point from it.

The Seasonal Approach

Have we been hoodwinked?

Not quite. The intent of the adjustment was to match the seasons separated into even quarters. With each quarter, we experience three separate forms of the season. In this way, the zodiac signs stand as a symbol for the characteristics of the four seasons. It is interesting to note that the current calendar is split up into twelve months. The twelve **zodiac signs** seem to fit right into this scheme of uniform organization.

However, the significance of twelve is best explained by the fact that there are 360 degrees in the arc of the zodiac belt. Who needs **Ophiuchus** and **Orion** when we can even up the edges at a solid 30 degrees? It is for the sake of symmetry that we split them up in such a way. After all, astrology is a mathematical process.

If we visualize the Earth rotating around the Sun in a year's time, the zodiac signs become road markers that map out this great journey. Except from the Earth's perspective, we witness this month by month, when the Sun creeps slowly through each of the twelve zodiac signs over the course of a year. This visualization is not due to the Sun's movement, but our own planet's rotation around it at the center.

With each sign at perfect 30 degree angles, we are able to assign characteristics to the location of Earth in each quadrant on its annual path around the Sun. With this dynamic motion we capture a glimpse at the complexity of the astrological influences along the planet's path with the additional interactions between Earth and the remaining celestial bodies.

III. The Significance of Angles & Aspects

Sacred Geometry

Why are some geometric shapes better than others?

    The very fabric of the universe is designed in distinguished patterns that bring continuity and structure to the external world we call reality. These patterns of existence — when most stable — replicate the **golden ratio** expressed in geometric forms that shape the exterior surface of our world. We often underestimate the power of symmetry, though any painter, architect, or musician would greatly benefit from a basic understanding in the aesthetic implications of the golden ratio.

    The Vitruvian Man is a perfect example of how artist and inventor **Leonardo da Vinci** applied his knowledge of the golden ratio to the symmetrical construction of the human body. Da Vinci's illustrations are found within *De Divina Proportione* by mathematician Luca Pacioli. As it stands, da Vinci's model is not just a theory but a truth in reality. The Vitruvian Man provides us with a visual representation to easier understand how the human figure itself is an expression of the golden ratio in the measurements of the **cubit**, palm, and foot. The beauty we find in the human form and in facial features is automatically determined in the mind with this illusion of symmetry in proportions.

This subtle perfection in ratio does not stop with man. Vitruvian was a name borrowed from another artist of the concept who outlined human symmetry in Marcus Vitruvius *De architectura*. **Marcus Vitruvius** used similar concepts of proportion to build grand architectural structures in his day. This Roman architect lived during the time of Julius Caesar and applied divine proportion to the construction of buildings to promote stability and aesthetic appeal.

It is said that the rediscovery of the golden ratio also contributed to the explosion of fine art during the Renaissance period, as golden rectangles (a shape developed through the application of **sacred geometry**) can be traced in the paintings and sculpture of this artistic era. The golden ratio is a constant theme throughout history and originates as far back as the ancient Greek world or earlier with the pyramids of Egypt.

The Parthenon is another classic example of ancient architecture that utilizes the principle of the golden ratio to accentuate the beauty of natural order. The Greeks had also found another application for "phi" (≈ 1.618) or the number value of the golden section that does not pronounce its presence in a tangible sense. That is, the philosophers of the Greek Classical period had discovered the beauty of harmonics behind the music of the world.

With the ancient concept of *Musica universalis* or *Harmony of the Spheres* — a mathematical and philosophical treatise on the proportions of the planets in harmony — great thinkers outlined the "sound" of the celestial bodies as they synchronize a song of divine proportion to match the meter of the golden ratio. With this information, the true importance of geometric proportions and mathematical ratios is revealed in the melodic number

The Significance of Angles & Aspects

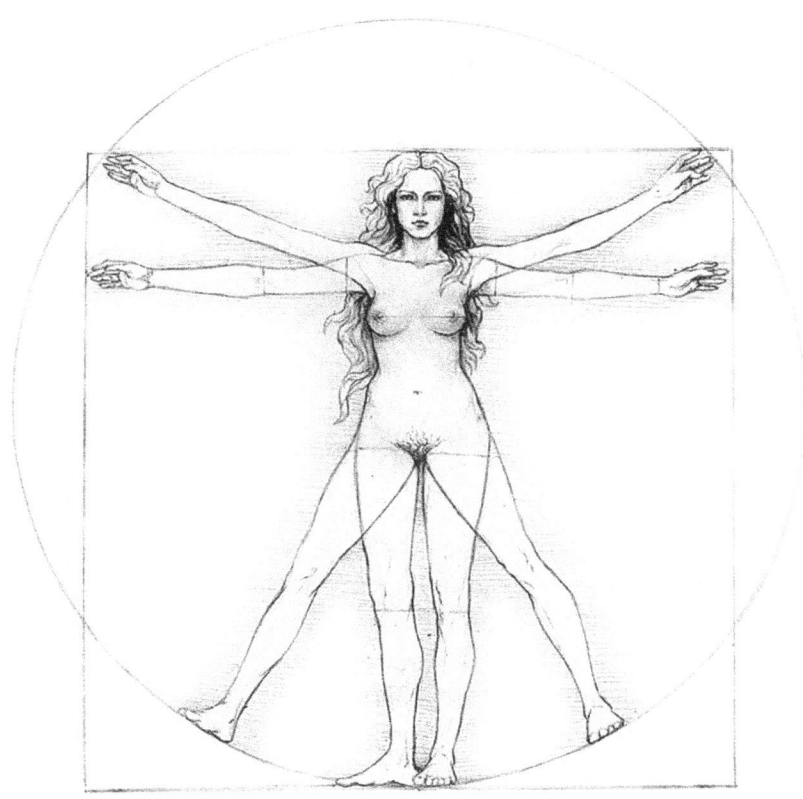

relationships that produce complimentary sounds.

When we look at not only the shape of an instrument, but the relationship between notes of the octave, we also find resounding patterns of the golden section. These patterns take the shape of a harp, a violin, a cello and a guitar and amplify sound in a harmonious way. That is why, the shape of the instrument is the instrument. Some will also stretch the application of the golden ratio in music so far as to say that Mozart or other great composers of the past used it in the timing of a musical piece.

> "It seems to some thinkers that bodies so great must inevitably produce a sound by their movement: even bodies on earth do so, although they are neither so great in bulk nor moving at so high a speed, and as for the

sun and moon, and the stars, so many in number and enormous in size, all moving at tremendous speeds, it is incredible that they should fail to produce a noise of surpassing loudness. Taking this as their hypothesis, and also that the speeds of the stars, judged by their distances, are in the ratio of the musical consonances, they affirm that the sound of the stars as they revolve is concordant."

—Aristotle, *De Caelo [On the Heavens]*

What is the significance of geometric symmetry?

With close observation, it becomes clear that these geometric patterns outlined by the golden ratio are universal to the creation of matter. They can also be found expressed throughout nature in self-replicating forms. When we see a nautilus shell on the beach, it does not often occur to us that we are looking at the golden ratio reflected in the repetition of the spiral pattern. The shape of a pine cone and unfolding petals of a rose also reveal patterns of divine proportion.

The origins of symmetrical order in geometry take us back to Pythagoras who first described the nature of "cosmos" as a "well-ordered and harmonious universe". Along with this information, he gave us the formula for the dimensions of a triangle known as the **Pythagorean Theorem** or the mathematical mechanics that fit the area of a right triangle ($a^2 + b^2 = c^2$). A similar discovery of the numeric value of **phi** helped the ancient Greek mathematicians to better understand the geometry of the cosmos. This divine ratio becomes the solution to the quadratic equation ($x^2 - x - 1 = 0$) or $[(1 + \sqrt{5}) \div 2 = x]$, when we are presented the answer "x" equals about 1.618 or the value of phi.

This number value of **phi** is a derivation of the formula for the golden ratio. A similar numerical sequence was brought from India and published in the west by Leonardo da Pisa or "Fibonacci". The Fibonacci sequence, as it was later named, builds upon a set of numbers, where the first and second numbers equal

The Significance of Angles & Aspects

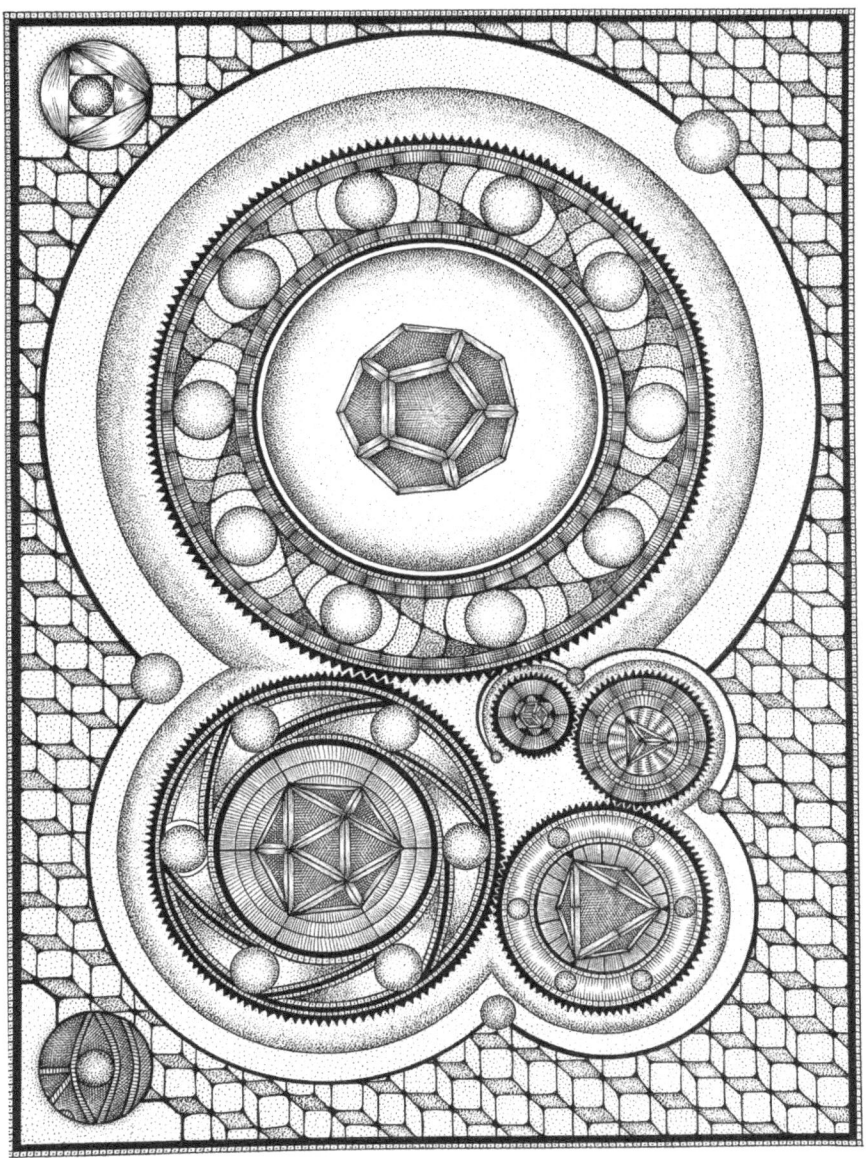

the third, the third and fourth equal the fifth, and so on (0, 1, 1, 2, 3, 5, 8, 13,…). These patterns of divine proportion point to an underlying mathematical symmetry of reality — the Fibonacci sequence of fractals and later **Pascal's triangle**.

Plato took a more visual approach to the fundamental

construction of all creation with his famous five **Platonic solids** that together form the most basic geometric shapes of matter — the tetrahedron, cube, octahedron, dodecahedron, and the icosahedron. These shapes demonstrate how nature fashions the visible reality in a three dimensional sense. Crystals form the shape of the tetrahedron, cube, and octahedron, minerals reflect that of the dodecahedron, while several viruses take the shape of the icosahedron.

Each geometric solid takes on a new form when the corners of the shape are cut, so that another shape is inserted where a corner once existed. Likewise, the shape can be modified by adding an arc to the straight lines that construct each edge to make the solid spherical — the difference between the philosophic categories of male lines (what is straight) and female lines (what is curved). Water becomes a great example for the presence of female, curved lines formed through molecular polarity — a natural magnetism.

A more recent fascination with divine proportion was presented to the world in the 17th Century by astronomer **Johannes Kepler** in the research he recorded in *Mysterium Cosmographicum,* also known "The Secret of the Universe". Within its pages, the polyhedral hypothesis describes the values for the number, distancing, and spheres of the planetary orbits as a reflection of the five **Platonic solids**. However, the data Kepler used for his calculations dated all the way back to the distant geocentric days of Ptolemy. Kepler took advantage of **Nicholaus Copernicus'** heliocentric model, but was uniformed of the planets Uranus and Neptune — beyond the veil of the visible sky. Despite his attempts to fit the solar system into its own category of divinity, the astronomical data of Kepler's calculations failed to yield accurate figures. Nevertheless, Kepler was aware of the harmony in music and aesthetic proportion outlined by the Greeks with the golden ratio. Following the ideas of Plato, Kepler also produced the **Kepler–Poinsot polyhedra** — a set of four star-shaped solids to add to Plato's five.

Just as the golden ratio is displayed as an external projection of universal pattern in harmony, so too does the model named the Flower of Life. Except, the Flower of Life does not symbolize the

pattern in a three dimensional sense as we perceive it as humans here on Earth, rather it indicates all possible geometric patterns within our current existence. In essence, the Flower of Life holds the key — a formula for all replicating patterns of geometric symmetry that fit within the established framework of the fabric of existence.

If we think about our reality in an objective sense, we can grasp this idea in simple terms. That is, the replication or creation of matter must fit within certain criteria — under the guidelines of what is 'possible'. Possible is the **Flower of Life**.

Fractals of Life

> "E'en in the single leaf of a tree,
> Or a tender blade of grass,
> The awe-inspiring Deity
> Manifests Itself."
>
> —Urabe-no-Kanekuni

One numeric extension of the **Fibonacci sequence** allows modern scientists to predict the manner in which life manifests, detect healthy living systems in the body, and develop intelligent technologies with an efficiency that excels beyond the platform of previous standards. This numeric sequence of micro and macro patterns or **fractals** branch off from the initial fractal pattern of numbers to express harmonious self-replicating forms and repeat the harmony of the main sequence in accordance with this pattern in time.

As these patterns unfold to the eye, we seem to continuously zoom in on a never-ending sequence of numbers shaping a visual pattern, which as it branches off to continue yet another extension of the whole, appears to regenerate this growth in a pre-existing dimensional fold of itself. This property of fractal replication known as **self-similarity** can be seen at work as it fashions the visual reality all around us. In short, fractal sequences in Nature reveal patterns of underlying microcosm in the macrocosm with subtle, yet perfect proportion; each branch reflects an echo of the whole.

When these smaller fractal patterns grow to great heights like the oak tree, they sprout branches that follow the original sequence passed down from ancestor tree to seed. Even the forest itself builds every tree and branch in fractal patterns that can be mapped out and measured using a single tree as the key for the entire blueprint of a colony. Researchers have come to apply fractal patterns to utilize the measurements of a single tree and leaf to estimate the amount of carbon-dioxide an entire rainforest absorbs.

Before they were tamed, these giant **fractal** patterns of numeric sequence were **Monsters** of the mathematical world. The work of mathematician **Benoit Mandelbrot** delivered the breakthrough that helped us to better understand these "monsters" of the past. With the research contained inside *The Fractal Geometry of Nature*, Mandelbrot gave us new insight into the subtle symmetry that defines what was once a manner of chaos. With this information, we peer at the pages of possibility that define the book of the natural world — from the look of a mountain and the flow of rivers on land to the float of clouds in the sky.

Perhaps one of the most useful implications of applying fractal formulas to practical human use came about when it was discovered that healthy biological systems, such as those which prompt the rhythm of a heartbeat or the formation of blood vessels and organic structures in the body, replicate and resonate in harmony with the geometric symmetry of fractal patterns. That is, the fractal patterns that are already encoded within the human body can be used to detect unhealthy cells by mapping the formation of chaotic blood vessels or also identify heart disease simply by examining the pulse.

We can use fractal patterns to predict the intelligent geometric symmetry of all that is Nature. But if we take fractals one step further, we begin to see the true power of **sacred geometry**. In the technological world, fractal patterns became the key to developing realistic computer generated landscapes and the hidden tool to fit a world of software features within the confines of the smallest cell phone.

In 1988, astrophysicist and inventor Nathan Cohen applied his knowledge of Mandelbrot's work to develop a more efficient antenna. By bending the antenna in the shape of a fractal pattern, Cohen found that the reception of his ham radio came in much clearer than before.

With this observation, Cohen discovered that fractals permit the transmission of a wide range of frequencies. In turn, the invention of miniature fractal antennas allowed modern cell phones to accommodate for a spectrum of functions in software applications. That is, fractal patterns are naturally occurring shapes that are highly efficient and flexible at transmitting and receiving frequencies or **electromagnetic radiation**.

In addition to its practical uses, the fractal sequence is held in high esteem in the aesthetic world. *Under a Wave off Kanagawa* by Hokusai is an artistic expression of **self-similarity** in the repetition of the breaking tsunami wave into smaller fractal replicates. This famous Japanese piece illustrates the fractal self-similarity observed in common patterns of Nature such as the break of a tidal wave.

Angles in Aspects

How does geometric symmetry relate to astrology?

All life is made up of carbon molecules found inside organic cells that bond in the shape of tetrahedrons. These building blocks always fit within the larger structure pattern — the Flower of Life. Therefore, simple tetrahedral bonds promote the creation of life through balanced replication and repetition. For this reason, similar angles of geometric symmetry are used in astrology to determine the influence of planetary aspects.

An **astrological aspect** occurs when two or more celestial bodies form a significant angle in relation to one another. These points are drawn on the individual's natal chart and derived from transiting planets at any given day. The significance of planetary angles is rooted in the functionality of basic geometric shapes in nature.

What does the angle tell us about an **astrological aspect**?

It comes as no surprise that the hexagonal structure — designed from continuous **60 and 120 degree angles** — constitutes a harmonious aspect. When light penetrates a hexagon, it illuminates the interior in equal lines of distribution to produce a repetitious pattern of constructive vibrations that stimulates continuous growth. The hexagonal shape of a snowflake produces this same effect as light bounces around its crystalline structure to be reflected back at the viewer with bright, white intensity. That is why the angles of both the trine and sextile are considered beneficial aspects in astrology.

The triangle in itself is one of the most stable and powerful shapes when applied to the architectural construction of buildings and bridges, while the hexagon or honeycomb is utilized by the bees as a structurally sound and efficient replicating geometric form.

On the other hand, right angle patterns are often associated with forces at odds and the crystallization of matter. In crystallization, materials are imprinted with geometric shapes that most often form **90 degree angle** and rectangular patterns. These crystal structures like Bravais Lattices are stacked in relation to right angles. These patterns do not promote replication, and because of this, right angles and rectangular shapes are not associated with growth. Rather, right angles or squares are associated with destruction and the release of energy that follows as a consequence. In this way, the square and opposition are astrological aspects that bring about change.

At a glance, it's easy to take the side of the ever-replicating and harmonious trines. Since these are benefic aspects — those from which we 'benefit'. But as with most things in life, balance is necessary. The creative and constructive forces of trines and sextiles promote growth, yet replication and growth without restraint has the potential to surpass the limits of excess. The second destructive form, the **malefic aspects,** the square or opposition, are needed to prompt a release of energy. So while the **benefic aspects,** the trine and sextile, nourish and replicate creative energy, they must encounter the malefic aspects to release it into existence. To the Hellenistic astrologer Vettius Valens, the malefic aspect appears with great power.

> "Malefics seem stronger than benefics. Just as a drop of black or brown, falling into a container of brightly colored paint, dims the color's beauty, and the large quantity of brilliant color cannot hide the dark stain, however small — so it is with malefics, stars which can attack men and rob them of the things in which they seem to be fortunate: family, livelihood, health, rank, beauty, and whatever is rare."
>
> —Vettius Valens, *Anthology*

Natal Chart Patterns

How are **natal chart** patterns used in astrology?

When three or more basic astrological aspects shape a precise geometric form, such as the triangle or square, the planetary influences involved in this aspect are deemed more powerful and directed. The overall energy that comes as a product of the geometric form is complete and much more significant. These symmetrical patterns can be considered a type of synchronization between planetary influences in a natal chart.

Basic **natal chart** patterns can be read by examining the type

The Significance of Angles & Aspects

of energy exchange that is promoted by the geometric shapes formed at birth. This is indicated by the degree of angles that connect to form these aspects. Natal chart patterns are also drawn up in relationship astrology or synastry to indicate the type of energy exchange expressed between two people.

What types of **natal chart** patterns are found in astrology?

When weighing the aspects and influences of each natal chart pattern, it is important to take into consideration the effects of both the benefic and malefic aspects. The nature of benefic and malefic aspects promote continuity and change for the querent, respectively. Most natal chart patterns contain one type of these aspects or connect the influences of both. When geometric patterns of symmetry involve both **benefic and malefic aspects**, the relation is considered to produce a more balanced influence.

Grand Trine

The **Grand Trine** natal chart pattern is formed when three or more celestial bodies create an equilateral triangle — three precisely connected trines.

Inside the perfect triangle, harmony seems to be ever-flowing between benefic aspects. The Grand Trine promotes creative expression and positive self-development. This complimentary natal chart pattern charms us with contentment. However, it can also limit the expression of change, since it lacks malefic aspects to release it from repetition. When defining the influence of a Grand Trine, it is important to consider the nature of both the planets and zodiac signs involved, as with all natal chart patterns.

T-Square

The **T-Square** natal chart pattern is formed when three or more celestial bodies create an equal right triangle — two precise squares connected by an opposition.

Inside the T-Square, the energies of malefic aspects, both the squares and oppositions, require immediate action and attention. These influences prompt a struggle to overcome adversity and result in achieved success when kept in balance; thus these patterns are associated with the manifestation of personal ambitions. When defining the influence of a T-square, the nature of the opposing planet plays a critical role in the challenge to gain stability with this aspect.

Kite

The **Kite** natal chart pattern is formed when four or more celestial bodies create a kite — a triangle cut with an opposition between two precise sextiles.

Inside the kite, an opposition stretches from the elongated triangle to the top of the kite tip to form a bow-like influence. The release of energy from the opposition is slingshot forward and dispersed between the two sextiles and then balanced with the final trines to create continuity. The cooperation of both benefic and malefic aspects in this geometric form direct energy in a highly constructive manner. Kites provide motivation and promote the realization of aspirations, but they can also lead to obsession when less significant aspects are neglected.

Cosmic Cross

The **Grand Square** or **Cosmic Cross** natal chart pattern is formed when four or more celestial bodies create an equal square or connecting T-squares — four square aspects intersected by two precise oppositions.

Inside the Cosmic Cross, energy is concentrated at the edges of these malefic aspects. This natal chart pattern presents a framework of rigid restraint. The limitations of the Cosmic Cross have the potential to build tension when not kept in check. The oppositions deter the impulses of the squares, which leads to an imprisonment in the passive. Effort is required to stabilize these aspects in order to transform what would otherwise be unfortunate influences into a sturdy foundation. When these aspects are balanced, the Cosmic Cross binds the planetary influences with stability.

Seal of Solomon

The **Seal of Solomon** natal chart pattern also known as the Star of David is formed when six or more celestial bodies create a six-sided star — two Grand Trines overlapped in opposite directions. It evens out to also form a Grand Sextile with six oppositions. The Seal of Solomon expresses the Hermetic adage, 'as above, so below' — a phrase that invokes the mystic's connection between the visible and invisible realms. In ancient tradition, the upper trine is white, points to the sky, and represents the divine masculine quality, while the lower trine is black, fixed downward, and symbolizes the divine feminine quality.

Inside the Seal of Solomon, the connection between two Grand Trines radiates the effects of creative harmony. This natal chart pattern is comprised of benefic and malefic aspects, which often promote cooperation between two sets of elements. To the ancient astrologer or mystic, this six pointed star spreads planets evenly across the exterior circle of a natal chart. The two overlapping triangles represent the visible sky connected to the world below the horizon, known to the ancients as the Underworld; thus the astrological symbol for the Seal of Solomon joins the obvious surface appearances with what lies in the invisible realm in the depths of the unknown.

The Brilliance of Light

Why is light such a unique form of energy?

When we see a beam of light, we are actually looking at two forms of matter — both a wave and particle. Visible light is formed from a concentration of electromagnetic radiation; thus it is made up of excited particles and travels in a wave. In the vacuum of space, light will always travel at a constant speed, as long as its initial path is uninterrupted by external forces. When a beam of light comes into contact with matter, it is often reflected at the same angle it meets the surface of solid matter. When light penetrates an object, it can also be bent through refraction.

When we drive past a moving train inside a car, the train appears to slow down as we speed up alongside it. Unlike the apparent slowing motion we see while matching the speed of the train, the speed of a beam of light will always remain the same — consistent with the speed of light. This is relative and true for all points of perspective. Light will always travel at the speed of light no matter how we look at it.

Another special property of light is that it travels in straight lines from the source. That is why it takes on the shape of the thing that created it. When we see the light from a star, it has sometimes traveled to our very position in space across many lifetimes, and because of this, the light that reaches us from distant stars and galaxies is often thousands of years older than the present moment. In this case, since the light source is found at such a deep location in space, it takes thousands of light years to reach us. With this information, we can conclude that the light released from celestial bodies opens a window to the past.

How does light carry information?

The special properties of light allow us to extract information from the energy source. Scientists can decipher the very elements that make up a planet or star just by the spectrum of light emitted.

That is to say, each chemical element emits visible light read across an **emission spectrum** — a sort of color signature defined by the frequencies of electromagnetic radiation in a planet or star's chemical composition. This spectrum gives us signatures made up of the "**ROYGBIV**" system of colors taught in school — red, orange, yellow, green, blue, indigo, and violet. White light is the reflection of all colors combined, and the color black, the absorption of all light in the spectrum.

In another way, light is important for calculating the distance between objects. It can also help us discover which objects are moving closer and further away. This process is determined by measuring the red shift or blue shift of the object. With red shift, the visible light appears red when the waves are elongated as the light source moves away from our point of perspective. On the other hand, blue shift appears blue when the waves are compressed as the source of light moves directly toward us. Although the wavelength of light appears to change, the speed of light always remains the same.

In modern times, the development of fiber optics has allowed humans to harness the power of light by encoding it with information. Pulses of light are transmitted through optic fibers in the form of an electromagnetic carrier wave to be decoded at its final destination — much like how we are able to tune into a music station sent along the AM and FM radio frequencies.

What is the significance of light in astrology?

In astrology, light was once the most important factor in developing the planetary system. Without light, the classical planets would not have been discovered by early astronomers. The **classical planets** refer to the Sun, Moon, and first five planets in the geocentric solar system — Mercury, Venus, Mars, Jupiter, and Saturn. These seven celestial bodies were considered "wandering stars" or *asteres planetai* to the ancients, and because of this, they were given the name 'the wanderers'.

The classical planets were visible to the naked eye in the ancient night sky only because they reflect the light from the

Sun. Without this level of luminosity caused by proximity and a reflective surface, these planets would be lost to the ancients — much like the invisible giants in the outer reaches of the solar system, Uranus and Neptune.

How does life perceive light?

The light we receive from the Sun, the energy we draw from the Earth, and that within us at all times has taken on many names in the past. It has been described as **Prana** (solar force), ruach (breath of life), or **qi** (chi or life force), and most recently **frequency** — our own independent wavelength of existence and perhaps the definition of our own personal paradigm in a non-visible sense.

The human response to light is seated at the center of the brain — the **pineal gland**. The pineal gland gets its name from the pine cone, as they both share a similar shape. This gem of a gland within the endocrine system interacts with the external reality by responding to the light received at the retina tissues of the eyes. Inside the pineal gland, cells respond to the presence of light and send this endocrine information to the **hypothalamus**. The hypothalamus secretes a chemical messenger — a hormone that communicates with the nervous system to incite an electrical synapse response within the brain or induce a chemical reaction inside other major organs of the body. Synapse responses cause immediate emotional or behavioral changes from within, yet the secretion of the hormone was initially prompted by an external force — often the rising or setting of the Sun.

Since we are all bioelectromagnetic creatures, our lives are regulated by light — a pure form of energy that we receive from the Sun. This natural cycle that exists within humans in response to the solar energy we receive from the Sun is called **circadian rhythm**, and it changes with the seasons.

The pineal gland is connected to the sleep and wake cycle of humans. The pineal gland produces melatonin in order to regulate circadian rhythm or the human biological clock. The ancients also considered the pineal gland to be the source of

The Significance of Angles & Aspects

creativity, spirituality, and mysticism, as well as the connection to our **third eye**. In the 17th Century, **Rene Descartes** went so far as to name the pineal gland the connection between body and spirit — where thoughts, imagination, and memory were born. Descartes' philosophy outlined within *Passions of the Soul* declared the pineal gland the "seat of the soul."

In the animal kingdom, most creatures that fall under the category of vertebrae possess a pineal gland. The pineal gland also regulates sleep cycles and seasonal behavior patterns such as hibernation. Plants, on the other hand, absorb light into chloroplast cells and convert this energy into fuel. In this way, we can consider the Sun's light a necessary resource for life on Earth. For without the plants, there would be no animals; thus no human civilization.

In fact, the origins of the beginning conditions for human to roam this Earth were brought about solely through our involuntary contract with the original pioneers that colonized land — the plants. Around a billion years ago, plants worked in cooperation with the magnetic field of the Earth to form the **atmosphere** through the production of molecular oxygen and nitrogen. Therefore, the existence of the atmosphere is biologically sustained. In other words, or those of astronomer and cosmic philosopher **Carl Sagan**, "the sky is made of life."

This atmosphere provided by the plants is our personal shelter from **ultraviolet and cosmic radiation** and protects all living creatures. That is, the air we breathe, the fruits we eat, the seeds of life we enjoy are the product of solar energy or light converted by plants into oxygen and nutrients in the form of carbohydrates. In turn, each time we exhale carbon dioxide, we breathe life back into the plant kingdom to complete the circle.

How does the Sun regulate the metabolism of a common potato?

As if a potato could reveal the secrets of the universe, it does just that. When biologists observed the **metabolism** of potatoes by measuring the rate of oxygen released throughout the day, they found that the potatoes kept their natural rhythmic cycles despite being locked inside a container shielded from the elements (fluctuations of barometric pressure, temperature, light intensity, and humidity).

The story unfolds with the rise and set of the **Sun**. The metabolism of the potatoes peaked at 7 am, noon, and 6 pm each day the experiment was conducted. At night when the Sun disappeared from the visible sky, these levels dropped down to the lowest oxygen consumption that hinted a regular slowing of metabolism every evening. In this case, the potatoes were blind in the dark, and the presence of visible light was unnecessary to initiate the recorded metabolic changes. Yet, the potatoes had no problem detecting the best time to metabolize.

Scientists also found that the season influenced this rate of change in the potato's metabolism, as the **zenith** or noontime peak of oxygen consumption pronounced itself more dramatically in the wintertime as opposed to the summer months. The potato then succeeded to baffle the mind, as it predicted its own correct adjustment of oxygen consumption in tune with the fluctuations of barometric pressure two days in advance! This blindfolded potato knew to make these metabolic adjustments two days before the conditions ever arrive, but how did the potato know? The question is one that perplexes the mind, though the time-sensing mechanism within the potato is no doubt attuned to the cycles of the Sun.

Does the Moon also have an influence over creatures of the Earth?

Similar to the potato's metabolic connection to the Sun, marine life is also influenced by waves of high and low tide. We know that the tides rise and fall with the orbit of the **Moon** in relation to the Sun around the Earth. The tides bring with them fluctuations in pressure, temperature, salinity, and other causes for change in feeding conditions. When biologists took a closer look at the behavior of marine life, they began to spot that the oyster preferred to open its shell with more frequency at high tide rather than low tide, since the feeding conditions at this time were more ideal.

To map a scientific explanation behind the source of sensing such a pattern, biologists displaced oysters from the bottom of New Haven harbor in Connecticut and brought them to Illinois to be housed inside a dark container of water taken from their original location. The oysters kept with their usual pattern by following the rhythm of the tides at New Haven harbor, but after a couple weeks passed, a remarkable thing happened. The oysters synched with the local tidal rhythm of Illinois — the appearance of the Moon above — despite the lack of ocean in the middle of the continental United States. With this information, biologists deduced that the oysters could sense these natural rhythms in time and adjust their behavior to reflect the cycles of the Moon.

IV. The History of Astrology

What did the ancients think about **astrology**?

In the era of our ancient ancestors, astrology and astronomy were one in the same — at least to the early Mesoamericans. Peoples of the past had not yet separated the empirical evidence of astronomy from the estimation and theory behind astrological influences, since neither of these concepts had become exacted in the way that we consider astronomy a science under scientific method in modern times.

For the peoples of ancient civilization, the celestial bodies reflected the soul of the heavens (ouranos, *gk*). Therefore, the interactions between these divine forces — beyond the reach of human influence — were considered to have a lasting effect on destiny. To the ancients, considering the astrological influences was an attempt to master destiny by adjusting one's own life with the flux and flow of the **ambient**. The movements of the 'wandering stars' were observed and fixed-star positions calculated as the celestial bodies shifted with the seasons.

Ptolemy on Astrology

What are the origins of the **horoscope**?

Today's method for evaluating astrological aspects was developed over the ages by incorporating ideas from earlier systems. Perhaps the most influential additions to Western astrology came from Greco-Roman astronomer and mathematician Claudius Ptolemy. Besides his astronomical model of the solar system in geocentric theory, Ptolemy also combined the earliest forms of Babylonian and Egyptian decanate astrology to form horoscopic astrology. In the book *Tetrabiblos*, Ptolemy relays the fundamental principles of the earlier systems of astrology with various borrowed concepts. At this point in history, these additions devised an astrological system for the individual nativity, **natal astrology**, and for the general conditions of mankind, **mundane astrology**.

In the ancient world, natal astrology predicted the effects of cosmic influences on an individual human. The astrologer estimated the fortune of a person by weighing the influences and aspects of nativity. Ptolemy later used both the date of conception and time of birth as the most important moments in an individual's astrological nativity. Despite the current emphasis placed on the natal chart, Ptolemy actually considered the time of conception as the most influential factor rather than the moment of birth or nativity as it is in modern times. In the days of Ptolemy, the **horoscope** was the term used to describe the **rising sign** or the first degree on the horizon at birth. Today, this rising sign in the east initiates the twelve astrological houses.

How did early **mundane astrology** work?

On a wider scale, astrology was used to predict the general conditions of weather patterns and planting seasons for the ancients. For this type of **mundane astrology**, the exact location — especially in terms of latitude — was essential in estimating the effects of the cosmic influences on human affairs. Throughout the year, the Sun appears to traverse between the Tropic of Cancer and Tropic of Capricorn due to Earth's axial tilt. For this reason, the Sun can be spotted directly above specific positions of latitude between the tropics throughout the year.

In terms of the celestial bodies influence over weather, the Sun and Moon were key factors. Ptolemy considered aspects of the Sun to be associated with a heating effect, while aspects of the Moon indicated a moistening effect. The principle behind this phenomenon is derived from the observed lunar phases of the Moon pulling on the ocean's tides.

Astrology in Navigation

Why did the ancients name the stars?

The stars proved the most useful tool in the early days of navigation. It was during the nights of wandering beneath the stars that the ancients developed celestial folklore connected with fixed constellations. There was no compass, only the light of the North Star to point our ancestors in the right direction; thus the stars were used as reference points like directions on a compass to guide the way on a long journey.

In navigation, a basic understanding of astronomy and astrological star-lore was essential, since the constellations that rise and fall each night change over the course of a year. This shifting of the night sky is caused by the tilt and wobble of the Earth, when the angle of the Earth dips up and down to focus the zodiac belt and celestial bodies over the latitudes between the **Tropic of Cancer and Capricorn** each year. It comes as no surprise that the location of the zodiac belt between the tropics is highly important in navigation, since the winds and tides circulate clockwise north of the equator and counter-clockwise south of the equator. When the celestial bodies hover above certain latitudes throughout the year, this motion prompts the return of storm seasons and seasonal patterns.

We see the visual effects of this phenomenon here on Earth, as the constellations that dominate the night sky shift with the seasons. With these shifting seasons, the change in weather patterns becomes associated with that particular zodiac constellation. Over time, the **ephemeris** table of planetary transits was documented in some of the oldest cuneiform records, and these tables were eventually published in later almanacs to track the celestial bodies for sailing and navigation.

How do **astrological aspects** have an effect on sailing the seas?

In early astrology, Ptolemy states that sailing conditions were derived from the influence of aspects between the Sun and the Moon. In particular, the seas are influenced when the Moon is full, quarter, or in its darkest phase at new moon.

Full & New Moon

As modern science tells us, a **full moon** indicates that the Moon is located opposite the Sun in relation to the Earth. In astrology, this phenomenon is called an **opposition**. On the full moon, the effects of this synchronicity between the Sun and the Moon pulls like a magnet on the Earth's oceans and rivers to create what is called a Spring Tide.

In the same way, the **new moon** or **conjunction** also creates a Spring Tide when both the Sun and Moon occupy the same location in the sky in relation to the Earth. In between each period of Spring Tide, there is a period of half-tide or Neap Tide.

Quarter Phase

Neap Tides occur when the Moon is at the **quarter phase**. Therefore, the effects of Neap Tide can be observed when the Moon forms a **square** astrological aspect in relation to the Sun.

It is suggested that Spring Tides create a recipe for the perfect storm when the Moon is found nearest to the Earth along its elliptical orbit. These tides stressed by the closeness of the Moon are called Perigean-Spring Tides. During Perigean-Spring Tides, storms on land are more likely to cause flooding due to the effects of this extreme high tide.

The Classical Planets

How do we structure our lives around the **classical planets**?

The Greek pantheon of antiquity was comprised of many deities that reflect the names of the seven classical planets. Perhaps one the most well-known Greek deities is Zeus (the king of the gods) who possessed the power of thunder and his weapon, a bolt of lightning. Today, we replace the name Zeus with the Latinized version Jupiter just like the Romans did before us, though both Zeus and Jupiter are Greek and Roman reflections of the same deity.

As we name off the seven days of the week, it does not often occur to us that each day was named for a deity once worshipped in the ancient world. When the seven-day week was adopted by the Romans with the Julian calendar, the names of the seven classical planets were the same names used in the pantheons of antiquity. Only we have replaced these Greek versions with varying forms of Latin rooted versions or the names of parallel deities in our modern languages. In English, the Latin forms of the classical planets resemble the Old English parallel of their Roman counterparts.

Naming the seven days of the week after the planets was likely derived from the perfect match with the number of seven classical planets. In the ancient past, each hour of the twenty-four hour day was ruled by a planet, and the first hour of each day was named the ruler of that day. The ancients ordered the hours by starting with the slowest traversing celestial body and

Modern	Greek	Roman	Babylonian
Sun	Helios	Sôl	Shamash
Moon	Selenê	Luna	Sin
Mars	Ares	Mars	Nergal
Mercury	Hermes	Mercurius	Nebo
Jupiter	Zeus	Iuppiter	Marduk
Venus	Aphroditê	Venus	Ishtar
Saturn	Kronos	Saturnus	Ninib

ending with the fastest — Saturn, Jupiter, Mars, the Sun, Venus, Mercury, and the Moon. The ancient day started with Saturn, and this slowest planet also ruled over the 1st, 8th, 15th, and 22nd hours. Such that the second day of the week belonged to the Sun, also known as the 25th hour.

What is the significance of the seven day week?

It seems odd that the ancients began splitting the week into periods of seven days, but in fact, the seven day cycle is one that subtly exists within the human body's biological rhythm. Modern chronobiology has revealed that small blood pressure and heartbeat variations can be traced back to a weekly cycle. This difference in periodic changes is also reflected in the body's response to infection, and the rejection of an organ after transplant is known to peak in intervals of a week.

The seven day week coincides with the four peak phases of the Moon — full moon, first quarter, new moon, and third quarter. It seems with the seven day week, we humans are on the right track.

Astrology through the Ages

English	Latin	Italian	Anglo-Saxon
Sunday	Dies Sōlis	domenica	Sun's Day
Monday	Dies Lūnae	lunedì	Moon's Day
Tuesday	Dies Martis	martedì	Tiw's Day
Wednesday	Dies Mercurii	mercoledì	Woden's Day
Thursday	Dies Jovis	giovedì	Thor's Day
Friday	Dies Veneris	venerdì	Frigg's Day
Saturday	Dies Saturnī	sabato	Seterne's Day

How did the ancient astrological systems work?

Babylonian Astrology

Some of the earliest astrological systems date back to the Fertile Crescent in Mesopotamia. It was in the ancient Near-East that the earliest astronomical records were written in cuneiform. A collection of constellations and stars can be found outlined in the *Mulapin* of ancient Babylon, and some of these star patterns we continue to use today.

One of the oldest discovered records documenting the astrological positions is known as the *Venus Tablet of King Ammizaduga* or *Tablet 63* of the wider collection named *Enuma Anu Enlil* — an old Babylonian text and collection of records that date as early as the 17th Century BCE. The ancient Babylonians were also the first astronomers to split the sky into 360 degrees and assign each hour one 24th of a day.

The **ephemeris** or astrological table was first created by the Babylonian astronomers in order to perform electional astrology or the branch that seeks to interpret the cosmic conditions to plan for events to come. With these 'celestial omens' the conditions of the future were weighed for the general populous and for use in state affairs; thus the Babylonians helped to develop an early system of **mundane astrology** by calculating the future positions of the celestial bodies and considering these influences to predict weather conditions, outcomes in political decision-making, or fortune on the battlefield.

The Chaldeans built the early astrological system by incorporating the idea of **triplicities** or that which is now referred to as the four sets of three zodiac found in each element. In modern astrology, the names Fire, Earth, Air, and Water give each of the early triplicities an elemental quality. This specialized Chaldean system was utilized by the state.

> "The rest which relates to astrology, and the effects produced upon human life by the twelve signs, the five planets, the sun and the moon, must be left to the discussions of the Chaldeans, whose profession it is to cast nativities, and by means of the configurations of the stars to explain the past and the future."
>
> —Marcus Vitruvius Pollio, *De architectura*

Egyptian Astrology

A record of the Egyptian sky was once outlined by the ceiling of the Dendera Zodiac in the Temple of Hathor, and this model of the constellations displays the 36 decans of the ancient Egyptian calendar.

The **decanic astrology** system was used by the ancient Egyptian astronomers as far back as 2000 BCE. Before Ptolemy combined aspects of the Babylonian and Egyptian systems with his own views to create horoscopic astrology, the Egyptians interpreted the effects of cosmic influences by assigning planetary rulership over the signs and houses. The purpose behind this practice was borrowed from the idea that some planets had a greater influence when placed in certain signs. There were strengthening positions known as **exaltation** or promotion to a dignity when a planet enters its place of **rulership**. On the other hand, detrimental aspects occur when a planet enters a sign opposite its place of rulership. In an opposite place of rulership a planet is said to be in a position of weakness or debility, also known as **fall** in modern astrology. This same practice of rulership and exaltation was also used by the Babylonian and Chaldean astrologers.

The early astrological houses were described as decans. Every zodiac sign was split into three arcs of 10 degrees named the first, second, and third decans. Each decan was ruled by a planet to make 36 decans in total. For some Egyptian astrologers, the first decan elemental quality and planetary equivalent ruled the zodiac sign, while the second and third decans took on the qualities of the respective planetary rulers of the two remaining signs in each **elemental triplicity**. For example, the zodiac sign Aries of the fire triplicity was ruled by the planet Mars in the first decanate, Leo or the Sun as the second decanate, and Sagittarius or Jupiter as the third decante to complete 30 degrees.

In ancient Egypt, astrology was not only utilized to weigh the cosmic influences on future events, but it had also been developed for medicinal use. Ptolemy mentions that the Egyptian astrologers had integrated the effects of the cosmic influence into medical practice. This early system of iatromathematics belonged to the branch of **medical astrology**.

Arabic Astrology

In the scorching Arabian Desert, merchants with camel caravans often traveled by night. Knowledge of the constellations was essential in navigating the desert with success. For this reason, both astronomy and astrology were widely common in the Arabic world. Though the earliest origins of the Arabic Parts is uncertain, it is clear that these invisible aspects were held in high esteem by various astrologers from antiquity up to the medieval Islamic period.

The **Arabic Parts**, also named 'lots', are a series of

mathematical aspects derived by adding or subtracting the degree of a celestial body with an aspect such as the ascendant. For example, the most commonly used Arabic Part in modern Western astrology is perhaps the Part of Fortune, also known as **Fortuna**. Many know Fortuna as the Part of the Moon.

Part of Fortune

The **Part of Fortune** or Fortuna is an invisible astrological aspect calculated by adding the degree of the Moon to the ascendant (0 degree) and subtracting the degree of the Sun for those born during the daytime. For night births the Sun is added to the ascendant and the Moon subtracted. In other words, Fortuna can be found for someone born in the daytime by rolling back the natal wheel so that the Sun is aligned on the ascendant at zero degrees. At this point, Fortuna would be the location of the Moon. For anyone born at sunrise, Fortuna is just the Moon.

Modern Astrology

By the 16th Century, the validity of astrology was called into question with the discovery of Nicholaus Copernicus' *De revolutionibus orbium coelestium* — an outline of **heliocentricism** that based the Sun at the center of the solar system. Early astrological aspects like those of Ptolemy calculated the influence of the celestial bodies using the geocentric model with the Earth stationary at the center of the universe. It was at this point in time that astrology lost its grounds among scholars. However, the reaction is less fitting than simply shifting the astrological model to a heliocentric perspective.

It's unfortunate to think that the heliocentric model was actually suggested thousands of years before Copernicus brought it into fruition. **Aristarchus of Samos**, a Greek astronomer who lived during the 3rd Century BCE, proposed the heliocentric model. Aristarchus is considered to be one of the last Ionian scientists.

> "But Aristarchus has brought out a book consisting of certain hypotheses, wherein it appears, as a consequence of the assumptions made, that the universe is many times greater than the 'universe' just mentioned. His hypotheses are that the fixed stars and the Sun remain unmoved, that the Earth revolves about the Sun on the circumference of a circle, the Sun lying in the middle of the Floor, and that the sphere of the fixed stars, situated about the same center as the Sun, is so great that the circle in which he supposes the Earth to revolve bears such a proportion to the distance of the fixed stars as the center of the sphere bears to its surface."
>
> —Archimedes, *The Sand-Reckoner*

These ideas were shared by the Hellenistic astronomer Seleucus and were initially imagined by the Pythagorean and Pre-Socratic philosopher, **Philolaus of Croton**. It was Philolaus, who proposed that the universe is composed of the harmony between the 'limiting and the limitless'.

v. Celestial Folklore

The Mystery of Ophiuchus & Orion

What are the origins of the constellations **Ophiuchus** and **Orion**?

    In ancient Greek mythology, the celestial figures Ophiuchus and Orion once crossed paths. Orion was the hunting partner of Artemis or Goddess of the Hunt. When Gaia overheard Orion boast to Artemis that there was no animal he could not slay, the goddess was angered at his arrogance. The demise of the Great Huntsman **Orion** was ordered by Gaia — Goddess of the Earth. The goddess sent a giant **Scorpion**, and after a vigorous battle with the beast, Orion died by the poison of its sting. Artemis pleaded with Zeus that Orion be placed among the stars. In the end, Orion and the Scorpion were separated at opposite ends of the zodiac. And as the Scorpion rises in the east, Orion dies and sets in the west.

    The myth continues on past Orion's death. Asclepius, the legendary healer, was able to extract the poison and revive Orion. After a complaint from the gods that Asclepius had defied natural order in raising the dead, Asclepius was struck down by the thunderbolt of Zeus. Impressed by the healing gifts of Asclepius, Zeus dedicated the constellation of **Ophiuchus** to this Great Healer. Every year upon the death of the Great Healer represented by Ophiuchus, the appearance of Orion is seen once again on the eastern horizon.

If we imagine both the signs of Orion and Ophiuchus placed at opposite ends of the sky in the zodiac belt — at a 180 degree separation — it is clear that the death of Orion upon the sight of the Scorpion is nothing more than an allegorical tale of this named region as it descends below the visible horizon for half the year. **Ophiuchus** is resurrected in the sky each spring and becomes present for the remaining half of the time. Upon the rise of **Orion** in the fall, Ophiuchus is struck down once again.

The Chinese Zodiac

What is the difference between Eastern and Western astrology?

The basis of Chinese astrology is more focused on nature than the mythology behind Western astrology. One of the twelve zodiac signs covers the course of an entire year. The Chinese zodiac are used to characterize the years, and each of the twelve Chinese zodiac signs is an animal, domestic or wild, as indicated by the qualities yin and yang, respectively.

In contrast to Western astrology, a new zodiac sign initiates the entrance of the year with the lunar New Year. This happens on the second **new moon** following the winter solstice, since the **Chinese calendar** tracks both the lunar and solar calendar cycles. The Chinese New Year usually falls at the end of January or early February of the Gregorian calendar.

In addition, an elemental quality of traditional **Wu Xing** — Wood, Fire, Earth, Metal, and Water — is assigned every two years and an energy quality of Tao, yang or yin, every other year. This sixty year cycle combines animal zodiac sign, element, and energy quality to define unique conditions for the annual turn of events to come. The last cycle began in the year 1984 with the 'Yang Wood Rat'. In the next year it was followed by the 'Yin Wood Ox'. Each annual Chinese zodiac also hints at the nature of a person's luck for a particular year. The Taoists believed it was futile to fight or resist a year of bad luck. One must only be aware that these conditions are temporary and will pass over the course of time.

Where did the Chinese zodiac originate?

Like all great things, the **Chinese zodiac** were invented in a story. In Taoist tradition, various versions of the great race between the animal zodiac signs have been told since ancient times, though many of the lessons and characteristics of the zodiac remain the same.

The Great Race

Long ago in the land of China, the Jade Emperor of the heavens decided there must be a way for mankind to track the passing of time. A calendar was to be constructed. The Jade Emperor called upon Rat to gather the animals together for a contest, so that he could name the years. The contest was to be a swimming race across the river from bank to bank, and each year of the calendar would be named in the order the animals finished. Rat returned to inform the kingdom of the Jade Emperor's plans for the great race. Rat also knew he must win.

On the day of the race, the Rat stood alongside good friend Cat at the river bank. Both knew they were equally the worst swimmers. The clever Cat noticed the swiftness of the river current and urged the Rat to take action. So, the Cat and Rat scouted out the strong and sturdy Ox, whose head — they were sure — would breach the water's surface. The cunning **Rat** flattered the Ox and asked if he and Cat could get a lift across.

"Of course," the kind **Ox** was easily convinced and agreed to let them up. Cat and Rat stepped onto Ox's back above the waves of the river current. They were both pleased to see Ox steadily take the lead.

Rat then realized he would have to share first place. As they neared the other side of the river bank, Rat insisted Cat go first. When Cat leapt across, Rat quickly pounced atop her head and took first place. Ox slowly emerged from the water, satisfied with second place. Cat was nowhere to be found.

The Jade Emperor was pleased at their arrival and named the first zodiac sign after the Rat and the second after the Ox. Soon they saw Tiger appear in the distance, challenging the flow of the river. They watched as brave **Tiger** fought ferocious against the current, until finally he reached land. As Tiger climbed up the river bank, the Jade Emperor praised his fortitude and named him the third zodiac sign.

Next, they spotted Rabbit, as he floated near the bank atop a log. The Jade Emperor was surprised at the sight. Gentle **Rabbit** explained how he had hopped across step stones, until he had come to a stop at the log. At this point, Rabbit was sure his luck had run out. He waited there, when a sudden gust sent the log sailing toward the finish. The Jade Emperor celebrated this news and named Rabbit the fourth zodiac sign.

Just then, Dragon dove from the sky and landed with grace beside them on the river bank. When the Jade Emperor questioned.

"You only just arrived, yet you can both swim and fly?" The diligent **Dragon** replied that the villagers were in need of water, so he took a detour to make it rain. On the way back, he saw Rabbit stranded on the log, so Dragon blew a breeze to float him across. The Jade Emperor applauded Dragon and assigned him as the fifth zodiac sign.

Horse was then seen trudging through the water. When the Jade Emperor heard the mighty **Horse** hooves on land, he turned to grant sixth place. But at that moment, Horse reared back — spooked at the appearance of the sly **Snake** who slithered down his leg. Snake took the sixth zodiac sign and Horse was given the seventh.

The Jade Emperor soon saw a raft floating Goat, Monkey, and Rooster across the water. When the raft had reached the river bank, the amused **Monkey** told the Jade Emperor how he had tied the logs that Goat pushed together with the vines Rooster found. The thoughtful **Goat** shoved the raft off land and Monkey paddled. The resourceful **Rooster** helped steer the wind with his wings, until they finally made it across. The Jade Emperor smiled, for they had worked together, and granted Goat the eight zodiac sign, Monkey the ninth sign, and Rooster the tenth.

When Dog was spotted splashing up the river, The Jade Emperor called out.

"You're late for one of our best swimmers!" The loyal **Dog** told the Jade Emperor that he was so impressed by the sparkling clean water that he stopped to take a bath, and so, the Jade Emperor named Dog the eleventh zodiac sign.

Alas, there was only one spot left and the Jade Emperor waited for the last animal to emerge. The Pig grunted as he swam up out of the river. The Jade Emperor wondered what took him so long, and the leisurely **Pig** announced that he was so excited for the race that he rejoiced with a feast. It made him so full that he stopped for a nap before crossing the river. The Jade Emperor was happy to give the Pig the twelfth and last zodiac sign.

As everyone turned to leave satisfied with all twelve signs, the Cat came into view. She dragged her soggy paws up onto the shore, as the Jade Emperor shook his head.

"Sorry Cat, but there are no more years left." The Cat had not made it in time and has since cursed the Rat — for she had been tricked.

Frames of Modern Thought

How does modern astrology make use of allegory?

In modern Western astrology, the celestial bodies are used as a framework to understand the subtleties of the human mind.

The planets help to describe the nature of what is considered conscious and unconscious by classifying each planet as an extension of these realms within the world of thought. This connection is made by characterizing the behavior of the rapid movement of the inner planets versus the steady extended orbital period of the outer planets along with each planet's proximity to the Sun. The inner planets represent extensions of the conscious mind, while the outer planets are of the unconscious realm.

The unveiling of the unconscious began with Friedrich Schelling in the 18th Century. It was at this time that 'unconsciousness' was written into literature, psychology, and philosophy to describe instinctive urges unbeknownst to the awareness of the conscious mind. Thoughts within the realm of the unconscious often go undetected, though this does not mean they are not ever-present within the conscious reality. It was Pierre Janet who used the term 'subconscious' to refer to those past experiences in memory that inadvertently influence present responses and attitudes. In more recent times, the idea of the unconscious mind became the backbone of Sigmund Freud's psychoanalytic theory.

It seems ironic that the theoretical development of the unconscious mind took shape around the same time that the outer planets were discovered. Since the planets Uranus found in 1781 and Neptune later in 1846 are associated with the deepest layers of the unconscious. Perhaps the connection drawn between these two influences is nothing more than a continuation of the allegory between the celestial bodies and archetypal astrological symbols in the realm of psychology.

The inner celestial bodies such as Mercury, Venus, and the Moon are considered to be the planets of the conscious mind. If we understand the **Sun** to be the ego, then these inner planets belong to our conscious thoughts and thence influence the ego or outward expression of self. These inner planetary thoughts are often personal and considered a product of the immediate conscious mind — nearest the ego. Inner planetary influences also express themselves directly through the ego. **Mercury** is our realm of intellect and personal faculties of cognitive reasoning. It is closest to the ego and prompts all forms of communication.

Venus holds our realm of morality and helps the ego attract and align our value system with the outside world. The **Moon** is tied to our realm of emotions which provoke conscious responses in the ego. The Moon is nearest to the Earth — the true self where we are grounded. In this way, the Moon helps maintain balance between the ego and the true self through emotional expression. The one remaining inner planet bridges the gap between the conscious and unconscious with a powerful notion — desire. **Mars** the realm of desire holds the deepest responses exhibited within the conscious mind that often induce involuntary reactions or immediate action.

Past this point, the outer planetary influences do not directly affect the ego or our outer role in reality, rather the outer planets can be considered an unconscious foundation from which we draw conscious responses. **Jupiter** refers to our realm of social philosophy that influences the manner in which we build relationships and expand beyond ourselves in the outer world. Also within the most immediate layers of the unconscious exists Saturn. It is from **Saturn** our realm of social responsibility that we draw our personal boundaries and adapt to the structural norms of society.

Deep within the unconscious, insatiable urges arise with such subtlety that each minor revision in the larger scheme of total thought goes unnoticed. Like the planets in the far outer reaches of the solar system, unconscious influences are just as elusive in nature as the world inside our dreams, until the planet Uranus appears to awaken us with a higher sense of self. **Uranus** influences our realm of personal awareness from which we define our unique quality as an individual and find freedom from society's structural limitations. And hidden beneath the layers of conscious and unconscious is the buried framework of our own ideology found in Neptune. **Neptune** our realm of global awareness has the power to shake our own world view. Since we naturally use what is unconscious as a guide for conscious thought, disturbances deep within the unconscious ripple heavy like a tide into the conscious reality. Therefore, it is with Neptune that we experience the dissolution of obsolete social structures in exchange for collective wisdom.

In recent years, Pluto finds itself demoted from planetary status, though it remains quite useful as the final planetary figure. Pluto is a fantastic generation indicator. Each quarter-millennium cycle of Pluto gives us insight into one of the most important factors — era of personhood. Time does not define our thoughts. However, it does have an effect on our immediate surroundings and quality of life; thus **Pluto** is our connection with time and portrays the unique social situation into which we are born.

> "No one can flatter himself that he is immune to the spirit of his own epoch or even that he possesses a full understanding of it. Irrespective of our conscious convictions, each one of us, without exception, being a particle of the general mass, is somewhere attached to, colored by, or even undermined by the spirit which goes through the mass. Freedom stretches only as far as the limits of our consciousness."
>
> —Carl Jung,
> *Psychological Reflections*

Celestial Folklore

VI. Astrological Symbols of Ancient Civilization

Tao of the Universe

What is meant by yin and yang in ancient Chinese philosophy?

In Chinese astrology and Eastern philosophy, the **Tao** concepts of yin and yang name the two natural states that together characterize the basic essence of existence. The idea in mind is to conceptualize a frame of universal wisdom that applies to reality in its entirety. In practice, the Taoist thinkers must remove themselves from thought in the personal perspective — motivated by the ego — and seek a universal and all-encompassing point of reference, one that satisfies the whole of eternity.

First to understand yang, it is easiest to classify its effect with what is often considered the masculine quality. **Yang** is the positive, the assertive, and rational. It is action. On the other side, yin is associated with the female quality. **Yin** is the negative, the passive and intuitive. It is inaction. These two manners of being, both yin and yang, carry the seed of one another to maintain a constant state of equilibrium. One cannot exist in harmony without the balance from the other.

In Tao, the interactions between yin and yang can be applied to the philosophies of nature and life. Because of this, all things in the ancient Eastern philosophy of Tao are considered either yin or yang. Each year in **Chinese astrology** is classified with an energy quality of yang or yin to reveal future conditions and the nature of events to come. Yang is also commonly used to express the character of the day, light, and the vitality of the Sun and yin, the night, darkness, and the mystery of the Moon.

Where does astrology fit into the wider concept of Tao?

In the modern era, the implications of astrology have been separated from the scientific investigation of astronomy. During the days of Ptolemy, astronomy and astrology were two sides to the same coin. Now, the only information deemed useful on the subject of the cosmos is that which can be observed or immediately rationalized with evidence collected through scientific method. The empirical exactitude of **astronomical observation** thus triumphs over the apparent whimsical quality of **astrological interpretation**. Though, it seems irrational to rule out any interpretation of a subject in which — with current scientific methods — we have yet to fully understand as a rational phenomenon; such is the nature of chaos.

When we take a closer look at astronomy or science in general, it is important to note that the process of scientific method relies upon human sensory perception and observation. After performing an experiment and collecting evidence through the senses, we then apply common logic, scientific law, and theory to deduce significance and predict future outcomes. Throughout the experiment, we do not notice how the process of scientific method constructs a fixed and limited viewpoint, and the further we delve in the scientific process of investigation, the narrower the view and more specialized the experiment becomes.

There is certainly a need for the rational. Scientific method in the science of astronomy is a rational process. It is built from logic and reason and is considered a **positive** mode of philosophical argument in that it utilizes fixed reference frames. In this way, **astronomical observation** is the positive or **yang** expression of the universe in cosmic order. With it, we operate within the bounds of systematic construction. Without a framework of practice or paradigm of thought to build upon, science is meaningless.

In science, laws are needed to simulate reality and create initial concepts. The paradoxical need to define the words that write the sentences in which phrase the laws that convey the concept in which portrays the universal principle and meaning in science must continuously be defined to no definite ends. This problem was recognized by the early Taoists. And after all this speculation, we lose sight of the purpose of initial inquiry and its practical application to the authentic reality.

Eventually, we wind up down such a narrowed and specified path of investigation into the universe, life, and the nature of order within the greater world of chaos that we forget to take a step back and view all aspects of reality working together in harmony. Can we ever hope to understand how everything works as a whole, if we fail to even connect each part in a meaningful way?

In the words of **Albert Einstein**,

> "Imagination is more important than knowledge. For knowledge is limited, whereas imagination embraces the entire world, stimulating progress, giving birth to evolution. It is, strictly speaking, a real factor in scientific research."

Rational knowledge must be accompanied by possibility. For in reality, logic is not fixed in time and relies solely upon circumstance. On the other side, astrology provides a medium for projecting possibilities. To infer about the future is to expand one's personal awareness with respect to time. The practice of astrology allows us to better understand the nature of chaos. For in chaos, we are not operating within a fixed system, and there are numerous outcomes for just one process. With scientific method, we manipulate the outcome to serve an observational purpose, though chaos is not contained to fixed outcomes. In the chaos that defines our universe, all probable possibilities exist.

The negative or **yin** has no need for a framework of operation. In fact, the process of yin involves ridding oneself of a fixed viewpoint to explore the implications of chaos from a universal perspective — aside from the personal viewpoint of the ego. The negative makes use of imagination and intuition to expand the plane of view, so that the initial inference encompasses all possibilities. In this way, **astrological interpretation** is the negative or **yin** expression of the universe in cosmic possibility. The yin aspect of scientific investigation is associated with theory. With it, we explore what it could be by distinguishing what it is known to be not.

The **negative** is not directly observed, but it is shaped through unconscious experience over the course of time, much like the subtle wisdom hidden beneath the elaborate scheme of imagery, themes, and exposition in a classic novel. If portrayed any other way, the message would remain unclear. For in this case, the complexity of the concept is made simpler through the intricate unveiling of an abstract plot, then in the midst of the climax and final resolution 'a-ha!' it all makes perfect sense. After much elaboration and expansion, we experience a moment of discovery — an intuitive insight in which we instantly understand its contextual significance.

The yin classification of chaos also allows us to infer into those processes of existence in which the cause cannot be observed in the effect. In the case of human behavior, the cause is often assigned to a thought, though a thought cannot be observed and fully understood by the action in which it provokes; for the action itself can have various sources based in multiple thoughts. Thus the presence of **yin** and **yang**, or the **negative** and **positive** approach to investigation are both needed in order to create a balanced process.

It is unfortunate to note that in recent times, the rise of

empirical exactitude has managed to suppress the notion of possibility to the point that we have thrown out the negative altogether, and since the negative or yin is the passive quality of inaction, the restless positive or yang overwhelms the stage with constant activity. With excess yang, the evidence becomes dominated by what is perceived by the senses — that which binds us in the third dimension, the realm where only freeze frame of a process is held in view, but it is clear now that we do not emulate chaos by isolating a variable and modifying outcomes. In fact, in this limiting process, we are demonstrating quite the opposite.

If we ignore the subtleties that make up the whole, we have yet to construct a framework that satisfies the entire picture. In this case, we cannot assume that anything we have discovered is sound, since we have not yet come to understand what exactly it is we are asking. Without an understanding of the question being asked, we cannot hope to fathom the nature of the thing in which we do not know.

> "Without stirring abroad,
> One can know the whole world;
> Without looking out of the window
> One can see the way of heaven.
> The further one goes
> The less one knows."
> —Laozi

Nativity in the Records

How did the people of early civilization use astrology in record keeping?

Throughout ancient history, the stars and planets have played a key role in religious ritual and practices of seasonal tradition. Some of the earliest religions born of the Fertile Crescent tracked astrological aspects in the sky and calculated the **ephemeris** to wage future events against celestial omens. Deeper into the branch of divination the ancient priests applied the foresight of celestial phenomena to the formation of prophecy — the idea that destiny must be written in the stars.

In the ancient religion of **Zoroastrianism**, the priests or Magi placed importance on astrology among other practices of esoteric wisdom. The **Magi** were often invited into the courts of kings to draw up horoscopes and predict the fate of newborn princes. This practice is written by the poet Abolqasem Ferdowsi inside *The Persian Book of Kings* or *Shahnameh* in an attempt to preserve this ancient Persian religion. This national epic is a poetic masterpiece that revisits the earliest Persian histories and cultural practices up to the 7th Century CE. Within the book *Bizhan and Manizheh*, the night is described by the wandering stars that fail to rise and the slender crescent moon that graces the evening sky.

> A night as black as coal bedaubed with pitch
>
> A night of ebony, a night on which,
>
> Mars, Mercury, and Saturn would not rise.
>
> Even the moon seemed fearful of the skies:
>
> Her face was three-fourths dimmed, and all the night
>
> Looked gray and dusty in her pallid light.

This verse is not only useful because it tells us the phase of the moon, but it also provides insight into a particular date given the positioning of the planets below the visible horizon. With this information, we can also deduce the season by which planets were above and so on to map the past with accuracy simply by tracing the planetary positions in the sky. Within the story *The Birth of Yazdegerd's Son*, the king's son Bahram is born.

> "Then, at the beginning of the eighth year of his reign, at the spring equinox, a son was born to him

under an auspicious star."

Both Persian and Indian astrologers were summoned, and they made use of the Greek ephemeris to unveil the fortune and fate of the new prince. The astrologers declared, "the heavens look kindly on this baby" and he will be, "a great and glorious king." Then sages were sent from far and wide to mentor Bahram so that, "the world will rejoice in his rule."

In another account within *The Reign of Hormozd*, the Emperor of China travels with his five daughters to meet the Persian King. The king favors the empress's daughter whose future is cast by the learned counsellors.

> "A child like a raging lion will be born from this girl and the Persian king; tall and strong-armed, in bravery like a lion, and in generosity like a rain cloud."

The Chinese Emperor is so pleased upon hearing her prophetic fate that he leaves his most favored daughter to marry the Persian King. The importance of astrology in Zoroastrian beliefs in the ancient civilizations of the Near-East is highlighted in *Shahnameh* with the significance tied to the casting of nativities and recording of significant astrological aspects.

The Magi also fashioned prophecy from rare familiarities such as **Great Conjunctions**, which were deemed amongst the most powerful aspects between celestial bodies. This very practice is demonstrated in *The Visit of the Wise Men* written within the book of *Matthew* in the Bible:

> "In the time of King Herod, after Jesus was born in Bethlehem of Judea, wise men from the East came to Jerusalem, asking, "Where is the child who has been born king of the Jews? For we observed his star at its rising, and have come to pay him homage."

The use of "wise men" refers to the **Magi** sages — those astrologers who had observed a bright star rising on the eastern horizon. The bright star was brought to the attention of King Herod, who called upon the Magi to calculate, "the exact time when the star had appeared." Then the Magi were sent to follow this great star, the Star of Bethlehem, to search for the child born beneath it:

> "...and there, ahead of them, went the star that they had seen at its rising, until it stopped over the place where the child was."

The tale refers to a significant astrological aspect rising, until it reaches the point of zenith. Then the aspect stops and begins to fall. At this point, the great star formed by its aspect descends toward the western horizon, and sets like the Sun. In early astrology, true 'noon' was considered the point in which a transiting aspect reaches its **zenith** or most powerful position in the sky on any given day.

After the Magi calculated the zenith of this **astrological aspect**, they used this measure in time to map the physical position on Earth with the latitude located directly below the aspect at its moment of peak influence. Since this latitude must lie on the Sun's path between the Tropic of Cancer and Tropic of Capricorn, the season becomes a great indicator of where the place-marker beneath the astrological aspect must be; thus they set off for this location for the child of prophecy, blessed by the star's power.

The Star of Bethlehem is often speculated to have been the observation of a **Great Conjunction** involving the outer planets Jupiter and Saturn in addition to a possible triple conjunction with Mars. It may have also simply signified the shape of the planets on the natal chart in a "Star of Bethlehem" shape. Perhaps the long orbital times of the outer planets stress the significance of such an aspect, since these transits rarely occur with such precision over the course of many years.

In addition, the story tells that the Magi watched the rise and fall of this "star" or transiting **astrological aspect** last for half the day or at least up to the moment it reached the point of zenith. If the star was based upon the combination of inner planets, the aspect would not hold long enough for such an observation; for the fleeting aspects of the inner planets are too quick to separate. In this case, the extraordinarily precise alignment or **Great Conjunction** of Jupiter, Saturn, and possible other planets is considered to have created the illusion of a brilliant star.

The ancient Greek astronomers paid close attention to each Great Conjunction and watched the planets Jupiter and Saturn align every 20 years to complete about 240 years in each **elemental triplicity** — the Fire, Earth, Air, and Water signs. The entrance of a new triplicity brought with it a dynastic shift. It was said that the first three conjunctions within each triplicity warned of destruction by conflagration and the last by flood.

In China, the **Great Conjunction** was tracked by the ancient astronomers and organized into the 60 year calendar. This number tracks the Jupiter-Saturn conjunctions in threes per calendar cycle. The Dogon people in Africa also made use of the 60 year cycle with each 20 year period to represent an important milestone to the next stage in life.

Elemental & Planetary Symbolism

What are the origins of the **Wu Xing** elements in astrology?

The five elements of **Wu Xing** are much like the yin and yang of Tao in that they act together to form a complete and balanced process in cycles. These elements were used in ancient China to symbolize the nature of each calendar year. The elemental cycles display processes of generation, restriction, and destruction. In the order Water, Wood, Fire, Earth, and Metal, the elements form the **creative cycle** depicted as a pentagon.

Water nourishes the **Wood** that feeds the **Fire** that results in ash to enrich the **Earth** that forms the **Metal** that enhances the Water with minerals.

In the order Water, Fire, Metal, Wood, and Earth the elements form the **restrictive cycle** depicted as a pentagram. The purpose of the restrictive cycle is to counter the excess creation and imbalance between elements through control or restraint.

Water extinguishes the **Fire** that melts the **Metal** that molds the tool to sever the **Wood** that parts the **Earth** that catches the Water in its banks.

The creative cycle of Wu Xing is the one used to mark the 60 year cycle in Chinese astrology. Each elemental quality can be determined by the last digit number of any given year:

Metal is zero and one

Water is two and three

Wood is four and five

Fire is six and seven

Earth is eight and nine

How was the pentagram used by Western and Mesoamerican astrologers?

The pentagram often appeared in various ancient systems of symbolism. The five pointed star is used in Hellenistic astrology to symbolize the apparent path of the planet Venus. The five points mark a process of Venus known as the retrograde cycle. Once every eight years, Venus completes a pentagram shape in the sky distinguished by its five retrograde points. The illusion of this pentagram is caused by the apparent motion of retrograde. During the retrograde period, Earth and Venus reach a point of conjunction in relation to the Sun, and Earth overtakes the position of Venus due to its shorter orbital path. Each time Venus turns retrograde, it has reached its closest position to Earth. Venus retrograde happens once over the course of 20 months and lasts for an average period of 40 days.

Venus naturally adheres to the five-tipped pentagram with another perfect ratio of time discovered by the Mayan astronomers. This number forms a perfect 8 to 5 ratio with the seasonal *haab* cycle of 365 days. In the Dresden Codex, Venus cycles of the **morning star** and **evening star** were traced with a pattern of 584 days. Every eight calendar years, each significant location of Venus or 'station' would be set to repeat.

The significance of each Venus 'station' is highlighted in the power of the morning and evening star. When Venus is either at morning or evening star, it has the potential to gleam with light that rivals all objects in the sky next to the Sun and the Moon. The brilliant glow of the morning and evening star is seen as a product of the retrograde cycle when an interior planet turns backward to hide behind the Sun.

Both Venus and Mercury experience morning and evening star 'stations', as each turns retrograde and corrects its path forward once again. Though the glow of a planet at the time of sunrise or sunset is but an illusion of the reflection of the Sun's rays against a sphere, as the light illuminates the planet by way of its atmosphere in contrast the backdrop of darkening skies at dawn and twilight.

> Days have passed since: but Evening-star
>
> Comes up againd and stays
>
> Just as before, spreading o'er her
>
> His clear, translucent rays.
>
> In sleep she would remember him
>
> And, as before, her whole
>
> Wish for the Master of the waves

Is clinching now her soul.

"Descend to me, mild Evening-star
Thou canst glide on a beam,
Enter my dwelling and my mind
And over my life gleam!"

—Mihai Eminescu, *Luceafărul*

Astrological Symbols of Ancient Civilization

VII. The Stars - Nature's Calendar

Stars of the Seasons

What are the origins of the Western zodiac constellations?

The development of astrology arose from early agrarian civilization, when knowledge of the seasons for sowing and harvesting was a key factor in the overall success of society; for famine, then and now, remains a very real challenge in agrarian life.

In the days of ancient Egypt, the stars were named to indicate the changes brought on by the shifting seasons. The Egyptians tracked not only the weather cycles and seasons by the stars but the length of daylight hours throughout the year. The constellations became a necessary tool to decipher events as they would unfold with the turn of the seasons. Folklore in the oral tradition brought to life the character of each constellation and star, since reading and writing were the most common skills for none but the scribes in ancient agrarian society. Thus the oral tradition of celestial folklore was contagious; for the necessity of such a time tracking device — to the farmer — was essential. In this way, astrology was both the calendar and the weatherman to the ancient farmers.

The brilliant star Sothis was given the spirit of a watchful dog by the ancient Egyptians. The rise of Sothis, the Dog Star, foretold the flood season of the Nile with the return of the 'spirit' of Isis; thus the rise of the Dog Star is its bark.

It just so happens that this effect is also enhanced by the Sun's relationship to the specific position of latitude in Egypt through the seasons, since its location is near the Tropic of Cancer where summer solstice rays are most concentrated. The Sun's traverse back toward the equator during the summer solstice caused the Nile waters to flood just after the sight of Sothis' rising on the eastern horizon. The Nile would then flood, after snow and heavy summer rain run-off from the Ethiopian-Mountains fell to the flat desert plains. It was the nutrients in these black silts flooding the desert that made civilization possible and brought rejuvenating life back to the Nile Valley.

Sothis is known to modern astronomers as Sirius, the brightest star in the sky that forms the dog constellation Canis Major. Even today the hottest weeks of summer are still **Dog Days.** The Egyptians also classified many of the original zodiac signs that we continue to use in modern astrological practice. The appearance of **the Balance** began in the ancient world to mark the constellation along the Sun's annual passage, where the hours of darkness and daylight became equal in length. The Balance has survived in modern astrology under the name Libra — the sign that once held the autumn equinox.

Following the Balance is the destruction brought on by the sting of **the Scorpion**. The death of autumn and coming of winter brings with it the reaping the final harvest. In winter, Nature loses its ability to generate life, and upon the sight of falling leaves, the seasons turn full circle, as all that has been created returns to the Earth. The long winter nights begin to fade, when finally **the Ram** (under the sign Aries) signifies the arrival of the Sun's generative heat. Then upon the entrance of **the Bull** in the sign Taurus, the Sun's creative power manifests into bountiful blooms with the buzz of springtime. When it reaches **the Lion**, all bask under the radiance of midsummer's Sun. These zodiac signs have all been versed in many ways since ancient times.

Astrology in the Almanacs

In the ancient Greek world, the text of Hesoid's *Works and Days* structures the basic rhythms behind agrarian life, making use of natural seasonal markers such as the stars and constellations. Harvest was initiated with the **heliacal rise** of the Pleiades, and the plow was to be used just after it set. Hesiod's advice extends not only to the farmer but to the sailor as well, when he warns of unfavorable winds following the disappearance of the Pleiades. The optimal time for sailing, as Hesiod suggests, is fifty days after the summer solstice. Hesiod also mentions that the **fall equinox** is the optimal time to pour wine into aging jars — an ancient wisdom still very much in use, even today.

How did the almanac help the **ephemeris** reach the farmer?

It is clear that in the past, astrology was always especially important to the farmer, so that when print was invented, the transit tables were recorded within the farmer's almanac. Agrarian societies made use of the stars and often published almanacs that were printed with weather predictions, tips for the planting season, and astronomical tables (the **ephemerides**).

In part, the almanac utilized astrology to wage farming and weather conditions against the movement of the celestial bodies with future aspects and transits found in the ephemeris. Nostradamus was perhaps the most renowned almanac maker of the Middle Ages, whose prophecies are still versed by people even today. From the ephemeris and other astrological insights, the almanac writer would draw prophecies and predictions for specific dates of the coming seasons.

It was a common indulgence of the almanac-maker to profess prophecy in these texts up until the 19th Century — at least for the almanacs published within the United States of America. Thus the **almanac** is an echo of the ancient practice of prophecy once reserved for a soothsayer, or perhaps, the oracle.

What did 'Poor Richard' have to say about astrology?

The almanacs were one way to help the farmer decipher the stars. *Poor Richard's Almanack,* written in the decades before the formation of the United States, lists the twelve zodiac and the way in which these signs were best remembered for the early farmers:

> "Gemini were originally the Kids, but called **the Twins**, as Goats more commonly bring forth two than one: These follow'd the Calves. Cancer, **the Crab**, came next, when that Kind of Fish were in Season."

According to Poor Richard, also known as Benjamin Franklin, the zodiac constellations were likely to have been named for the rural affairs of each particular month, and so, the twelve zodiac marked the events that would unfold with the seasons as they pertained to the farmer.

> "Then follows Sagittary, **the Archer**, to show the Season of Hunting; for now the Leaves being off the Trees and Bushes, and Game might be more easily seen and struck with their Arrows. **The Goat** accompanies the short Days and long Nights of Winter, to shew the Season of Mirth, Feasting and Jollity; for what can Capricorn mean, but Dancing or Cutting of Capers? At length comes Aquarius, or **the Water-bearer**, to show the Season of Snows, Rains and Floods; and lastly Pisces, or the **two Shads**, to denote the approaching Return of those Fish up the Rivers..."

Poor Richard states that, "Astrology was before Letters." This much is true. Without astrology — a way to track the seasons by the stars — the farmer would not have survived the centuries before reading and writing were common practice; for the stars can be read without the use of letters, and the oral tradition of the zodiac flourished long before the development of written word.

> "Astronomy instructs him in the points of the heavens, the laws of the celestial bodies, the equinoxes, solstices, and courses of the stars; all of which should be well understood, in the construction and proportions of clocks."
>
> —Marcus Vitruvius Pollio, *De architectura*

The Astronomical Clock

How are the stars and celestial bodies used to track time?

In the city of Prague, there exists a relic of the past that provides the most useful time-telling tool. It is known as the **Astronomical Clock** — the only one left of its kind, which continues to track the time systems of ancient civilization. Mounted to the tower of Old Town City Hall, the Astronomical Clock displays the twelve **zodiac signs** that form a simple astrolabe to track the movement of the celestial bodies across the sky. The oldest part of the astronomical clock named the Orloj dates back to the year 1410 at the time of the late Middle Ages, just before the turn of the Renaissance.

The **astrolabe** itself is an invention of classical antiquity used by one of the last great philosphers **Hypatia of Alexandria** at a time when both the Sun and Moon were tracked in relation to the Earth at the center known as **geocentric theory**. That is the very reason why the Earth is displayed at the center of the astrolabe. The Orloj was created by clockmaker Mikuláš of Kadaň with the help of Jan Sindel, a mathematics and astronomy professor of Charles University.

The genius of this medieval astronomical clock not only tracks the Sun and Moon's position in the sky throughout the year, but etched in the colorful backdrop, it also displays the time of sunrise, sunset, and the **zenith** at the point of true 'noon' time. The Orloj rotates with both **solar and sidereal time** and tracks Central European, Old Bohemian, as well as ancient Babylonian Time.

Along the outermost rim, the twenty-four gold, Gothic numerals display Old Bohemian Time, also known as Italian Hours. Old Bohemian Time shows the number of hours past sunset as indicated by the position of the golden hand pointer in which shifts with the time of sunset over the course of the year.

Working inward, the next rim of twenty-four gold Roman numerals displays Central European Time. The hand that holds the Sun pointer moves across the Roman numerals to indicate local time or the solar day, and the hand that holds the star pointer tracks sidereal time with the stellar day. The completion of one stellar or sidereal day is about four minutes shorter than that of the **solar day** (one complete rotation of the Sun's apparent path around the Earth). This is because the backdrop of stars that measure the sidereal day rise and set relative to the Earth's rotation and shift over the course of time with the **precession** of the vernal equinox.

Within these first two outer rings of gold numerals is the next set of time increments etched in twelve black Arabic numerals. The ancient system of 'unequal hours' or Babylonian time is tracked by the golden lines that fan out from the center of the dial. Each Arabic numeral marks one of the curved gold lines to indicate the hour. The gold lines divide the hours between sunrise and sunset into twelve equal parts. The phrase 'unequal hours' comes from the measure of this time through the seasons; for in the ancient world of Babylon, the hours at the height of summer measured 81 minutes in duration, while the hours in midwinter are shortened at only 41 minutes. This ancient Babylonian system of time is indicated by the hand with the Sun pointer.

The astrolabe of the **Astronomical Clock** tracks the movement of the Sun, Moon, and **vernal equinox** through the twelve zodiac constellations. The zodiac dial shifts with the year to display the Sun's motion as it reaches the Tropic of

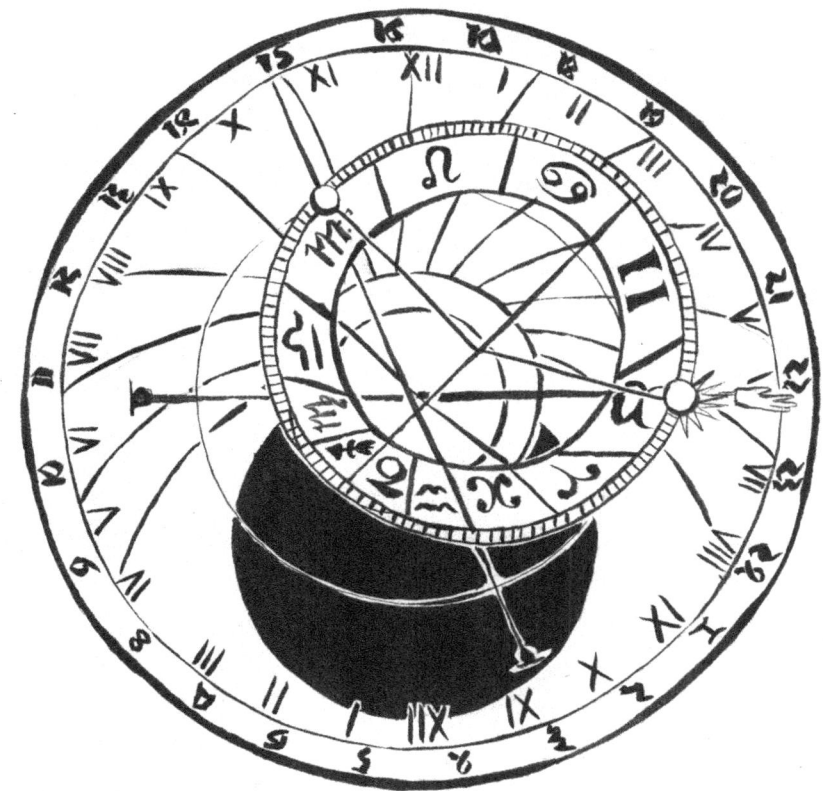

Capricorn, crosses the equator, and climbs to the highest latitude at the Tropic of Cancer. The Sun pointer slides up and down the hand to indicate this motion. When the Sun arrives at the Tropic of Capricorn indicated by the outermost gold ring, the winter solstice has arrived. As the Sun approaches the equator indicated by the middle gold ring the **autumn or spring equinox** is underway. By the time the Sun reaches the Tropic of Cancer indicated by the innermost gold ring, midsummer is marked with the summer solstice.

The colorful backdrop of the **astrolabe** creates a visual representation of the sky during the day and night. The day is painted in blue across the top, and the night is shown in black at the bottom. Between the periods of light and dark, the areas shaded in orange and grey display the ascension of dawn into sunrise and declination of dusk into sunset. On the left, the dawn is shown in Latin as *aurora* in the orange shaded portion and sunrise as *ortus* in the grey shaded portion. On the right side, the sunset reads *occasus* in the grey and dusk as *crepusculum* in the orange. The Sun pointer is used to indicate each of these events over the course of one day.

The last feature of the **Astronomical Clock** is the spherical medallion used to represent the Moon. The medallion at the end of the Moon hand is divided in half, so that one side is silver and the other side, black. As the hand rotates through the lunar month, the moon phases are displayed within the sphere of the Moon pointer.

> "For Levania [the Moon] seems to its inhabitants to remain just as motionless among the moving stars as does our earth to us humans. A night and a day, taken together, equal one of our months, since at sunrise in the morning almost an entire additional sign of the zodiac appears on any day as compared with the previous day. For us in one year there are 365 revolutions of the sun, and 366 of the sphere of the fixed stars, or more accurately, in four years, 1461 revolutions of the sun but 1465 of the sphere of the fixed stars. Similarly, for them the sun revolves 12 times in one year and the sphere of the fixed stars 13 times.... But they are more familiar with the nineteen-year cycle, for in that interval the sun rises 235 times, but the fixed stars 254 times."
>
> —Johannes Kepler, *Somnium [A Dream]*

Calendars through the Ages

How are the stars connected to the development of the calendar system?

The sophistication of the medieval astronomical clock is made possible with the invention of the calendar itself. In ancient civilization, various calendars were adopted to coincide with the day (rotation of the **Earth**), the month (motion of the **Moon** about the Earth), and the year (movement of the Earth about the **Sun**). Though in due time, things can get rather complicated, and the calendars and clocks that we once used to track these time systems were often as flawed as are the imaginary time systems invented by the clockmaker under the structure and support of the wider whole of society.

Luckily, time is written in the stars. So, there's no need to feel anxious over the thought of losing track of time. It seems when all falls out of sync — when the clocks and calendars fail to portray the natural rhythm of the celestial bodies — we can always turn to astronomy to set the records straight.

That is why in the ancient world, astronomical observations were used to measure the accuracy of time. For time is only an afterthought — the perception of our own apparent motion around the Sun, a star caught in orbit of a vortex, the **Galactic Center**. Through the ages, the Earth's wobble causes the backdrop of stars in the sky to shift with subtle ease in time with what is known as the **precession of the equinox**. This motion of the slow shift in backdrop of stars marked by the vernal equinox has played a key role in the creation of calendars, and in turn, of time-telling errors.

How did the position of the **vernal equinox** help shape the calendar through the ages?

The Babylonians initiated the human systematic illusion of time as the first people to track the day in twenty-four parts. In ancient Babylon, the calendar year commenced with the reappearance of the **vernal equinox**. At this point in time, the annual eleven-day festival of Zagmuk took place to honor the deity Marduk. The ancient Egyptians also kept a calendar that consisted of twelve months, each assigned with thirty days, but an additional five days was added to each twelfth month to make up for the inaccuracy of these increments. As it remained, the Egyptian calendar would retrograde with the equinox and the pace of true time every 1,460 years.

Unlike the ancient Babylonians, the Egyptians, Persians, and Phoenicians celebrated the New Year with the **autumn equinox** up until at least the 5th Century, when the Greeks arrived on the scene with the **winter solstice** reserved for the New Year's festivities. The Jewish calendar initiated on the first new moon after the vernal equinox — similar to the New Year of the ancient Babylonians. However, the civil year was tracked with the new moon that followed the autumn equinox — similar to that of the ancient Egyptians.

The Jewish calendar also began to track the lunisolar year on the day inscribed thereafter with the date 3761 BCE. There were three distinct years in the Jewish calendar — those that were defective with a total of 353 days, regular at 354 days, and perfect with 355 day. Though, the system still required compensation for its inaccuracy over tim, and so, a provisional or intercalary month was tacked to certain years to form what was called the **Metonic cycle**.

Other **lunisolar calendar** systems, such as the Hindu calendar tracked the months in a similar way, but the intercalary month was added when astronomers observed two lunations of the Moon in a single month; thus the intercalary month in the Hindu calendar was added once about every three years.

The early Romans continued in step with the Greeks to celebrate the New Year with Saturnalia just before the **winter solstice**. The Roman calendar once spanned for 10 months from Martius to December with just 304 days in total, until Numa Pompilius placed January and February at the beginning of the year. Still, an intercalary month was needed every second year to make it even.

The Romans deciphered the date by counting from three specific day markers in a given month. These three days were known as the calends to name the first day of the month (1st), the ides the midday of the month (15th or 13th), and the nones the ninth day before the calends (5th or 7th).

CAESAR

"Who is it in the press that calls on me?

I hear a tongue, shriller than all the music,

Cry 'Caesar!' Speak; Caesar is turn'd to hear."

Soothsayer

"Beware the ides of March."

CAESAR

"What man is that?"

BRUTUS

"A soothsayer bids you beware the ides of March."

"Beware the ides of March," appears in reference to Julius Caesar's infamous death on the 15th of March — the words for whom we have Shakespeare to thank. Finally, Julius Caesar decided it was time for a new calendar — one in which all the world touched by the Romans would adopt in the first great calendar reform. The formation of this new calendar was put into the hands of Marcus Fabius and Greek astronomer Sosigines. At the end of the reform, the Julian calendar took effect in the year 45 BCE.

With the **Julian calendar**, the average year was set at 365.25 days with 30 days for even months and 31 days for odd months. The name of the seventh month Quintilis was changed to Juli — for Julius Caesar — and Februarius (February) was set to hold an extra day every leap year. It was at this time that the civil year and vernal equinox took the date 25 Martius (March 25th). As a result, the year 46 BCE became the "Year of Confusion", as three whole months of intercalation had been added. The year lasted a grand 445 days.

During the reign of Augustus, the Julian calendar was modified, so that like Julius Caesar, Augustus would also claim his own month; thus the eight month Sextilis was named August. According to Johannes de Sacrobosco, since the Emperor Augustus would not be outdone by the former Caesar, he declared August must also be 31 days and knocked February down to a total of 29 days. Alas, now we must recite a poem to memorize the number of days in each month for the arrogance of this ancient usurper of time. Although the details of Sacrobosco's account of the irregularity of the months is challenged by modern historians, it allows us to understand the immediate shift of time in possession of the hands of a powerful few.

The years progressed under the Julian calendar and so did the **precession of the equinox**, until the date had shifted from the 25th of March — where it was upon the creation of the Julian calendar — to March 21st by the time of the Council of Nicaea in the year 325 CE. This discrepancy, of course, was recognized and corrected at this time, so that the **vernal equinox** reflected the date March 21st. Under the direction of Constantine the Great, the New Year was shifted to the religious holiday Easter, and by the 16th Century, the Julian calendar had fallen off the track of true time by about 10 days — just in time for another calendar reform.

The **Gregorian calendar** was created by Veronian physician and astronomer Aloysius Lilius, who was sure his new calendar system would satisfy all the faults of the Julian calendar. As a result, the Gregorian calendar was instated in the year 1582 under Pope Gregory XIII, and as a consequence, the date shifted from October 5th to October 15th in an instant to make up for the error of the Julian calendar.

The new calendar quickly took hold across the Roman Catholic communities of the world. The solar year of the Gregorian calendar was now replaced with the more precise estimation of 365 days, 5 hours, 39 minutes, and 12 seconds. It was with the Gregorian calendar that the leap year began to be determined by divisions of 400 and the New Year moved to January 1st. Great Britain and the people who lived in the early colonies that now make up America did not convert from the Julian to the Gregorian calendar until around the year 1752. For this reason, George Washington celebrated his own birthday on February 11th instead of February 22nd as it is today.

The **Gregorian calendar** managed to reach much of what is now known as Europe along with Protestant sectors of civilization by the 18th Century. Finally, it was adopted by nations of Eastern Orthodox influence and Russia at the time of the Bolshevik Revolution in 1917.

The Mayan Calendar

The Mayan sky-watchers of Mesoamerica were astrologers, first and foremost. The Maya devised advanced astronomical techniques and elaborate astrological implications for a number of planetary and star transit cycles. The Pleiades rose with the rainy season, while **Venus** ruled rhythms of Earth and Sky.

The ancient Mayan people of Mesoamerica developed one of the most intricate and elaborate interlocking calendar systems of the past. The **Mayan calendar** is set with a period of 20 days as a basis for further counting. On each of the 20 days, a different god is revealed in consecutive order depending on the number of the day. The addition of the *tzolkin* cycle or sacred count added to this pattern and repeated the 20 day cycle for up to 260 days. This cycle of (20 days x 13) = 260 days per each *tzolkin* dates back to around 200 BCE.

What is the significance behind the sacred count of 260 days?

Perhaps such importance behind the sacred quality of the number 260 comes from its prominence throughout nature in the average human gestation period of about 266 days, the appearance of Venus as the **morning star** every 263 days and the possibility of eclipse at a three to two ratio with the *tzolkin* 260 day cycle.

The Mayan Calendar Round was modeled after the expression of these natural cycles of celestial and local rhythm in order to define the flux and flow of all that is revealed in time with an eventual synchronicity. In this way, the ancient Mayan timekeepers sought to find harmony in the overlap of natural cycles and structured a cyclic interlocking calendar to mimic the order of not only the **Sun**, but its connection to the **Moon** and most importantly, the planet **Venus**.

Besides the *tzolkin* 260 day count, the Mayan people made use of the 365 day year or *haab*. Continuing with the base unit of 20 days, the *haab* was built from (20 x 18 = 360) to form 360 days of the year. At the end of each cycle, an unfortunate month of 5 days was added to complete the annual seasonal count. Every 52 years, the *tzolkin* (260 day) and *haab* (365 day) cycles aligned.

How did the Mayan civilization develop the Long Count calendar?

After further timekeeping advancements of the Mayan world, a new calendar began to take shape by about the 2nd Century CE. This reformed calendar system saw to the destruction and rebirth of the world as we know it at the end of each Long Count calendar cycle. This ability to track all time in a cyclic manner was less to describe an 'apocalyptic' scenario — the end of time — and more for the purpose of establishing prophecy each day and recording events of the past that transpired before the 'turn-over' of last cycle. For the Mayan people, this cyclic time reflected the belief that the past repeats itself; in essence, the past holds the key to the future.

To come to such accurate predictions of natural cycles, the Mayan astronomers were set with the task of observing the skies to draw up the **ephemeris of Venus**. We can view these past observations written down in the Venus calendar found within the Dresden Codex. To the Maya — who found the Venus cycles of utmost importance — the planet Venus symbolized war and took the form of the male god Quetzalcoatl. This figure is sometimes associated with a real person exiled from Tula (the Toltec capital) in the 10th Century CE. This exiled individual who once represented Quetzalcoatl, fact or myth, also prophesized his own return that would later coincide with the appearance of 'pale' Spanish conquistadors arriving on the eastern sea in the year 1517.

In the early myths of Quetzalcoatl, the deity disappeared for a time — four days he was invisible and four days he died to wander the Underworld — only to ascend to the throne on the eighth day.

This early rendition of Quetzalcoatl refers to the observed behavior of Venus, as it is last viewed in the western skies at twilight. At this time, Venus disappears in front of the Sun for a total of eight days, then it rises again as the **morning star** in the east. Venus grows fainter with each passing day that it drifts further from the Sun. When it reaches the end of a 263 day cycle of 9 months, it disappears for a total of about 50 days, and at the end, it is revealed again with great brilliance as the **evening star** of twilight.

This total Venus cycle takes a period of about 584 days divided in four 'stations' — the appearance of the morning star, evening star, and two intervals at 8 and 50 days for two uneven periods of disappearance. This pattern is also synchronous with the 9 month cycle of lunar phases for the Moon.

Interestingly enough, the 584 day Venus cycle also interlocks with the seasons at 365 days of the *haab* to form a ratio of 5 to 8 — each Venus station will reoccur in the measure of eight solar years' time. Many of the modifications for the Mayan time-keeping system, like the solar calendars of the Old World, reformed the former calendar over the years to conform to a more accurate depiction of the Venus cycle. The Venus calendar was first and foremost to the ancient Mayan astronomers.

The Primes of Antikythera

How did the Greeks make use of prime numbers in calendric mechanical design?

Buried beneath the rubble of a Roman shipwreck, an oddity of former civilization displays an ancient, yet refined understanding of the cosmos with the most intricate time-telling machine. The Antikythera Mechanism found off the coast of Syracuse in Sicily is a device built from bronze with an interlocking gear design that predates the Orloj of the **Astronomical Clock**. The device was first uncovered in 1901, and it is estimated that (as early as 65 - 50 BCE) this mysterious mechanism with brass gear-wheels sank to the bottom of the Mediterranean — where it remained submerged off the coast of the old Greek island colony of Antikythera amongst the prized treasures of an ancient Roman galley.

The Antikythera Mechanism is thought to be of Greek or Hellenistic origins and displays the most complete time-calculating machine ever uncovered from antiquity, dating back to before the turn of the Common Era. Gears to track the seven **classical planets**, the phases of the Moon, and the measure of **solar, lunar, and sidereal time** were included in the blueprint of the device. Although the most astounding feature of the Antikythera Mechanism is its ability to forecast not just the sight of an eclipse, but the hour, color (black or fire red), and shadow it projects on the Moon with absolute precision.

By comparison, the second oldest time-telling instrument built of gear-wheels dates back to about 520 CE, and documented evidence of similar gear-locked calendric designs extend as far back as the Middle Ages. Yet the second oldest surviving device was developed in the Byzantine world and reflects a much more simplistic design to track the Moon phases.

After further investigation into the inner-workings of the Antikythera Mechanism, the symbols depicting various months were revealed to match the very names of months recorded in ancient Corinth. The complexity of the device would not have been made possible without thousands of years of previous astronomical observations scribed into cuneiform

ephemeris tablets. For this reason, the origins of the astronomy and mathematics behind the calculation of the **Antikythera Mechanism** predates its mechanical design and take us back to the oldest records of the Babylonian sky-watchers.

In the time of the Kings and Queens of ancient Babylon, omens of a celestial nature were used to predict unfortunate periods for citizen and state. Amongst the most unfortunate astrological aspects was the eclipse. The sight of an eclipse was a bad omen — so much in fact, that the King of Babylon abdicated his throne and granted his position of power over the kingdom to a substitute ruler — one who would in turn, ride out the remainder of this unfortunate period. For this reason, the ancient astrologers observed the coming of an eclipse and developed an 18 year prediction period in which the eclipse cycle was set to 'repeat'.

Inside the Antikythera Mechanism, the multitude of gear-wheels tick in time with this same 18 year eclipse cycle period (about 223 lunar months) established by civilizations of the ancient world. Using the value of 223 months to simulate the 18 year prediction cycle, the 223 toothed gear within the mechanism tracks and forecasts the hour of the dreaded eclipse. To simulate the scale of **solar time**, 19 solar years at 235 lunar months were added. Therefore, to compensate for true time, the Greeks added a 19 toothed gear of 235 months to keep in step with the changing of the seasons.

Both the 223 and 19 toothed gear-wheels reflect the value of primes — those numbers that are no longer divisible by any number but 1 and their own value. Interestingly enough, two of the remaining gears, the 127 and 53 toothed gears, are also prime numbers. The 127 toothed gear-wheel interlocks with the gear of 19 solar years to track 254 orbits of the Moon about the Earth according to **sidereal time** (254 sidereal days $\div 2 = 127$).

The last prime, the 53 toothed gear-wheel turns with the 223 lunar month gear (18 year period) to simulate a 9 year variation in the ellipse of the Moon. The value of 53 is perhaps the most impressive of them all, since its ratio compensates for the variable motion of the speed and orbit of the Moon across a period of 9 years by adding an interlocking pin-and-slide mechanism to the gear; in other words, this additional pin-and-slide gear-wheel predicts the shape of an ellipse in the days of Archimedes.

This idea of elliptical orbit was later outlined in **Kelper's laws of planetary motion**: first the shape of a planetary path is an ellipse, second the speed of orbit is quickest at **perihelion** and slowest at **aphelion**, and third the duration of orbit is at a ratio with its mass. Even if the thought of **elliptical orbit** ceased to grace the mind of science up to the instance of its realization with **Johannes Kepler** in the 16th Century, the hint of its discovery in such an ancient invention as the Antikythera Mechanism allows us to question the true depth of what our ancestors understood about the mode of the cosmos as a derivative of Time.

The Stars – Nature's Calendar

VIII. Equinox & Solstice

Quarters of the Zodiac Cross

What is the significance of the **equinox** and **solstice**?

    The equinox and solstice were once celebrated in ancient times with elaborate ritual and festivities in order to signify the four quarters of the annual seasonal cycle. At these four quarters, the Sun's passage from the equator to the Tropic of Cancer and then back to the Tropic of Capricorn becomes more apparent to the observer here on Earth by the length of daylight hours. On the day of **equinox,** the Sun and ecliptic are directly overhead or 90 degrees in relation to the equator of the Earth at 0 degrees latitude, though on the solstices, the Sun is directly overhead or 90 degrees in relation to either of the tropics at about 23 degrees latitude north and south of the equator. This is the furthest the Sun's path varies between positions of latitude, from 23.5 degrees north and south of the equator.
    The heated days of increased sunlight during the summer are the result of the presence of the Sun, just as the long evening

hours of the winter indicate the absence of it. This movement of the Sun across the tropics is caused by the tilt of the Earth, and so, the ecliptic moves between these positions of latitude over the course of a year. From our point of perspective, it would seem the Sun is traveling north for the summer to the **Tropic of Cancer** and south for the winter to the **Tropic of Capricorn.** That is, if we gazed from a position of latitude in the Northern Hemisphere; for in the Southern Hemisphere, the tropics used to mark each season must be swapped with the Tropic of Capricorn south of the equator to bring the summer winds and the Tropic of Cancer north of the equator to welcome the winter season.

Why were the **equinox** and **solstice** important to the ancients?

On the equinoxes, both the spring and autumn, the day and night balance with equal hours. In the Northern Hemisphere, the autumn equinox falls on the sign of the scales or Libra and the spring equinox with the ram or Aries for a running charge into the new cycle; thus the cycle resets itself with the return of the

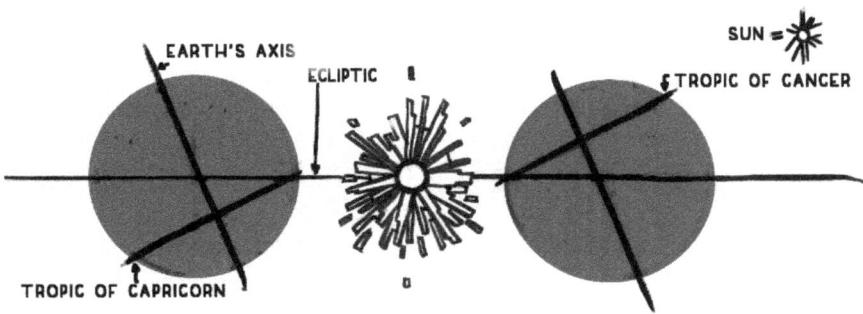

spring equinox.

The **spring equinox** demonstrates where the spring season begins, when the hours of daylight lengthen to exceed the hours of darkness. At this moment, the Sun's position lies at the equator and continues to approach the observer's latitudinal position with each day after the spring equinox, then finally, the Sun reaches the Tropic of Cancer at the **summer solstice** on the longest day of summer. From this point, the Sun turns back toward the equator, and without its light, the darkness emerges with each passing day. When the Sun once again reaches the equator, the daylight and darkness reach a point of equilibrium with the **autumn equinox**. As the Sun passes the equator this time, the hours of darkness surpass the hours of light, until the season sets in with a chill on the shortest day of winter or the winter solstice at the Tropic of Capricorn.

This motion of the Sun between the tropics was of high importance to the ancients, because it ensured an accurate method for tracking the seasons. The observance of the **winter solstice** was once a blessing to ancient agrarian people, since it marked the day the Sun turned back to pay them a visit with the coming year. And, the long winter nights would slowly come to a close, as the daylight once again triumphed over darkness.

In ancient Rome, the winter solstice was celebrated with the festival Saturnalia on the 17th to the 23rd day of the Julian calendar. At this time, a human sacrifice was dedicated to the god Saturn (the ruler of agriculture). Other peoples of the past found the winter solstice highly important, since it marked the shortest day of the year.

How did the ancients use icons to signify the **equinox** and **solstice**?

When we look at the Great Sphinx monument next to the Pyramids of Giza, it is difficult to place the significance of such an enormous lion with the head of a human. When we investigate further into the origins of the **sphinx**, it is thought that this particular statue guards the eastern and western gates of the heavens. If we look to the zodiac for an explanation, it becomes clear that the eastern and western gates of the sky resemble the zodiac constellation Leo and Aquarius, the lion and human placed at opposite ends of the zodiac.

We can continue down this astrological connection to define the true meaning of the sphinx — a creature part human, part lion, part eagle, and part bull. The mystery of the **sphinx** is nothing more than an iconic representation of the zodiac cross. When we look to the ancient night sky for answers, it becomes clear that these four parts of the sphinx refer back to the four corners of the **equinoxes** and **solstices.** These are the cardinal points on the zodiac compass. The wings of a bird seem out of place, until we are acquainted with Aquila — an ancient constellation just above Sagittarius represented by the eagle. Taurus represents the bull and together these constellations all separated by 90 degrees on the zodiac belt form the zodiac cross.

The **sphinx** is not the first rendition of such a mythical creature. The lamassu was the Assyrian version of the sphinx, an early celestial being. Within the book of *Ezekiel* in the Bible, the four cardinal points characterize the cherubim with faces of the human, lion, bull, and eagle. These 'faces' are symbols that together represent the compass of the zodiac cross.

> "There are four cardinal points to the sections of the equator's and the zodiac's circles. We call these points equinoxes and solstices, and from these sections is the start of the zodiacal circle."
>
> —Johannes Kepler, *Somnium [A Dream]*

Plato's Great Year

What is meant by the Great Year or the **Platonic Year**?

The **Platonic Year** also known as the Great Year refers to the motion of background stars over the course of thousands of years. Plato himself actually considered the "Great Year" to be the point in which all the celestial bodies return to their respective positions of initiation. Since Plato's time, the original idea of the Platonic Year has been developed to describe one full equinoctial cycle through the twelve zodiac signs. This **precession of the equinox**, as it is named, completes one full retrograde period at the moment in which the background of fixed stars returns to the point of initiation at the close of the Great Year.

The ancient Greek astronomer and mathematician Hipparchus is credited as the first to discover the precession of the equinox in the 2nd Century BCE, though it is often thought that his calculations were a continuation of earlier methods developed by the Chaldean astronomers. Hipparchus measured the precession of the equinoxes by tracking the fixed star **Spica** (the ear of grain held by **the Maiden**, the constellation Virgo) against the autumn equinox.

During his investigation, Hipparchus noticed a variation in the degree of Spica against the degree noted in the records by the astronomers before his time. He put together the facts and came up with **precession**. Hipparchus estimated the precession of the fixed stars to retrograde at no less than one degree every century. This estimation is actually not far off, since current scientific methods have fixed the rate of precession at about one degree every 72 years, and since we know that the sky is divided into 360 slots at one degree each, (72 years x 360 degrees) ≈ 25,920 years equals the Great Year.

Later in the 17th Century, Sir Isaac Newton 'the father of classical physics' took on the Great Year to assign a scientific explanation to **precession of the equinox**. Within Newton's *Mathematical Principles of Natural Philosophy*, he outlines the interaction of gravitational forces between the celestial bodies — especially the **Sun, Moon**, and to a lesser degree **Jupiter** — that play a key role in the axial rotation of the Earth. These forces cause the Earth to bulge at the center to create a variation in the tropical or solar year (equinox to equinox) and sidereal year (the time it takes the Sun to revisit the same fixed star position).

The relationship of the Earth in the midst of these celestial bodies affects the direction and angle of Earth's wobble through the ages. On the date of the vernal equinox, the Sun's passage progresses into a new zodiac sign with each age, as if the backdrop of stars move without the Sun's consent over the course of about 2,160 years; thus the ages measure about 2,160 years on average.

Estimation of the Ages

Taurus	4500 BCE	2200 BCE
Aries	2200 BCE	0 CE
Pisces	0 CE	2200 CE
Aquarius	2200 CE	

During the Age of Taurus people worshipped the bull or golden calf. The Age of Aries arrived with Moses atop Mount Sinai, and the Age of Pisces initiated Christianity with the entrance of Jesus. In astrology, the ages are observed by the Sun's location in the zodiac on the **vernal equinox**. Many believe we are in transition from the Piscean Age — initiated with the Common Era — to the Aquarian Age, as the vernal equinox retrogrades into Aquarius to mark the dawn of a new age of invention. During each age, the Sun is thought to take on the quality of the zodiac sign in which it occupies on the vernal equinox. With the Sun's precession through each of the twelve **zodiac signs**, astrologers observe the course in which mankind will follow on its social and spiritual evolution over the centuries unfolding with the passage of time.

Vedic Astrology

How does sidereal astrology bypass the **precession of the equinox**?

In modern Western astrology, the vernal equinox is fixed at a date that marks the entrance of the zodiac sign Aries. Over time, the precession of the equinox has caused this ancient fixed position to drift backward, until it reaches a point at which the Sun's location on the **vernal equinox** is no longer at the cusp of Aries with the entrance of spring. Now on the vernal equinox, the Sun can be found within the sign Pisces. Western astrology based on the tropical zodiac is calculated using the **precession of the equinox**. However, the tropical zodiac does not satisfy the true position of the stars in the sky. When these systems were first established in the ancient world, both the sidereal and tropical zodiac systems once aligned. Over the centuries, the background of stars has drifted, and for this very reason, astrologers must rely on the sidereal zodiac to construct a true map of the stars.

Vedic Astrology or Hindu Astrology outlines a separate system of estimation based on the true fixed star positions apart from the systems of Western astrology, which initiate the sequence of zodiac signs on the location of the **vernal equinox** or the cusp of 0 degrees Aries.

The *Vedanga Jyotisha* is the oldest astronomical Sanskrit text of the Vedic Age in India (from about 1400 - 1200 BCE) that outlines the teachings of sage Lagadha. The Hindu astronomical and astrological systems explained within the *Vedanga Jyotisha* were defined for agrarian use in the form of **ephemeris** and assisted in the development of the early Indian calendar. Within the Jyotisha — the study of light — calculation and prediction methods were defined in an attempt to understand the subtitles of the whole that influence our particular position in the universe.

The Jyotisha outlines the early systems of astrological estimation that focus on the phases of the Moon, the location of the Sun between the tropics and other basic astrological aspects such as planetary eclipses and conjunctions. With this information, the *Sastras* or scripture used astrology to track the celestial bodies for both monthly and seasonal rites. Toward the end of the Vedic period, the use of astronomical systems flourished with the expansion of civilization and agrarian life. At this point the Indian calendar had developed into two separate systems — one to track the civil year that served as an outline for the other more precise system to track the appropriate shifting of the celestial bodies for religious and ritualistic purposes.

Within the *Vedanga Jyotisha* the Indian year initiated with the 'joining or coming together' of the Sun and the Moon at the zodiac region named *Sravishta*. The Indian civil year consists of 1830 days (five annual cycles at 366 days each). A year consists of six *rtus* (seasons) and two *ayanas* (courses of the Sun) that mark its annual journey northward and southward to each of the tropics. The six *rtus* grant each season a total of 61 days and the *ayana* are fixed at 183 days. Every 60 typical months, a penalty for proprietary rites is added as an intercalary month — *prayascita*. One *prayascita* falls at the end of the 5th *ayana* and another follows the 10th *ayana*. These segments of time belong to the Indian civil calendar system used in day to day activities.

The Indian civil calendar was constructed with even segments of time that made early calculation and division between the days, months, and years an easy process. However, the system that tracked the civil year was also accompanied by another, more precise representation to keep the positions of the **luminaries** in relation to time; thus the civil year acted as a framework to guide these calculations which were used in the *Brahmanas* (sacred texts) to determine the proper time for ritual.

In the astrology of the Vedas, significant stars were noted and used to track conjunctions with the planets. As the Sun moves forward through the zodiac, these fixed stars that paint the backdrop of our visible universe retrograde behind at a faster rate than the Sun's progression. Per each five year period, the stars actually rotate about the Earth at the usual rate plus five additional days (1830 + 5 = 1835 sidereal days). This slight separation illustrates the difference between **sidereal and solar time**. Within the Sanskrit text of *Surya Siddhanta*, the nine *manas* or systems of time outlined that of Brahma, the Gods, the Pitrya, and the Prajaptaya, as well as those commonly used by the Vedic priests, that of **Jupiter**, the **Sun** (solar), the **Moon** (lunar), the Stars (sidereal), and the **Earth** (terrestrial time).

The *lagna* (the ascendant or ancient **horoscope**) was used in Vedic astrology to signify the planetary period that determined the individual life path and configurations — *dasha*. According to Surya Siddhanta, a conjunction aspect between two celestial bodies provoked the *ansu'uvi marda* — the mixture of the rays. Each aspect represents a point situated along the ecliptic that consists of continuous and endless time. From these aspects, Vedic astrologers drew fortunes of both good and evil.

The **retrograde** motion was broken down into segments in time that classified the frames before and after the planet came to a standstill. A separate set of zodiac was also built upon the shifting stars of the sidereal sky. These planetary positions along the sidereal zodiac were named the *Nirayana* (the sidereal day and night), *Nakshatra Ahoratra* (the measure of sunrise to sunrise), and *Nakshatra Masa* (the sidereal month). Like systems of Chinese Astrology, early Hindu Astrology outlined a system of 28 lunar mansions named the *nakshatra*.

Astrology in Architecture

How did the ancients use architecture to track the **solstice**?

The location of the Sun's passage from tropic to tropic throughout the annual seasonal cycle was once a celebrated event for the ancient people of Ireland. In and around the isles of the north Atlantic, an important event fell in the month of December to accompany the shortest days near the winter solstice.

In the sacred Boyne Valley, just above the city of Dublin, there exists a series of prehistoric passage tombs in the sites of Brú na Bóinne — Knowth, Dowth, and Newgrange Monuments. The largest is Newgrange built in the Neolithic period before the construction of the Great Pyramids, and even Stonehenge. This grand passage tomb was constructed with incredible precession and accuracy before the development of written language.

It is the sight of a **solar alignment** with the sunrise on the winter solstice. To this day, the interior is still sealed from the elements, untouched by the downpours of Irish storms that have swept the Boyne River Valley in the past five thousand years, and the tomb itself still functions as it has since the time of construction around 3500 BCE. It was at this time that the Sun first entered the interior tomb to light up the winter solstice.

Each year on the **winter solstice**, sunlight illuminates the passage tomb, and as the Sun breaks the horizon and rises in the East, the interior walls of the passage glow with an orange brilliance. Newgrange was no doubt the site of ritual worship for the ancients, though the nature of these forgotten traditions remains unclear at the present time. However, it is clear that the ancients built the tomb of Newgrange to signify the light at the end of the tunnel and the close of the long and difficult winter nights. The winter solstice marked the entrance of the lengthening day after the chill of midwinter, when the Sun began its return journey back from the **Tropic of Capricorn**.

How did the Egyptians make use of **solar alignment** in

architectural monuments?

The architectural complex of Abu Simbel located in Nubia dates back to the rule of King Ramses II in ancient Egypt. The site was constructed during the reign of 'Ramses the Great' in the two decades following the year 1264 BCE. At this time, the twin temples were carved out of the mountain to honor Ramses II and place his own figure on a pedestal among the early Egyptian deities.

The Temple of King Ramses II also known as Abu Simbel was carved into the side of the mountain with a facade of four colossal statues — the king among the Sun gods *Re-Horakhte*, *Amon-Re*, and *Ptah*. It was dedicated to his queen Nefertari. The temple entrance was built at a precise angle that aligned with the rays of the Sun at the time of Ramses II's birthday and coronation (every year on February 22nd and October 22nd), when both the hours of light and dark reach an equilibrium. On each of these dates, the interior tomb once again lit with the rays of sunlight, so that the statues within the temple became visible by day.

This temple of Abu Simbel was dismantled and moved in 1964 to escape being submerged beneath the reservoir Lake Nassar. For this reason, it was cut into smaller blocks and brought from its original site, piece by piece, to a more suitable location outside the flood range. Upon the construction of Aswan High Dam in 1968, the temple was successfully extracted from the flood zone, lifted from the site, and rebuilt in an area beyond the water.

How did the Inca of the South America observe the **equinox** and **solstice**?

The Inca, who lived in the capital of Cuzco, once celebrated the New Year with the appearance of the Pleiades. In the high mountain peaks of the Andes, the city reserved for *Sapa Inca* (The Great Inca) and the "Virgins of the Sun" can be found just above the Sacred Valley in the Cusco Region of Peru. This sacred city is known as *Machu Pikchu* or the 'Old Peak'. It is now know that sunlight played a key role in the construction of *Machu Pikchu*.

Machu Pikchu is a 15th Century Incan complex thought to hold the site of an earlier sacred place. Within the temple complex, the 'Sacred Plaza' opens up to the west at an alignment of 245 degrees. The 'Room of the Three Windows' on the eastern side of the 'Sacred Plaza' frames the sight of the sunset on the June solstice (the **winter solstice** of the Southern Hemisphere). Inside the *Torreon* or the 'Temple of the Sun' a stone glows with rays of sunlight that enter from the east window on the June solstice. This suggests the June solstice was a ceremonially significant date used by the Inca to track the solar year.

It is clear that the angles of orientation throughout the structures of *Machu Pikchu* connected the shrines and plazas to the location of celestial bodies and sacred mountain peaks in order to honor the spirit of these sacred mountains or *apus*. Atop Huayna Picchu or 'New Peak', a stone shaped into an arrow points the way south to the Intihuatana Stone at the *apus* of Mount Salcantay.

Named the 'hitching post of the Sun', the *intihuatana* is a stone carved into the natural pyramid summit of *Machu Pikchu* that operates much like a calendar of the Sun. The Intihuatana Stone points directly toward the Sun's position in the sky during the **winter solstice.** This tool is used to 'to tie, or hitch up the sun' in its rightful place in the sky. Many *intihuatana* stones could once be found throughout the Kingdom of Cusco and the old Inca Empire, though after the invasion of the conquistadors, only a few remain intact. The particular *intihuatana* in at *Machu Pikchu* dates as far back as 2300 BCE.

On the **equinox**, the Sun sits atop the pillar with all his might and for a brief time in passing, he is 'tied to the stone'. At this particular day in time on March 21st and September 21st, the Sun casts no shadow from its position upon the *intihuatana*. The *intihuatana* also aligns with the December solstice (**summer solstice** of the Southern Hemisphere). At the moment of sunset on the summer solstice, the Sun in relation to the *intihuatana* descends below the *Pumasillo* (Puma's Claw) or the sacred peak upon the Vilcabamba mountains to the west.

Equinox & Solstice

IX. Zodiac Archetypes

The universe or "the Absolute" is depicted in mythological stories to help mankind grasp concepts of eternity as well as aspects of the eternal. Both the myths and **cosmogony** of the ancient world take the shape of primordial tales that help explain the original essence of existence and the instance of initiation, when all came into being — the creation story.

The oldest creation stories of many religions assign characteristics to these underlying primordial aspects of Nature, which would otherwise seem too abstract to grasp. Within these myths of the ancient world, the characters are represented as deities to explain conceptual ideas, phenomena, or forces beyond human control. In this way, the gods and goddesses of the ancient world gave qualities to the most basic forms of Nature to help understand each extension of **the Source** — from which all things apparent and invisible manifest.

Deities of the Ancient World

How did the ancients explain the creation of the cosmos?

The ancient Egyptians constructed grand temples to the worship of a wide range of deities in various forms within a company of gods and goddesses known as a *paut*. Throughout the land of the Nile, each member of the *paut* granted abstract ideas a name, such as the primordial aspects of creation, the fundamental elements of Nature, and the underlying essence of being.

Words were particularly important and useful to the ancient Egyptians that — when used correctly — held a mysterious quality; for the name in itself works just like magic. When the name is spoken, the reflection of the words comes into being. Without a name, the essence of the thing resides in non-existence. For this reason, the names of those things that were later opposed were physically destroyed from monuments and records; thus the existence of the thing in question was erased alongside the name.

Among the oldest company of gods were the *paut* of eight that formed the Ogdoad of Hermopolis or *Khemennu* (the city of eight Gods). These eight gods and goddesses embodied the eternal in the form of **primeval states** or the original form of all being — the infinite that takes the shape of eight — much like the symbol for **infinity** (∞). Of the eight in the *paut*, there were actually only four that were split into male and female form.

Before all there were *Nu* and *Nut*, the god and goddess of the abyss — the deep and boundless watery mass from which all things came into being. *Hehu* and *Hehut* were next to be defined and rather undefined as indefinite or the limitless factor in accordance with time, as hinted by the use of 'Heh'. This pair was also thought to indicate the atmosphere between Earth and the heavens or the male and female form of Fire. *Kekui* and *Kekuit* were the male and female form of darkness that envelopes the abyss. *Kekui* is the time of night just before the dawn known as 'the raiser up of light' and *Kekuit* is the time of night just after the sunset or 'the raiser up of the night'. The final pair, *Kerh* and *Kerhet*, sometimes referred to as *Amen* and *Ament*, were the latent powers of the abyss, also known as hidden powers of the night.

The **Ogdoad of Hermopolis** is often described as the

elements Water, Fire, Earth, and Air. Though, it is also known that these eternal eight must describe attributes of the **primeval states** from which all existence comes into being. For this reason, the *paut* of eight has also been associated with aspects of Space, Time, Form, and Power — that which gives birth to all of creation.

The local deities of Hermopolis held *Thoth* as the "lord of the temple", whose influence was held above all others as the personification of divine intelligence. Thoth was accompanied by feminine counterpart *Maat* — that which is kept straight. All deities of Egypt associated with "right" were said to uphold Maat for she was truth. The dominion of Maat extended across both moral and material realms to emphasize the extent of what is just, genuine, unalterable, and with regularity, and so, we have the phrase "God will judge the right" or the exact equivalent of the Egyptian phrase "a neter apu pa maat." Together Thoth and Maat — the embodiment of intelligence and regularity — form the foundation of divine law and order.

Thoth was the heart, mind, and reason or "soul of Ra" from whence came the words that carried out the wishes of *Ra* — most often depicted as the creator, that which is visible, or the Sun-god. Ra took many forms in creation, and all created things that he leaves in the train behind him were his limbs, and therefore, a part of him. Thoth and Maat each directed the vessel of Ra in which the Sun-god traversed on his journey to fight against Apep — the force of chaos — every dawn since the beginning of time in this kingdom under the Sun.

How does consciousness fit into cosmic creation?

In ancient Hindu myth, the birth of the cosmos can be explained by the tale of *Prajapati* and the **Hindu Trimurti** of devas — *Brahma*, *Shiva*, and *Vishnu*. Before the spark of initial creation, there was Prajapati, "Lord of the Universe", also known as "the Absolute".

Prajapati had no use for time and no need for a beginning and an end; thus Prajapati was the essence of eternity. When Prajapati began to focus and meditate, a seed appeared out of the chaos and sprouted a lotus tree from his naval. The lotus tree grew, and as it did, light shone and surrounded the lotus. From the lotus tree and light, Brahma was born. Brahma is the first born of the Hindu Trimurti and represents the creator. As the light expanded with the cosmos, so too did the existence of Brahma, and they mixed to create the essence of being. Brahma became the power contained within all things in time.

In addition to the creator Brahma, the destroyer or transformer Shiva was born to bring balance to Brahma's creation. The deity Shiva is characterized by qualities of knowledge and strength and represents the union of opposites as well as destruction and transformation — the natural force in which will eventually bring an end to all that has been created. The last of the triad Vishnu signifies the preserver or the force that maintains and sustains the whole of existence. Vishnu is a symbol of the avatar.

Other versions of this tale assign Brahma as the original deity that exists within the primal void. In this form of the myth, Brahma takes on the role of Prajapati. When Brahma sleeps, the world is in the state of Prajapati or indefinitive nonexistence. When Brahma wakes, the whole of reality or illusion of the cosmos comes into being for a 'day' in the life of Brahma. At this time, order is born out of chaos. When Brahma rests, the essence of being and the cosmos are also laid to rest until the moment at which this deva awakens again to provoke another round in the infinite cycle of creation. With the **Hindu Trimurti** myth, the whole of the cosmos seems to have been fashioned and formed from the presence of consciousness itself. The very act of meditating brought the whole of creation into existence.

How did mythology help the ancients explain aspects of consciousness?

In one particular sect of the ancient **Zoroastrian** religion and myths of Persia, the cosmos was created by the one from which all light, darkness, and destiny transcends — *Zurvan* or "time". Only Zurvan the essence of space-time and matter existed at the beginning within the void of nothing. In time, Zurvan longed for a son and sacrificed time in exchange for the ability to create one. Zurvan began this endeavor with optimism, but as time passed, doubt overtook the deity's creative power. When Zurvan was finished twins emerged, one pessimistic and one optimistic as a reflection of Zurvan's thoughts. The twins took the form of *Ahura Mazda* (the wise creator) and *Ahriman* (the destructive spirit). Ahura Mazda planned to create the perfect universe in the name of truth and light and formed the Sun, Moon, and the stars. Ahriman with qualities of darkness and deceit sought to add chaos to Ahura Mazda's perfect world. After humans came into being, Ahriman poisoned the first human with the 'Dying Life' or mortality in death.

The battle between *Spenta Mainyu* (the spirit of good) or "Holy Thought" born of Ahura Mazda, and *Angra Mainyu* (the spirit of evil) or "Evil Thought" of Ahriman enveloped eternity. Ahura Mazda could not defeat Ahriman and instead sealed the spirit of darkness inside creation itself and set a limit to time; thus the struggle between good and evil will exist until the end of time. With the help of the light— Mithra, the Sun, or truth — Ahura Mazda and the seven deities counter the force of Ahriman. In this story, the forms of Ahura Mazda and Ahriman embody archetypes — the extremes of being or consciousness that manifest in all of creation in the form of good and evil.

How does humanity fit within the realm of deities and initial creation?

In ancient Chinese myth, creation was set into motion, when both the forces of yin and yang reached an equilibrium at the beginning of time. Pan Gu then awakened after 18,000 years of slumber and began to take chaos into his hand. With a mighty blow, Pan Gu sent the elements swirling about the cosmos. As the Earth and Sky grew, so too did Pan Gu — until all that was heavy sank to form the rocks of the Earth, and all that was light floated up to make the Sky.

After another 18,000 years, Pan Gu had separated the Earth from the Sky, often with the help of the **celestial beasts**: the

Vermilion Bird, the Black Tortoise, the Azure Dragon, and the White Tiger (or sometimes the Qilin). When Pan Gu was certain chaos was overcome, the great creator fell back asleep and took the shape of the rest of the cosmos. When Pan Gu breathed, it was the gust of the wind and clouds, and his voice, the boom of thunder. His right eye became the **Sun** and his left eye the **Moon**. His bones became the minerals of the Earth, and his bone marrow, the most sacred diamonds. His blood formed the rivers and streams and the hair of his face, the stars above.

Nüwa looked upon the landscape and was delighted at all Pan Gu had created, though she thought the Earth seemed a lonely place. Nüwa found a soft yellow clay and molded it into shape. When she placed it on the ground, the figure came to life. Nüwa began to dance in celebration and ran about giving life to more figures. In seeing that they would grow old and die, Nüwa made the figures into men and women granting them the ability to bear children.

In the **Shinto** mythology of Japan, the creation of the world was initiated by *Inzanagi* (he who invites) and *Inzanami* (she who invites) or the embodiment of yang and yin. The couple descended from the heavens and stood upon the Rainbow Bridge. The two *kami* held the 'Heavenly Jeweled Spear' and stirred the waters of the primordial ocean. In doing so, they created the first island Onogoro. As they witnessed Love, the Love between the two *kami* grew into desire. Izanagi and Izanami walked in opposite directions around a pillar and merged in creation each place they met. In this first wedding the outcome was flawed, since Izanami spoke first. In time they bore a child, Hiruko (leech-child), who they sent away atop reeds on the water.

The gods urged them to repeat the wedding. This time Izanagi spoke first, and so, the islands of Japan were born from Izanami. Her *kami* became the spirit of the trees, rivers, wind, and mountains. In Shinto belief, *kami* is the essence of all life and existence that can be easily recognized as the **Spirit** within all of creation. Even after death, *kami* lives on in one form or another.

It seems after creation was set into motion, only then did the creator decide it must be lacking something — the color of animation, the chatter of life. In this way, the creation of humanity is much more an afterthought than the purpose of creation in these early Eastern cosmologies.

Ancient Abstracts of a Modern Nature

How does myth allow us to put ancient abstract concepts into modern perspective?

Upon revisiting the primordial tales of the infinite eight — the **Ogdoad of Hermopolis** — we can begin to draw parallels between ancient allegory and modern cosmology. The four **primeval states** that were set into motion at initiation take us back to our origins in the cosmic explosion of the Big Bang. The Ogdoad of Hermopolis is a *paut* of eight Egyptian deities thought to represent abstract concepts of eternal forces that harmonize and distort to create the universe. These primeval states depict the basic essences of reality in the order each were originally revealed — Space, Time, Form, and Power.

Space was first and describes the **abyss** — that which existed before the universe came into being. After the explosion of the Big Bang or the initiation of Time, the universe was lit and sent spiraling into motion. Brilliant white light sprang out from the seed of the **cosmic egg**. This was the separation of "Earth and Sky" — recounted time and place again across the many civilizations of the ancient world. The fabric of Space stretched, and as it began to cool, the established forces of plasma and radiation shaped the first **primordial matter** into Form. In Time, the radiation slowed to invisible X-rays then ultraviolet light.

Just as the **primeval forces** of Izanagi and Izanami, male and female, or the opposite polarities ascended the Rainbow Bridge — the spectrum of colors fashioned light in various wavelengths to reflect all that was creation. The rainbow of colors was the Form born, when the polarities brought light to the **visible spectrum** — in Violets, Indigos, Blues, Greens, Yellows, Oranges, and deep, dark Reds. In turn, this visible light slips away, as the slowing caused by the expansion of Space and progression of Time sends it back down to the lower frequencies of the invisible realm as infrared or radio waves.

At this point in the universe's history, the differentiation between plasma and radiation grew with order, as the polarities encoded in the universal pattern (lotus tree) pulled in opposing directions to grant Form geometric symmetry. Each place the **polarities** locked the established primordial matter in harmony, the latent Power of the universe was unleashed, building the geometric shapes of matter and exerting energy to echo the initiation of the **creative principle** established at the origins of Time.

The Pantheon

How do **archetypes** of human consciousness fit into the wider scheme of creation?

At the root of all creation stories lies the original question of which the answer inspires us to discover in the first place at the moment of initial inquiry. The question along the lines of, "what is I?" or, "what is the essence of being?" which so often leads us to an answer that explains the root of all creation and its connection to humanity. It is as if we must know where 'human' fits into the wider realm of creation, and to know the long sought secret answer unencrypted within writings of a former time must somehow redefine us and dictate the entirety of our lives or control the direction of our force of will in this realm of being. Though we can never be too certain if we have come to understand the meaning of it all or simply the meaning of the answer or the meaning of an answer to the question; for some questions have several answers.

The ancient Greeks especially sought to insert such inquiries into the nature of existence and that of humanity in story-telling tradition. The Greek Pantheon places the twelve gods and goddesses of Olympus at rulership over the affairs on Earth to reveal the irrational qualities of nature and humanity. In the highest archetypal form, many abstract concepts of conscious thought and that of natural processes — such as aspects of weather, phenomena of the elements, and the changing seasons — are presented through the interaction between characters in Greek myth. These extreme **archetypes** depicted as deities embody the attributes or expressions of the underlying **Spirit** of conscious thought and create a more concrete 'mode of thought' to explain the forces of nature and extensions of consciousness itself.

In the realm of Greek myth, the gods and goddesses of Olympus take sole responsibility over the affairs of the Earth and often intervene in the lives of mortals. High up on Mount Olympus, the great rulers reside alongside the mighty Zeus, crowned king of the gods. Zeus is a master shape-shifter who could craft himself into many forms, throw his voice like thunder on the wind, and strike the Earth along with its inhabitants with his most famous weapon — a lightning bolt. Zeus ruled over the heavens and is often considered creator, as he had an eternally unsatisfied lust for the act of creation.

Flanked by his two brothers, Hades (ruler of the Underworld) and Poseidon (god of the sea and streams), Zeus maintained the affairs of humanity and kept all aspects of the Earth in proper order. Zeus also had three sisters, Hera (his wife and queen of the gods) who ruled over marriage, Demeter (goddess of the harvest), and Hestia (goddess of the hearth and home). Hera made quite the jealous wife. She often acted out in anger and resentment in light of Zeus' many affairs with mortal ladies, and she took revenge on his children just to get even. It is rumored that Hestia (ruler of women and domestic affairs) eventually withdrew her position amongst the quarreling gods of Olympus.

How do the Greek myths account for abstractions such as natural cycles?

Demeter ruled over the harvest with her only daughter Persephone, and together the two brought life to the fields and ripened the fruits of the Earth. It is said that Hades caught wind of Persephone and immediately became fascinated by her beauty. Hades decided he would take Persephone for his own and waited one day for her to make an appearance. When Persephone bent down to tend to the garden, Hades reached out of a gaping hole in the Earth and dragged Persephone down with him to the **Underworld**.

Demeter was distraught at her daughter's disappearance and traveled across the land in search of Persephone. In the absence of her daughter, Demeter neglected the crops, and the harvest began to fail. When Zeus noticed the shriveled plants and flowers crumpling back to Gaia, he decided to set things straight. A compromise was necessary if natural order was to continue.

In the end, Persephone was allowed to return to her mother Demeter but not before her fate was sealed in the Underworld. It was a known fact that those who ate the food of the Underworld would be trapped there for eternity. Hades had already tricked Persephone into eating pomegranate seeds, and as a consequence, she would thereafter be made to return to the Underworld for a third of the time each year. Persephone was made Queen of the Underworld.

Upon the return of Persephone, Demeter welcomed her daughter home with bountiful blooms in the spring. Each year when Persephone left for the Underworld, the leaves would fall as winter arrived when Demeter cried over the loss of her daughter.

How does humanity fit into the realm of creation in ancient myth?

The origins of humanity are mentioned within the Greek myth of Prometheus, who stole Zeus's **Fire** to bring life to the first man. The man's name was Epimetheus. In turn, the lame god Hephaestus — often depicted amongst the gods of Mount Olympus to take the place of Hades (who actually dwelled in the **Underworld**) — used his abilities of fire and forge to fashion

Zodiac Archetypes

another figure from Water and Earth; thus the first woman Pandora was born. All was right with the world, until Zeus decided to get involved.

Zeus brought a special surprise to Epimetheus, a mysterious jar with gifts from each god and goddess, often depicted as a box. Zeus told him it was a gift for his lady or Pandora's Box. Epimetheus had been warned not to take gifts from Zeus, but the great king of Olympus knew he had already won and curiosity would get the best of them one way or another. Either Epimetheus or Pandora would surely open the box. Of course, it was Pandora who first lifted the lid to see what was inside. Out flew Envy, Hate, and Disease, which escaped into the world in an instant.

Pandora in a panic hurried back to Epimetheus to show him what she had done. When she opened the box again, one tiny bug appeared from the darkest depths of the bottom — out came Hope. From that moment forth, all ills had escaped into the world, but Hope would rise up out of the shade of sorrow caused by such suffering.

How do the gods and goddesses present **archetypes** of conscious thought?

> "The concept of the archetype, which is an indispensable correlate of the idea of the collective unconscious, indicates the existence of definite forms in the psyche which seem to be present always and everywhere. Mythological research calls them *motifs;*"
>
> —Carl Jung,
> *Archetypes and the Collective Unconscious*

In many of the stories presented in Greek myth, consciousness itself is classified in archetypal format through the presentation of extreme personal qualities found in the gods and goddesses of Olympus. Athena (the goddess of wisdom, truth, and battle) is one such figure. Athena was celebrated throughout the ancient world within heroic epics such as Homer's *Odyssey* — guiding the warrior Odysseus with trickery on his return journey home. As patron of Athens, Athena bestowed upon the city the most valuable resource — the olive tree. She not only represented the qualities of divine wisdom, but the ability to speak the truth and debate these points by asserting force of will.

To know is only half the battle, but to conquer with words of truth one cannot lose. Her origins of birth are more a clue into the archetype of Athena. Zeus met a sea-nymph Metis or "thought" and took to her with passion. When Metis became pregnant, Gaia first predicted the child would be a girl, but she later changed this to a boy who would ultimately surpass Zeus and become the new ruler of the heavens. In a panic, Zeus swallowed his love Metis with child for fear his son would take his place. In doing so, Zeus acquired her knowledge in "thought", and the child Athena then sprang from Zeus' head fully armored and ready for battle — and her words of wisdom, divinely inspired.

Hermes was the son of Zeus and messenger of the gods. Hermes is often associated with quick-wit and expression of the mind featured in numerous tales of Greek myth. Hermes makes an appearance in a wide range of myths as the messenger and mediator between opposing parties. For this reason, Hermes is quite the popular character; for the gods and goddesses were nearly always feuding. Hermes embodies the archetype of communication and reason, who was always the quickest to respond. Though this messenger of the gods was a loyal figure, he also had a mischievous side much like the logic of the mind.

On the other hand, personalities of the gods and goddesses were not always so pure in form. In the case of Ares the god of war, a darker side of human nature is expressed. Ares was self-centered and the most violent of gods who often kept the chaotic Eris (the spirit of strife) in his company. Ares was not necessarily determined to win the battle, but instead took pleasure in the sight of bloodshed. Most of the gods stayed far away from Ares; for this wrathful god brought nothing but trouble with the exception of Aphrodite (the goddess of love and beauty).

Aphrodite was the fairest of all the goddesses and wife of Hephaestus. Despite her husband, Aphrodite fell in love with Ares and the two engaged in an affair. It did not end well for these lovers when they were finally caught in the act, but the overall message is quite clear. Love and violence share the same bed. To bring beauty into the mix only complicates matters, and so the Trojan War and abduction of Helen — the most beautiful queen — was recorded in myth to have been caused when her abductor Paris chose the goddess Aphrodite (beauty) over all other qualities.

How do ancient myths present lessons for differing types of conscious thought?

Many assign a dualism to consciousness of good and evil, light and dark that leaves no room for a 'grey area'. These dual **archetypes** of abstract thought presented in myth help to explain 'consequences' or outcomes of each type of consciousness at its most extreme expression. However, what is good and what is evil has been redefined by one moral code or religion preceding the next in step with each face of **the World** across the ages in time. In the case of the Egyptians, chaos in its non-conscious form has been reduced to the epitome of evil or Apep the serpent who battles Ra — the upholder of order.

In the ancient world, chaos as an extension of consciousness took another form embodied in the Greek god Dionysus. The myths involving **Dionysus** (the god of wine or intoxication) presents those thoughts driven by the senses and higher or altered states of conscious thought that expand the human experience outside the frame of logic or reason. Dionysus is instinct, emotion, and intuition — to what we name the transcendence of self as one within the whole of nature associated with the feminine principle of the mind.

It is no wonder in recent times, Dionysus has often been mentioned accompanied by **Apollo** (the god of the **Sun** and light), who bears a striking resemblance to Ra, since the god Apollo stands for all that is rational, logical, and with control.

Apollo is the perfectionist of consciousness and looks to create within the framework of natural order. In this way, Apollo is narrowing one's self to define individuality, and thus represents the masculine principle of the mind. With blatant contrast in motive behind the consciousness of Dionysus and Apollo, it is much easier to grasp the archetypal dualism assigned in modern times to these two opposing frames of thought.

Zodiac Archetypes

Just as the deities of the ancient world denote archetypal expressions of consciousness, the **classical planets**, which are always found within one of the twelve zodiac signs, further define the nature of these conscious filters.

The planets can be viewed as a reflection of the light that emanates from the **Sun**, though not all planets reflect this light in the same way. The light which is absorbed to produces the spectrum of color that we see on the surface of each planet is only half the story. For the very reflection of color in the **visible spectrum** also denotes those colors that we do not see or that which are being absorbed by the specified planet. In a way, these visible and invisible colors reflected across the visible spectrum or chemical composition signatures also give us a clue into the nature of consciousness itself; for there is both an exterior expression of consciousness and an invisible realm of internalized consciousness.

There are many distinctions between the planets, not only color but size and proximity to the Sun or our position on Earth, and so, the classical planets fittingly named just the same as many of the deities that belonged to the ancient pantheons also reflect archetypal consciousness. As all the planets or extensions of consciousness are united, we have the personality. In a way, the allegory of early archetypal symbols was literally written into the stars by the constellations in the sky.

Where do the zodiac signs fit within the idea of archetypal

consciousness?

There are many ways to distinguish the difference between each zodiac sign. These unique patterns and signs in which the planets can be found along the zodiac belt at birth help to define the conscious filter through which the specific extension of archetypal consciousness is perceived and expressed. Then how are these filters in which we perceive the world defined? Through the designation of basic elemental qualities and animal versus human signs — representative of instinctual urges and the rational mind. The zodiac signs are also assigned a **cardinal**, **fixed**, or **mutable** position in relation to the remaining signs.

Just like the basic elements of ancient mythology, the assigning of **elemental triplicities** — Water, Fire, Earth, and Air — holds more significance than the surface meaning of each of these words. To define what is truly meant by these archetypal elements is to understand the distinction between conflicting thought patterns that exist within the mind. We first must look at an even more refined form of **archetype** — conscious filters so often referred to as Apollonian or Dionysian. That is to say, the patterns that form the extreme perception or expression of divine masculine and feminine consciousness or those conscious filters that resound with these opposing archetypes.

How can we expect to assign such dualism to our thought processes?

It becomes easier to make such a connection when we look at the anatomy of the brain and its two conflicting hemispheres, the source of Apollonian or Dionysian thought in us all — that which restricts to identify and that which expands to encompass the whole.

To better understand what is meant by **Water**, **Fire**, **Earth**, and **Air**, we can find a useful source within the **archetypes** of the tarot. A typical tarot deck is comprised of four suits — Cups, Wands, Pentacles, and Swords depicted as such or in a similar altered form. Though the root of each suit points to the four basic elements, the Cups (Water), the Wands (Fire), the Pentacles (Earth), and the Swords (Air). The interpretation of each tarot card in a reading is highly dependent upon the presentation of these suits. Cups are representative of emotions and intuitive intelligences, Wands are assertion of will and creative potential, Pentacles exhibit production of practical surface matters, and Swords are tied to communication and rational expressions of the mind.

These patterns also hold true for the basic elements each suit represents. In the case of Cups and Swords (Water and Air), these expressions or perceptions of consciousness are archetypes of the divine feminine principle. Likewise the Wand and Pentacle suits (Fire and Earth) represent the counterpart filters of the divine masculine principle. Within the wider frame of the zodiac belt, even numbered signs are considered feminine and odd numbered signs, masculine. For the **Chinese Zodiac**, the years of the calendar numbered **yang** signs were wild animals (the male, active principle), while **yin** signs were domestic animals (the female, passive principle).

How can our own cosmic conditioning be defined by archetypes?

The zodiac signs act as the twelve **archetypes** of human personality or filters for each realm of thought through which consciousness is initiated. If we add the **classical planets** into the mix with each planet representative of a certain nature of consciousness, we begin to build personality based upon the realms of thought and filters through which these thoughts are expressed and perceived. For those outer planets Uranus and Neptune, which are unseen or invisible to the eye, we define the invisible realm of what is unconscious, and so, we have the twelve archetypes of personality, the seven forms of conscious thought, and the pair of subtle tricksters deep within the unconscious realm of the mind.

If we track the planetary positions with a natal chart — the human personality or initial essence at birth — each location becomes a source of later transits that influence the original nativity. Just as the personality is challenged and built upon through life experiences atop our own inherent essence of being, so too is the horoscope influenced by its beginnings when the initial pattern of nativity is touched by transits throughout the course of the querent's life.

Archetypes in Psychology

Does archetypal classification in astrology have any basis in psychology?

It is possible to draw parallels between universal **archetypes** of modern day psychology and the twelve zodiac personalities. The basis of archetypal thinking resides in the power of symbols. It is true that symbols are open to interpretation relative to the viewer's perspective. In this way, it is possible that all interpretations of one symbol hold true depending on who is asked. Symbolism speaks to the invisible realm of knowing and unconscious recognition, where intuition is activated without the need for conscious thought. In short, symbols bridge the gap between the material and invisible realms with no conscious effort needed. Then there are those archetypal **symbols** that seem to invoke a linear response across the whole of humanity. These particular symbols in human personality can be classified as psychological archetypes.

Psychological archetypes are resounding extensions of consciousness that hold true for all possible perspectives. The raw classification of one's personality can be defined as an archetypal filter of conscious thought born from basic patterns of instinctual behavior. Personality is our own unique perception or personal paradigm that denotes how we perceive and react to external and internal circumstances. It defines our individuality and the very nature of the reality we construct. Basic types of archetypal personalities include the broad classification of the optimist and the pessimist.

Further into the realm of psychological analysis in the form of archetypal personality, we find the introvert or extrovert along with those who use sensing or intuition, those who think or feel, and those who judge or perceive as a continuous and dominate mode of thought. Each of these possible filters of the **archetype** are included in modern day personality definitions such as the Jung or Myers Briggs Tests with which we have begun to classify each individual's personality type by defining four distinct categories.

The categories are usually along the lines of INFP the introverted, intuitive, feeling, perceiver (the idealist) or ESTJ the extroverted, sensing, thinking, judger (the guardian). Interestingly enough, if we look closer at the four categories, of which there are two options each, we can quickly see how each pair of options is an expression of the broader feminine and masculine mode of thought.

In psychology, thoughts born out of the **left and right brain** can be defined as two separate filters of conscious thought. The left hemisphere is often labeled as our logic, ability to rationalize, analyze, distinguish concepts, and apply critical thinking, while the right hemisphere would much rather rely on sensitivity, intuition, creative insights, visual pattern recognition, and associate with an all-encompassing perspective. These two parts of the brain continuously chatter in the concentration of nerves situated in the middle of both hemispheres — the **corpus callosum**.

Through the expansion of our point of view, we distinguish universal patterns, and by narrowing this view, we define the universe. There is a latent power that exists in the harmony of left and right. In the case of mythology for the left and right brain, the difference between the right eye of the **Sun** (masculine hemisphere of the brain) and the left eye of the **Moon** (feminine hemisphere of the brain) helps to understand the conflicting functionality between the two sides. It is when mankind learns to unite both hemispheres of the brain that progression in life will resemble the dawning of a Golden Age.

> "A more or less superficial layer of the unconscious is undoubtedly personal. I call it the *personal unconscious*. But this personal layer rests upon a deeper layer, which does not derive from personal experience and is not a personal acquisition but is inborn. This deeper layer I call the *collective unconscious*."
>
> —Carl Jung,
> *The Archetypes and The Collective Unconscious*

How do **archetypes** allow us to classify the invisible realm?

All human beings exist within the material plane, and what we call the physical reality is the common ground. Likewise, the source of all consciousness also resides in what is known as the **collective unconscious**. All intelligence is drawn into our being from within this collective and universal consciousness. The existence of the collective unconscious allows us to connect our own paradigm of conscious thought to that of others and instantly relate through the mutual understanding of concepts.

In this invisible and immediately imperceptible realm of the mind, we store all information collected throughout our lives, even if the information was never consciously perceived or recognized. Just as a savant holds the extraordinary talent of reading the entire page of a book at a glance, so too does the unconscious mind perceive the whole of the apparent reality. This whole picture is narrowed through the conscious recognition of archetypal **symbols**.

If we look at a photograph of a forest, all individual parts of flora and fauna seem to blend into one scene, yet the unconscious not only sees the trees and animals but absorbs the subtleties such as the color and texture of the leaves. When later asked what was in the picture, the conscious mind will often give a flawed answer when it comes to the minute details; for we have already narrowed our view to a symbol that satisfies the overall picture. However, this information we lack is ever-present deep inside the unconscious realm of memories. We must learn only how retrieve it.

For this reason, symbols and archetypes have more of an impact on our daily lives than we would like to admit. Every exposure we are introduced to in this world shapes the very reality we continuously create for ourselves. Our invisible reality can easily be manipulated for the worse and is often neglected as the source from which we fashion conscious thought altogether. We have forgotten how conditions within the physical realm are not the only factors that exist within the all-encompassing reality in which we experience life.

The **Magi** and seers of the cosmos recorded archetypal **symbols** as tools of remembrance in the days of ancient astrology. That is, the zodiac symbolized a concept or extension of archetypal conscious thought. We need not invent the wheel over again, if we can retrieve the blueprint for the idea in mind. Therefore, the symbol allows us to discover the universal secret in an instant.

The initiation of a specified thought only requires the proper catalyst to bring about instantaneous understanding, but what truly allows us to recognize the concept is the meaning of the symbol that remains linear across the whole of human consciousness.

The Eternal Trinity

How does current calculation and theory build a scientific form of **cosmology**?

In the modern definition of our own initiation — the **Big Bang theory** explains how all that we see exploded into existence from a single point at the beginning of time to form the visible universe. Much like the separation of Earth and Sky as outlined in ancient myth, the Big Bang divided the universe into matter and radiation. This act of creation is viewed as a process of nature, when all the elements and conditions for such an event settled into place, just so. The Big Bang explains the beginnings of what we call reality — the explosion of massive proportions that sent the universe and space-time expanding with such immense force that it still continues in motion from its moment of initiation, even today.

We can begin to classify this interpretation of existence as **the Source** from which all things visible and invisible manifest. The Source restricts and assigns stipulations to the order in which chaos takes with what we conceptualize as underlying ratios, mathematical constituents and geometric shapes that rule out what is possible and impossible within the material reality. The Source is the mechanics behind natural law and order. In this way, the Source is the framework behind the paradigm we call existence. Its order defines the outcomes of probability and restricts the bounds of what is possible. This initial 'cause' set off a chain reaction that has reached all effects of past happenstance.

These effects were brought about by the initial 'cause' described by the Big Bang, when our universe was set into motion at least as far as the eye can see in accordance with time.

Despite its power to shape the visible universe, the ever-unfolding patterns of the Source — reality in physical terms — is not the only factor that influences the development of the material plane. It must also be accompanied by the **Spirit** of chaos and conscious interaction. The Spirit of chaos — limitless possibility — lurks in the background of all that is creation. Without the existence of chaos, there would be nothing for order to restrict. Perhaps, chaos always existed and remains the underlying **quintessence** of reality. It is the missing element of random chance — the thought of possibility — while the structure of the universe — that we often trace with scientific calculation leading back to the Big Bang — is the order born from the chaos that continues to build our paradigm of existence. Now we have a structure to restrict the bounds of the abyss into the shape of reality.

If we begin to unite these elements, the essence of existence is a dance between the Spirit of chaos and the unfolding processes initiated at the Source. When chaos meets this universal order, manifestation of reality becomes the merging of the two in the act of creation. **Manifestation** thus becomes the formation of a paradigm.

How did the ancients classify existence in terms of eternal trinity?

Many of the ancient religions and myths of the past have attempted to describe an eternal trinity to classify the essence of all existence. With the Hindu Trimurti, Brahma is the creator who brings order to reality, while Shiva remains the source of chaos to balance the flow of existence. Vishnu is the third element of manifestation that preserves and maintains the two.

Trinities were often established with patron deities to guard the religious complexes of cities in the ancient Egyptian world. Later, the Christian trinity describes our connection to the eternal in a similar, however unique version as the Father, Son, and Holy Spirit.

If we were to take this thought of trinity to shape the basis of reality in a **Pantheistic** sense — describing all parts as an extension of a single story of existence — we find that the trinity can be useful to describe the interacting behaviors that shape the nature of the cosmos in its entirety. We can connect the bounds of undefined possibility outlined with the **Spirit** of chaos to the restrictive framework established by the order of **the Source** with the act of **Manifestation** or the creative principle as an interlocking process that defines the one all-encompassing reality. This idea of Manifestation can also be described as **Maya** — the illusion of a vision that reflects the invisible upon the surface of reality.

> "Our psychology is, therefore, a science of mere phenomena without any metaphysical implications. The development of Western philosophy during the last two centuries has succeeded in isolating the mind in its own sphere and in severing it from its primordial oneness with the universe. Man himself has ceased to be the microcosm and eidolon of the cosmos, and his 'anima' is no longer the consubstantial *scintilla*, or spark of the

Anima Mundi, the World Soul."

—Carl Jung,
Psychology and Religion: West and East

How does the **Spirit** of chaos and order of **the Source** apply to Nature?

Nature is the force that brought about life in the form of flora and fauna. Nonetheless, the might of Mother Nature is also seen in the weather, the tides, and shifting landscapes. To the ancient civilizations of the Earth, the sudden shade of a whipping sandstorm, the sight of a tsunami, or the eruption of ash and dust pouring from high above the mountain top were proof of one side of Nature — the chaotic, destructive, and unpredictable side.

But the thought of Nature alone is one that continues to bring humanity comfort. Despite its chaotic consequences, Nature continues to fashion the visible reality of plants, animals, delicate biological kingdoms, and major geological networks with organization, efficiency, and intelligence in harmony with the underlying order established at the Source. Just as **Carl Sagan** once wrote, "Nature is not entirely unpredictable."

In fact, when the **Spirit** of Chaos and the Order of **the Source** meet, Nature is expressed by the opposition of these principles with creative force or destructive consequences. Perhaps our love of Nature comes from the creative principle, knowing that it too has an affinity for harmony — that which manifests in Love and Life.

Zodiac Archetypes

x. The Limiting & the Limitless

What the Ancients Knew

How did the ancients define nature as a process?

In the ancient Chinese philosophical tradition of Tao, the forces of yin and yang together formed the very essence of nature — a process based upon these interlocking polarities at the heart of existence. The yin holds the seed of yang that shows himself when too much of her is present, and when yang overpowers the odds, yin appears once again to take his place. Between the eternal interacting forces of yin and yang, balance is continuously overturned and maintained. One is the seed of the other, and we must observe both, not as separate entities, but as a process of eternal balance between the two.

In a similar sense, great thinkers of the ancient Hindu world once gave up on the idea of "cause and effect" altogether. Instead, they came to consider that each was the observance of the other from the view of a different vantage point.

Somewhere along the road, the observance of cause and

effect gave rise to scientific method. It was the thought that one could penetrate the "mind of god" that inspired such enthusiasm for the sciences, mathematics, and astronomy.

Though according to the ancients, this practice also introduces a world of subtle folly that may be too disguised to spot. By simply narrowing our viewpoint, we lose alternative meanings of the thing in question. For this reason, an objective observation cannot be narrowed to just one definition. Just as **Albert Einstein** stated, all things are relative; that is to say, all things are relative to the viewer's perception of the thing. This concept works in cosmic observation as well as conceptual inference. If we do not recognize this fact, we lose the ability to apply what it means not just to us in our own perceived observance but to the perspective of the wider world as a whole outside the frame of cause and effect.

For example, if we give something a name such as an element or chemical compound, we are taking an objective stance and seeing the thing for only the narrowed definition we have given it, when in fact, this is just a freeze frame of the process.

> "If a faithful account was rendered of man's ideas upon Divinity, he would be obliged to acknowledge, that the word God has been used to express the concealed, remote, unknown causes of the effects he witnessed; he uses this term only when the spring of the natural and known causes ceases to be visible…"
>
> —Baron Von Holbach, *Syteme de la Nature*

What is a hormone such as melatonin?

When we define a hormone as a substance in the body that gives rise to a chemical reaction in the bodily organs, we have already begun to narrow our viewpoint of the thing in question. We have not yet come to the realization that to name 'hormone' as such and apply our narrowed definition, it has become an objective observation rather than an active and changing process of nature; for when the hormone is decoded by an organ, it creates a chemical reaction that incites an electrical synapse response that prompts a change in natural bodily process and results in the direct modification of behavior. By connecting the beginning to the end, or the endless beginnings of ends, we can see that all things hold the seeds of other things, just so.

Then where does the hormone come from? Some would say it is released in the body from the endocrine system, though this outlook is only an objective and material stance. When we look closer, the hormone is often, but not always the result of an outside force that did not already exist within the body. Melatonin, the hormone that regulates sleep cycles, is a direct result of the setting Sun; thus our body's metabolism is in part directly affected by the rising and setting of the Sun, and so too is our behavior as a final result.

How can the cosmos be defined by the limiting and the limitless?

In the theory of ancient Greek philosopher **Philolaus of Croton**, the most basic forms the universe takes are limiting and unlimited. When we apply this idea to our modern description of the essence that forms the cosmos, it becomes clear that what is meant by limiting can be described as matter, the source of gravity, and universal constant that restricts through order, and what is meant by limitless is the opposite of the universal constant, the eternal expansion of space, and chaos of undefined possibility in time. Both of these forces would not exist without the presence of the other, and for this reason, we must apply Philolaus' idea of the harmony that exists between the limiting and unlimited factors.

> "Concerning nature and harmony the situation is this: the being of things, which is eternal, and nature in itself admit of divine and not human knowledge, except that it was impossible for any of the things that are and are known by us to have come to be, if the being of the

things from which the world-order came together, both the limiting things and the unlimited things, did not preexist. But since these beginnings preexisted and were neither alike nor even related, it would have been impossible for them to be ordered, if a harmony had not come upon them, in whatever way it came to be."

– Philolaus, *Fragment 6*

In another sense, limiting can also be applied to the obtainment of knowledge; for if we did not create a limited frame of view, we would have to throw off all understanding of the thing in question and mark it as limitless or unable to understand for the sake of infinite implications past, present, and future. In order to avoid this paradox, we must apply a narrowed viewpoint or framework that becomes a point of reference. That is why in science, we must limit to observe an outcome and thus understand, until what is observed becomes known.

Science is a process of predicting, which relies on the observance and collection of data received through the human senses and the application of this knowledge found through implication in theory. In this case, only the material plane is being observed, and all data collected is a product of sensory perception, hence the old adage, "seeing is believing."

In the *Tao of Science*, R.G.H. Siu wrote that consciousness is influenced by different forms of knowing, "intuition of the mind to some essence and the other of faith and of action from a symbol in the mind to the outside object". Siu states that essence is 'perceived' through intuition and the substance is 'known' through means of awareness.

When conducting an experiment using scientific method, the scientist reaches conclusions by averaging all the data received each time the experiment is conducted, though we often fail to notice that the very subtle window of error in a few units of the answer concluded with each trial averaged into the next is lost through the process of exacting probability for the sake of predicting the next outcome. Instead of inferring that all answers that have been reached are true or all outcomes are probable through the experiment conducted, the scientist finds that the average of the sum of outcomes is more useful than the true differentiation between possibilities.

The entire process replicated through the experiment has been generalized to reach only one solid conclusion rather than the multiple outcomes that are true in nature with numerous possibilities, which would otherwise seem random. Science must rely on observation through the senses and narrowing exactitude for the sake of simplification, but the philosopher of the cosmos seeks an all-encompassing and eternal point of reference. For this reason, when we classify everything under the limiting perspective, we forget the possibility of the limitless.

As much as we may try, it is not up to humanity to restrict possibility; for that function is left to the natural patterns and framework of existence. Then how do we come to understand the greater picture if we cannot rightfully restrict our own view? As Siu wrote, we must come to understand, "Nature's secrets are matters of probability." To encompass the whole of existence in which we reside, we must come to the realization that there is order in patterns and chaos in possibility.

What creates or defines the thoughts in which we perceive?

A conscious thought or perception of reality is only an observance of chaos, the product of **possibility** and **probability** due to circumstances bound by time. In this way, thoughts do not have an observed cause and effect because conscious perception is a matter of undefined chaos which takes the form of multiple outcomes and in a sense 'in-comes' or initiations — the product of perceived circumstance — and circumstance is ever-changing like the tides of the ocean. Thoughts are influenced by our filters of perception, such as the personality, that shape the individual's observance of apparent reality — the product of the natural passage of time and present framework of order built upon the chaos of existence.

Circumstance is the condition in which we meet when we are introduced into chaos. It is a point of reference and current perception of the reality around us. Therefore, the world of thoughts seems almost as enigmatic as chaos itself. For there seems to be no real grounds to relate cause and effect to thoughts despite the inference of behavioral patterns that define 'tendencies' described by each individual's personality.

That is why we must ask, what is the source of thought creation? If the personality is a filter through which thoughts are inferred, then we must question what is inherent or ever-present in thought patterns due to personality and what is influenced by external circumstance.

It seems almost absurd to predict the cause and effect of thought when considering the endless possibilities born from consciousness or the perception of circumstance or even the endless possibilities of circumstance itself. When viewing consciousness from this end, thoughts become the outcome of multiple circumstances and perceived possibilities. Thoughts are more like chaos in that they do not conform to the law of cause and effect. They defy mathematics in that one idea given to another does not subtract the idea from the first owner. Both people, instead, now share the idea.

We can define **chaos** as the manner of thought influenced by the perception of possibility as it interacts with the hidden probable outcomes of circumstance.

The Science of Tao

How do the eight concepts of Tao relate to modern scientific theory?

Tao is as much a cosmology as it is a **metaphysical** view of the universe. Tao is the "way" to the fundamental principles that arrange the whole of existence. This concept of Tao splits the primeval aspects of the universe into eight trigrams or concepts. These eight concepts are similar in nature and reveal latent powers of positive and negative (+ and -), light and dark, male and female, and electricity and magnetism. If we were to combine the sum of all these primeval aspects into one definition, we could use **yang and yin** (the divine masculine and feminine principles).

Before the universe came into being, there was **Wuji** — the boundless abyss of the limitless primordial universe. At the initiation of the visible universe, **Taiji** or the limiting polar elements of yin and yang were instilled. Yin, the divine feminine, defines the essence of the underlying negative principle of the universe — it does not act, but attracts — and yang, the divine masculine, denotes the positive principle or the epitome of force and action. The divine masculine (yang) is what the divine feminine (yin) attracts outlined in **Taiji**.

These polar qualities have also been symbolically depicted as snakes spiraling up the **rod of Asclepius** — one black and one white. This symbol is widely common in modern medicine and is named the **caduceus**. If we apply the symbol of the caduceus to our knowledge of Tao, it becomes an allegory of the harmony between opposing forces yin and yang, as they dance about the pillar of Time.

Likewise the original symbol of Tao, **the bagua** displays these two snakes of the caduceus as dots, points in time, forms of space or forces, as they are appearing (+) as light (the **positive** polarity) in visible form or disappearing (-) as dark (the **negative** polarity) in non-visible states.

These basic polarities of Taiji encompass all acts in nature, interlock together and pull apart in intricate patterns to create the elements of **Wu Xing** — the shapes and states that define the geometric symmetry of the universe.

Deep into the Milky Way

How are we connected to the Milky Way Galaxy?

As humans living on planet Earth, we find our place within the wider solar system of a star — our **Sun**. This concept connects us to the planets we see trekking the sky above as being a part of our own orbital system, and all too often, we stop right there.

In doing so, we neglect to see that our Sun itself does not take up a static position in the wider scheme of things. That is to say, the Sun does not sit stationary in the infinite expanse of space-time. Instead, the Sun like our own Earth moves at a predetermined passage set by the order of the cosmos, as it orbits around an even greater celestial body situated at the center of the Milky Way Galaxy. The Sun itself is in orbit around this massive object situated at the **Galactic Center**.

What is the source of mass that attracts the Sun to the **Galactic Center**?

The spirals of stars that draw the arms of the Milky Way Galaxy are bound by the pull of a massive object that resides at our Galactic Center. At the **Galactic Center**, a thick presence of stars condenses around the mass to form a giant globular cluster. Beneath the light emitted from the tightly bound cluster of stars, some would argue that a super-massive black hole exists. This super-massive **black hole** is given the characteristics of an object so dense and so compact that it defies the laws of physics. The super-massive black hole is an invention of modern science that helps to explain the object that holds all the stars in the galaxy together.

Outside our own galaxy, we find worlds some alike and some very different than our own. In scientific theory, it is often proposed that there also exists a super-massive black hole at the center of all other galaxies that make up the universe. In this way, there is a world of microcosm connecting us to the macrocosm in this realm we call home — the infinite expanse. Here we are interconnected through means of gravity in our passage around the Sun orbiting the Milky Way Galaxy that exists in the company of all exterior galaxies to make up the totality of the universe.

When we begin to look at things from afar, it becomes much

easier to see that our own place at the edge of a spiral in the greater Milky Way Galaxy is comparable to the life of a clownfish hiding within the sea anemone just at the edge of a safe cliff reef in the vast ocean blue. In our position, we are shielded from the influence of greater objects that would otherwise be a danger to all life on Earth. The black hole itself is an excellent example of the power of the cosmos and the forces of nature at a more eternal state.

We take up this position at the edge of a spiral, because it offers us the possibility of Life beyond the influence of harmful energies from deep space objects that would otherwise wreak havoc on the small blue-green planet we call home.

> "But from afar, a galaxy reminds me more of a collection of lovely found objects — seashells, perhaps, or corals, the productions of nature laboring for aeons in the cosmic ocean."
> —Carl Sagan, *Cosmos*

Why is the theoretical **black hole** such an enigma in modern science?

The idea of a **black hole** comes from the radio emissions we receive from a particular region in the sky. Not only do the stars seem to spiral around this center as if nearing its **singularity**, but the theoretical object that resides in its place gives off a noisy signature, which astronomers can trace with the use of a radio telescope. The signature noise of a black hole produces a particular gamma ray spectrum — some of the fastest traveling photons or electromagnetic energy in the galaxy.

Although we may have facts in data that point to the presence of such an object as the black hole, it is difficult to distinguish what actually exists at the **Galactic Center**. We cannot very well point a telescope in that direction and visually perceive this black hole, but the presence of stars swirling about this point at the center hint of its existence.

Given the stars that form this globular cluster are sometimes

The Milky Way Galaxy

1. Norma Arm
2. Galactic Center (Sagittarius A*)
3. 3 Kilo Parsec Arm
4. Scutum Crux Arm
5. Sagittarius Arm
6. Orion Arm
7. Perseus Arm
8. Outer Ring

even greater in size to that of our Sun, it becomes even more difficult to fathom the object that resides at this position to cause such an enormous pull that it attracts all the stars in the galaxy. Some would say the force of a black hole's pull is gravity itself. Although, its super-massiveness in theory causes quite an enigma for modern physicists given the density of such an object pulling with such an immense force of gravity cannot be satisfied by the scientific laws we abide by today, considering all the weight of a black hole is compacted into such a minute area. The super-massive black hole creates such a huge dent in the fabric of space-time that we are unable to account for the colossal presence of such an object in our current three dimensional frame of view.

The Limiting & the Limitless

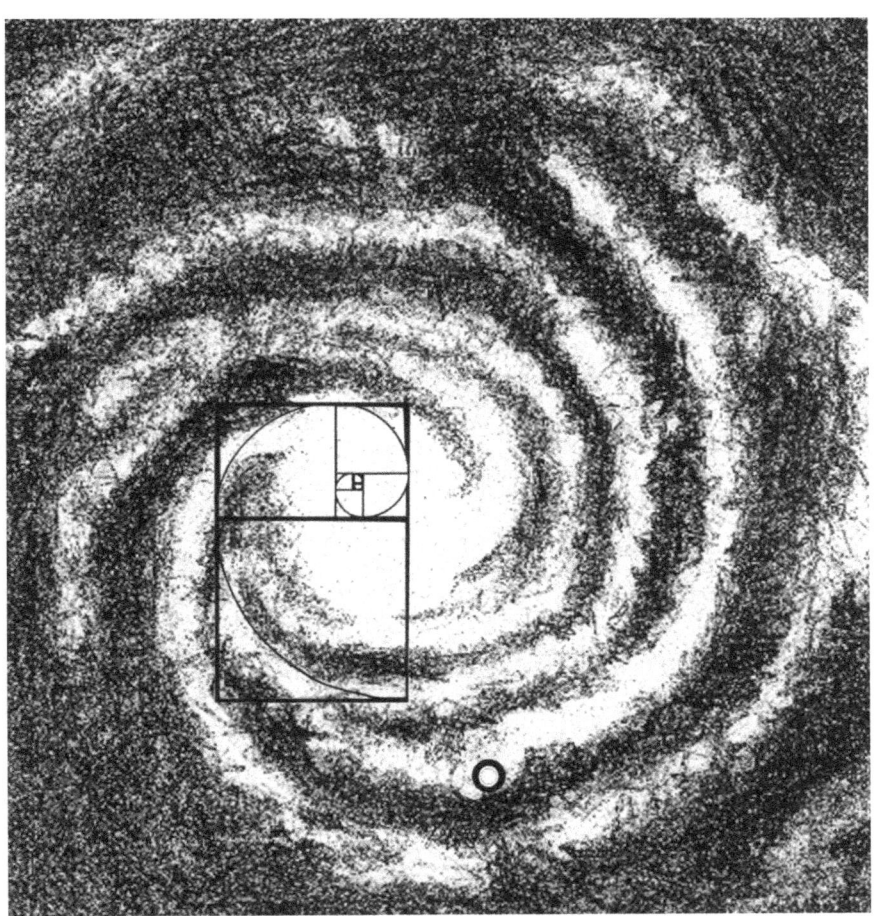

Even more puzzling the enigma becomes when we consider what happens as an object enters the **singularity** of the black hole. Some subscribe to the theory of **Einstein** in that matter can neither be created nor destroyed but only changed in form. So, what happens to a star that falls into a black hole? Does this matter simply disappear, does it emit its energy in the form of radiation, or are we simply considering the puzzle from the wrong frame of reference? The puzzle itself seems to expand with each fact, much like the seemingly infinite expanse of space-time.

Many theoretical physicists consider that time itself is connected to the presence of a **black hole**. When a star nears the singularity, the star seems to slow as if it could be viewed from

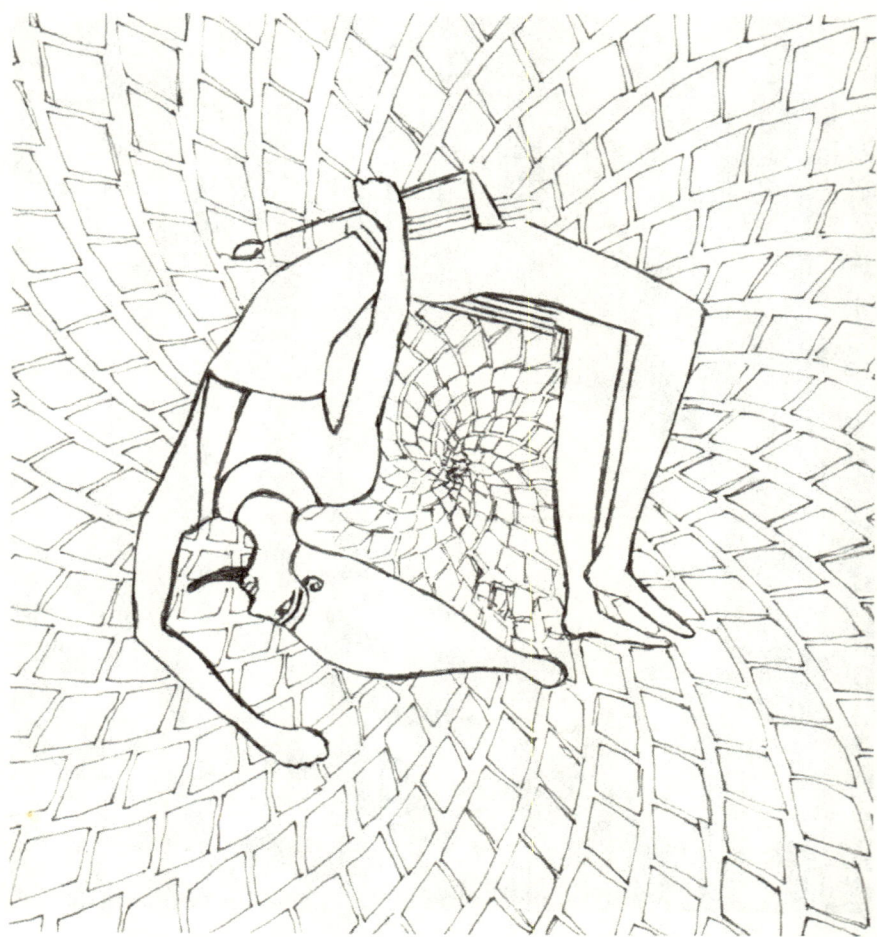

its own perspective at a standstill on the edge, falling infinitely into the abyss of the black hole. That is, if the force of pressure from the extreme heat and massive density of surrounding stars did not completely destroy it before it had the chance to reach the center. If this were a human being with our awareness of time, we would feel as if time itself has stopped dead at the edge of the **singularity**. At this point, our bodies would appear to elongate as if being stretched like string taffy, as we fell further into its endless edges.

Does this mean that the black hole is not an object at all but instead a warped position in the fabric of space-time — much like the opposite of a star, but rather the inversion of expanding space-time? The point where no light, no matter, nothing, not even time in the sense we perceive it can exist. Could it be that our own three-dimensional eyes deceive? As mentioned in *Surya Siddhanta*, the Buddhas considered that the Earth had no support, and as nothing heavy is fixed stationary in the air, Earth must fall eternally downward in space.

It is interesting to consider that the passage of time itself may be defined by the presence of a **black hole**. For if as suggested — we are falling at an infinite rate into the vortex, while the fabric of space-time expands eternally around us — perhaps our own memories or even the memory of us falls away with time to be lost in the belly of the black hole fixed at the center of the Milky Way Galaxy. Perhaps, the black hole denotes the end or the **Underworld** of time and our thoughts, Osiris himself, or the **Akashic Records** of all past emotions experienced within the *Anima Mundi* (the World Soul), the collective unconscious, or **aether** of consciousness itself.

Reverting Back to a Pulsar

How do scientists map a timeline of the cosmos?

When the original explosion of the universe initiated the formation of this paradigm, its force glowed with a brilliant white intensity. This light eventually shifted to make the universe translucent and released the **cosmic microwave background radiation** still swirling about the cosmos today.

As the interlocking polarities contained within the plasma and radiation of the universe began to slow, overlap in time, and cool, neutrons and protons emerged. By way of **primordial nucleosynthesis**, these particles interlocked to create the first elements of hydrogen, helium, and lithium.

About 400 thousand years after the initiation of the Big Bang, the universe dimmed into what scientists sometimes name "The Dark Ages." During this epoch in the History of the Universe, the fabric of space-time had stretched to disperse the light and branch energy out into cosmos.

It was around 400 million years after the initial explosion that star formation began, when these elements reached a more stable state. The elements came together to form the first stars. Some of the first stars of immense mass expanded into what is known as the red giants. Inside these red giants, the pull of interlocking polar patterns caused by the constituents of the universe and the force of energy were made to refashion the fabric of cosmos into more complex structures and shapes which baked the lightest elements into heavier elements by way of nucleosynthesis within the high temperature furnace of radiating plasma — an event called **stellar nucleosythesis**. These nucleosynthesizing stars created the "primary elements" for Life — carbon, oxygen, and nitrogen.

This process of star formation permits dense elemental occupation into a position of space-time to build heavier nuclei at the core of gravity's influence. Following the birth and death of these stars, more complex particle pairings dispersed in the aftermath of the collapse with the release of enriched clouds of **planetary nebula** and formation of white dwarf stars. In time, white dwarf stars exhausted into brilliant nova. This observation of continuous star formation can be seen from the moment of its origins with the very first stars.

Stars of extreme mass and proportions evolve into red supergiants that ultimately result in a supernova explosion. During a supernova explosion, these colossal stars eject radiation in the form of a shockwave that shakes space and outshines all other light sources in the galaxy. This process also prompts what is known as **supernova nucleosythesis** or the force behind the formation of the heaviest elements.

After a supernova explosion, the collapse of mass under the weight of gravity forms the remnants into a neutron star, or if the mass exceeds the Schwarzschild radius, a black hole follows. A neutron star cools to condense into a highly magnetized and rotating pulsar. Pulsars spin and emit a ray of electromagnetic radiation in the form of a beam of light. Like a lighthouse it flashes and turns with the steady beat of a pulse. The rotation of a **pulsar** is amongst the most accurate time-telling instruments in the universe.

Stars upon stars born from the remnants of ancestor stars and entire colonies of interacting stars became the galaxies. Each of these galaxies is held intact by the forces of a super-massive black hole.

When we look toward the beginning stages of a galaxy, we spot a quasar or the brilliant center of a young galaxy that emits a beam of energy nearing the speed of light. Quasars are extreme explosions — the largest since the Big Bang — and are thought to be the result of the interactions situated at a young galaxy's center. The end stages or death of a galaxy lies at the Galactic Center in the belly of a black hole. As time goes on, the paths of galaxies cross and galaxy clusters continue on the evolution of this construction project of massive proportions across the universe, indefinitely.

The Galactic Year

What use is the **galactic year** in astrology?

Just as the Earth orbits around the Sun to form one year, the Sun orbits the massive object at the Galactic Center to form the **galactic year**. The galaxy is so colossal in size that it takes the Sun more than 225 million solar Earth years to travel once around the **Galactic Center**. Despite the similarities, the Sun's orbit is not-so linear as the Earth's yearly transit; for as the Sun advances through the stars that form each spiral arm of the Milky Way Galaxy, it travels in a bobbing or oscillating motion rising north and falling south of the center of the galactic plane.

As the Sun transits north or south of the galactic plane it is moving away from the thick concentration of stellar matter at the center. If we consider the spiral arms of the Milky Way to also increase the probability of interactions between passing stars and objects that disturb the **Oort Cloud**, then we can conclude that the Sun's journey around the Galactic Center has a direct influence over circumstances for Life here on Earth. The Sun's transit above and below the galactic plane open its conditions to changes in probability and circumstance; for when it is nearest to the center of the galactic plane or within the spiral arms, the Sun guiding our solar system is introduced to a denser collection of nearby stars due to natural proximity.

Perception of Time

How is reality perceived by humans through the senses?

The physical plane in which humanity resides is called the **third dimension**. That is because as humans, we can perceive the physical realm in three dimensions with a length, width, and height. Everything that we know and see through firsthand experience — all that can be 'proven' through observation — resides in the third dimension. In order to absorb and interact with the third dimension, humans must rely on the senses (sight, sound, smell, taste, and touch). Without these senses, we are bound within the paradigm we create inside the mind or our own personal extension of the **collective unconscious**.

For this reason, human sensory perception narrows our view to the third dimension. Although we can only physically experience our lives unfold from the perspective of the third dimension, this does not mean that time (the fourth dimension) is nonexistent. For the slow progression of the unfolding of life's events is proof for the existence of time. Instead, we are only shown a freeze frame of the **fourth dimension** at any given moment that can easily be referenced as our current consciousness. The present is our current residence of being — the plane of our personal viewpoint.

What is it that empirical evidence lacks?

Through the ages, science is built on one great discovery trumping the next; thus the old is made obsolete, and the new sets the meter for all. This framework or mode of observance provides a structure to build upon, and without a sound basis of theoretical implication for each observation, the experiment is useless. We may have the data and tangible facts, but what does it all mean — or what is now 'known'? Without the proper understanding of what it is that we see, empirical evidence yields no true statements just like our early interpretation of the sky in geocentric form.

It becomes clear that humans are guilty of constructing an entire theoretical framework around what is 'known' in science only to find that one extra bit of information added to the mix sends the whole thing crashing to the ground. This outburst, *Eureka!* moment causes a sudden paradigm shift in viewpoint, much like **the Tower** card in a traditional tarot reading. With a flash of insight — lightning strikes the tower — and the foundations upon which all had been previously built crumble to the ground in an instant. When the dust settles, we have only the core — the new "known" we must now use to build the tower back up brick by brick.

How did we find ourselves in such a circumstance? Where did it all go wrong? It was not the facts or the observation that was flawed — it was the very basis of what we thought we saw. Human sensory perception has the potential to lead us astray in such a way, since it only completes a sound argument if theory is also correctly applied. And living in the third dimension — a mortal life bound by time — we often forget that the infinite has no use for cause and effect.

There is no beginning and end, and outcomes themselves are procedures that we have the honor of observing through the senses and interacting with at our own humanly pace. But speed things up into the realm of the fourth dimension, and we catch a glimpse of our own beginning and end.

How then do we jump to the **fifth dimension**? Chance would have it that the fifth dimension envelopes all probable possibilities for our viewpoint in time. So that if we must choose between a pair of books to read, the current possibility in the fourth dimension is that we have chosen this one. Consider if we had picked the other book. The paradigm just stated exists within the fifth dimension, because it was probable, possible, and still exists despite our not choosing it.

When we begin to step up to even higher dimensions, we learn that all things that are probable and possible inside the realm in which we dwell must also be true, even if these things exist outside our own fixed viewpoint. That is to say, all probable possibilities found within the given order of chaos have the potential to manifest. When we take the sum of these probable outcomes and paradigms of possibility from beginning to end, we have the universe.

But suppose our own universe is not alone, and there are more planes of manifestation each with a different set of laws that assign order to chaos. The sum of all these realms of manifestation or universes is the **omniverse**. At this point, we can consider the omniverse all probable possibilities of existence. The omniverse, thus, is just a fancy word for **the Source** from which all things apparent and invisible manifest. It is the totality of the order of existence — it is the beginning of ends.

The ancient Greek philosopher Plato understood the dilemma of human sensory perception in such a way that his 'Allegory of the Cave' now seems an ode to our ignorance in the third dimension.

Allegory of the Cave

Imagine a group of prisoners chained inside a cave — left to stare at shadows on the wall born from the firelight behind them. A bridge also exists between the prisoners and the fire. Items that pass on the bridge catch the firelight and shadows dance on the wall before them. They cannot turn round and have no knowledge of the source casting the shadows, but they decide to name the shadows on the wall as things. The sounds they hear when each item appears, the prisoners associate with the shadow it forms.

As they sit and stare, many things pass and disappear. The prisoners compete for the title of who can spot each thing and that, and they predict what will come next or next to the appearance of another thing. The game quickly becomes a source of pride for the prisoners, and those who best play it are envied.

One soul is yanked up from her position on the floor. She has been released and lays eyes on the source of the shadows for the first time. Each item is a puzzling sight, and the brilliance of the firelight causes her to turn away. Still, the shadows remain more 'real' than the items before her used to shape them. Now she is forced to ascend the passage up to the light and resists in distress as she rises to the top.

The light outside the cave is such a blinding white that 'surreal' is this new world and 'real' remains the shadows. When her eyes no longer ache from the exposure of what is bright, the visible world begins to take shape. The shadows are easiest for her to observe then the images of things reflected upon the water. Finally, she discovers each thing itself and quickly becomes entranced by what is now 'real'.

Rather than absorb everything under the Sun, she prefers to examine the heavens by night and begins to fix her gaze at the Moon and the starlight; until finally the sunrise, and she sees it is the Sun — and then the light, it also must be the Sun. She recognizes that this Sun touches all that is real, and this light is the source of all that she saw.

When she is made to return to her former seat within the cave, she finds difficulty in focusing on the shadows once more. The other prisoners notice her struggle with each blink and laugh as they declare, "your eyesight is shot!" They see only danger in ascending to the light, and instead pass the time predicting shadows on the wall. She seems almost threatening with her strange new sight, and they consider her demise might put them at ease.

In time, they fear the one who will snatch them from the floor and drag them from the shadows that dance upon the cave. Still, she remembers what she discovered in the light. She must adjust again to the world of the shadows once more, yet this time enriched with knowledge unbeknownst to the awareness of the prisoners — those who have always dwelled beneath the light. Now she understands what it is that she predicts and triumphs over the others with her new found insight.

The Allegory of the Cave is one way to define how our perceptions rely on the senses to define the things that we see. If we are observing, but our apparent three-dimensional viewpoint is all that we take into consideration, then we have the potential to be led astray; for the third dimension is not the totality of all experience. The realm of the mind must also be taken into consideration — for the mind of consciousness itself is powerful enough to shift the world in an instant.

How do we define the dawn of space-time — the beginning of the universe?

In the modern world, we often use science to define the origins of existence as being a product of the Big Bang — the initial explosion that sent the fabric of space-time expanding at an infinite rate eventually to grow with order and complexity so great that it shaped matter into living, breathing, rationalizing organisms. These inferences come from data received through astronomical observation and implication in theory. To understand the beginning, we look toward the edges of time on the outskirts of space.

Time itself gives us a clue into the origins of the universe from nothing into something. We do not often realize it, but time itself reaches us in the form of light. The further out we see into space, the older the light from the star. Since light is also fixed at a finite speed (2.99×10^8 meters per second), we see the elder reflections of the stars' and galaxys' light. Depending on the distance between the object and the viewer, it will take years for this light to travel to the position of our eye; thus is the definition of a light-year.

But in truth, the observation of this light shedding object has the potential to be flawed, for the object itself — the source of the light — may no longer exist! Therefore, our observation is somewhat of a hologram or an echo of a past form of the thing in question.

The farther we gaze out into the cosmos through the telescope, the older the stars and deep space objects appear. This is due to the time it takes for light to travel to our position of perception in the wider universe. Then we reach a barrier called "the edge of the visible universe", where space and time are nonexistent. Some say this is proof that all things began at one point, for the expansion of all objects that exist within the bounds of space-time are younger than what is visible. No matter the case, the edge of space-time is considered to be proof of the beginning of the universe — the birth of a paradigm — and this very beginning is subject to infinite expansion after activation.

Some scientists consider that our own viewpoint is fleeting, and all that was ever existence will expand and cool in time to the point in which the very fabric of the universe no longer holds and snaps back in a colossal collapse as the grandest implosion to match the caliber of our beginnings with the Big Bang. However, there is no absolute proof of what happens to the universe in time, for this is yet undefined.

Other modern scientists consider that when expansion begins to contract — when the **red-shifted** spectral signatures of distant galaxies all become **blue-shifted** — the unfolding of events will invert the flow of space-time or the sequence of causality will reverse, until the cause is revealed after the effect.

If we traveled through time in a straight line from the point of our position here on Earth, we would eventually bend with the curvature of space to loop back and revisit ourselves. The shape of the universe does not translate so easily to our three dimensional understanding of reality. Just because we cannot physically observe what exists outside the **cosmic background radiation** barrier at the edge of the visible universe does not mean that it is non-existence. Or simply because our own lives are measured by time in the **third dimension** does not mean that the universe in which we reside has the need for a beginning and an end. Perhaps, the beginning was simply the end of another stream of conscious existence.

Eternal Singularity of the 0th Dimension

How can we use our knowledge of myth to describe the value of a **singularity**?

Is the initial singularity just a point of equality or a value of zero between the opposing **primeval forces** of existence? If so, the definition of our own universe's origins can be described as the point at which we crossed over the zeroth dimension, where and when the forces of space and time came together in equilibrium, if only for a brief moment.

Perhaps the origins of our own Big Bang or the zero point of singularity just before all came into creation contained the seed of our universe's interlocking dimensions that unfolded with the elegance of the lotus flower to fashion the undefinitive cosmos. And this seed acted as the very blueprint for the manner in which matter and energy separated to form the visible reality, which we now know as continuously manifested and established by the underlying polarities that guide the geometry of our universe — the positive and negative, the light and dark, the limiting and unlimited, the electric and magnetic.

Singularity is best described as a position in space-time where and when the unequal forces reach a point of equilibrium in which, granted by the constituents of the **omniverse**, the force of **positive** (+) equals the reaction of the **negative** (-) and the result initiates a value of zero in relation to space-time; that is, the thought of humanity was born as a reflection of the **cosmic egg** or the seed of our universe stored before our light and vessel crossed the zeroth dimension. The positive exceeded the negative **primeval force** and caused the seed of the lotus to sprout up from the zeroth dimension — we consider this very moment to be the birth of our universe.

With this information, we can conclude that the initial cause of all the effects contained within our universe was rooted on the other side of the original singularity at the time of the Big Bang. That is, the cause to our effects lies on the other side of a singularity.

How does zero carry us from our beginnings to our ends?

Like the look of a zero (0), the **Pantheistic** universe is not the value of one point, but a circle in time. If we bend the circle of a zero (0), we have the shape of eight (8), which loops us back to our origins in the eternal cycle that is continuously prompted and conceptually initiated at the point of **singularity** fixed at a moment in between at the overlap of non-geometrical existence in the zeroth dimension.

> "Know that the world is uncreated, as time itself is, without beginning or end, and is based on the principles, life and rest. Uncreated and indestructible, it endures under the compulsion of its own nature."
>
> —Jinasena, *Mahapurana*

XI. Evolution & Extinction Cycles

Patterns of Extinction

What causes have been presented to explain mass extinction events?

In recent years, researchers in the fields of biology, geology, and physics have attempted to track down a correlation between the natural rhythms of the Earth and changes in climate and diversity of the plant and animal kingdoms across the globe. To track such cycles of extinction and evolution, we must compare ice core data, sediment layers, and marine fossil records to piece together a timeline of Life in the past.

The History of Earth and all its flora and fauna is one riddled with times of 'testing' and 'adaptation' in the form of evolution and extinction cycles. Each sudden shift in extinction led to evolution that was brought on by the natural fluctuations of Earthly cycles or the interference of **extrasolar** objects that caused a cataclysmic event. Over the last decade, there are some who would propose that mass extinction events unfold with a pattern that can be traced. Regardless of whether or not this is fact, these mass extinction events seem to occur in step with rapid evolution events in the form of booming species adaptation and bio-diversification, and because of this, many theories have been presented to explain the reason for such a pattern at the root of the pattern.

A large portion of biological adaptation takes place due to change in scenery, and the **ice age** is one such time when climate shifted to drop the temperature with rapid pace. Plants and animals were forced to adapt to the freezing effect or otherwise face extinction. Ice ages are thought to be caused by natural fluctuations in the Earth's orbit or Milankovitch cycles tracked by weighing several factors — the **eccentricity** of Earth's orbit, the degree of axial tilt or **obliquity**, and Earth's wobble or changes in **precession**. In order for climate change to set in, temperatures must also fluctuate across a global scale.

In another way, adaptation is forced in the fight for survival outlined by Charles Darwin in the theory of natural selection as the relationship of one species to another, "organism to organism". As stated within *Catastrophes and Lesser Calamities of Mass Extinction*, adaptation must occur when the fight for existence is stronger than the immediate environment. If we take this into consideration, we can also connect how adaptation occurs at the expense of another species due to natural barriers, such as predation and starvation. For this reason, the health of the great Circle of Life, also known as the 'food chain', plays a key role in the adaptation of species to environment.

Additional causes of environmental change in the form of climate shift include fluctuations in **atmospheric gases** (the level of water vapor, methane, sulfur-dioxide, and carbon-dioxide) affects global temperature as well as the amount of solar radiation reflected off of Earth's surface, also known as **insolation**. Changes in carbon-dioxide levels in the atmosphere are often intertwined with meteor impacts and **volcanic activity** that show up in geologic layers.

In the year 1784, Benjamin Franklin mentioned in a lecture that he had experienced an unusually cold summer while journeying to Paris on diplomatic service. Franklin's observation of mild temperature was correctly ascribed to the eruption of Grímsvötn volcano and Laki fissure that destroyed over half of the livestock in Iceland, as it released high concentrations of poisonous hydrofluoric acid and sulfur dioxide into the atmosphere.

But the final cause, **cosmic radiation** is perhaps the most difficult to track. However, we do know that solar maximum or frequent sunspot activity reduces the amount of cosmic rays and **ultraviolet radiation** we receive due to the boost it gives the Earth's magnetic field as a product of high solar activity, thus radiation.

Some have tried to attach a companion star to the Sun in order to make sense of natural climate cycles as the effect of our Sun existing in a binary system. Others speculate that the Sun's path around the Galactic Center may be linked to variations in cosmic radiation, since the Sun travels in an oscillating motion as it proceeds above and below the center of the galactic plane.

Some researchers speculate whether the Sun's location in orbit causes an increased vulnerability to cosmic radiation or **extrasolar** disruptions by way of gravitational disturbances within the solar system's **Oort cloud**. This event theoretically causes asteroids in the furthest reaches of the **heliopause** to be redirected toward the interior solar system, and in turn, the surface of Earth. Within *The Galactic Theory of Mass Extinctions*, a timeline of geological records of mass extinction and evidence of crater impacts are suggested to coincide with the rise of Oort cloud comets that peaks every 30 to 36 million years.

On top of these listed causes for climate change, **plate tectonics** and **shifting magnetism** are also factors to take into consideration. For if an entire continent were to break apart, the animals on either side would drift slowly away, until they were separated by a vast ocean and became almost unrecognizable to one other.

Wilson cycles refer to patterns of destruction and growth of the ocean basins due to the shifting of continental plates. As of now, the Atlantic Ocean is the location of the Atlantic Ridge, where molten rock escapes from below the surface to create new ground at the bottom of the sea floor; the Pacific Ocean holds subduction zones such as the Marianas Trench, where land submerges back into the Earth. If this were ever to shift, it is theorized that the planet would face potentially catastrophic changes. Although plate tectonics play an important role in local climate change, the shifting of continents must also be accompanied by another cause to trigger a cooling effect as vast as the **ice ages**.

During the early Miocene collision, the plates of Africa and Arabia were forced into the plate of Europe, while the plate of Australia and New Guinea ran into the plate of Indonesia. This effect of plate tectonics saw to the separation of the Pacific Ocean from the Caribbean by the middle Miocene with the rise of the isthmus that is Central America. This collision event also prompted bio-diversification and mammal speciation during what is known as the Cenozoic Era or "new life".

The ocean currents also become a quickening tool to climate change, since the clockwise rotating tides north of the equator and the counterclockwise rotating tides south of the equator regulate local weather and migration patterns. When the waters warm, the current disperses this warmth to the edges of the poles naturally, and then as the waters cool, become more dense, and fall to the ocean floor, these chilled waters are forced to turn back once again for the equator — much like a conveyor belt. The minutest upset of temperature has the potential to shift the entire system through this vast circulation of ocean currents.

How does the Sun's orbit affect life on Earth?

Cosmic as well as ultraviolet solar rays are thought to play an important role in the habitability of life on other planets. For this reason, a planet's atmosphere and magnetic field are important factors to consider in the case of mass extinction and evolution cycles. Cosmic radiation is twice as high on Mars due to this planet's lacking magnetic field and thin atmosphere. The cosmic radiation we receive here on Earth is born of cosmic rays or high speed, high energy particles that reach us from outside our own solar system. We know that if a supernova were to explode near enough to Earth, then we would feel the effects with a massive dose of cosmic radiation — a tide of concentrated electromagnetic energy waves traveling near the speed of light.

Although this topic is still being debated, there are several scientific theories as to how the Sun's path around the **Galactic Center** affects the frequency of **extrasolar** interference and the level of cosmic-created particles present on the Earth. One such theory seeks to track the marine extinction and evolution patterns with the Sun's apparent movement through each of the Milky Way Galaxy's spiral arms. In theory, the location of the Sun traversing through the dense arms of stars would bring about a higher probability of extrasolar interference and asteroid impacts.

Another theory questions the Sun's apparent movement above and below the plane of the Milky Way Galaxy. At the center of the galactic plane, the Sun is threatened with more frequent extrasolar disturbances due to the density of stars and objects that reside at the center of the galactic disk. Some speculate that when the Sun reaches its northernmost point above the plane of the galaxy that the solar system is exposed to harmful cosmic radiation in the form of shockwaves emanating from the **Virgo Cluster** — one of the largest collections of galaxies just outside the Milky Way spirals.

> "Shockwaves may have contributed to accretions of matter at every scale. The epic of cosmic evolution had begun, a hierarchy in the condensation of matter from the gas of the Big Bang-clusters of galaxies, galaxies, stars, planets, and, eventually life and an intelligence able to understand a little of the elegant process responsible for its origins."
>
> —Carl Sagan, *Cosmos*

The Cause for Evolution

As the instructions encoded inside our DNA become mutated, the diversification of species is made possible. It is mutation that prompts the shift to evolution, but not without the conscious favoring and selection of particular nucleotidal sequences do we have evolution. Therefore, evolution is the result of a harmonization between mutation and conscious selection; for without the surrounding environment or even species itself to favor a modified trait, mutation would not be permitted to survive past its initiation.

Mutations occur when the nucleic acid instructions contained within our DNA are tied up in knots after we come into contact with harmful radiation. Radiation that has the potential to cause mutation is emitted across a spectrum of frequencies, although the most prevalent categories of harmful rays include **ultraviolet and cosmic radiation**.

It is a rare occurrence that mutation is caused by DNA polymerase mistakes during replication. For the most part, these mutations are the result of cosmic rays, ultraviolet rays from the Sun, radioactivity, or chemical compounds in the environment, and these external forces are the cause for nucleotidal changes that give rise to the evolution of a species or **speciation**.

But not without conscious selection does the modified trait become the new norm. Therefore, the presence of mutation alone does not give rise to evolution; thus there is an intelligence to all life. It is the consciousness contained within all living things, Nature who selects which adaptations will be favored and flourish here on Earth. Diversification in the form of mutation is a result of **the Source**, while natural selection is a result of consciousness — the **Spirit** within all Life.

Cycles of the Sun

How do **sunpot cycles** affect the conditions for Life on Earth?

The Sun endures a period of low and high sunspot activity,

solar maximum, and solar minimum, once about every eleven solar years with each cycle peaking in halves to complete the **sunspot cycle**; the solar cycle is twice as long at about 22 years and indicates a shift in the orientation of the magnetic fields in the Sun's northern and southern hemispheres.

During each **solar maximum**, a measurable variation in solar activity is attributed to the high number of sunspots on the Sun. As more sunspots appear on the Sun's surface due to heightened solar activity, we expect a higher probability of ejections, flares, and solar storms. For this reason, we can conclude that years of solar maxima have an ionization effect on the upper levels of Earth's atmosphere. The result of this effect can be seen first-hand by the solar winds that reach us in the form of charged particles absorbed as infrared emissions, which paint the night sky with the most spectacular lights show, the **aurora borealis** or 'Northern Lights'. At the same time, solar maximum or high solar activity also strengthens the pull of Earth's magnetic field, so that harmful ultraviolet radiation is more easily kept out.

By contrast, **solar minimum** is a period of low solar activity in which the surface of the Sun is devoid of sunspots. Although the solar minimum sets in across a period of only about eleven years, there are longer lasting grand solar minima cycles observed outside the usual set of twenty-two orbits about the Sun. Just a few centuries ago, the world endured a long-term period of low solar activity known as the Maunder Minimum. At this time, weather was recorded to have been unusually damp and cold from the mid 17th up to the 18th Centuries.

How does **heliocentric astrology** predict the **sunspot cycle**?

When we take a closer look at the **heliocentric astrology** of the Sun, the secret rhythms that fuel the heat of solar maxima reveal themselves. The colossal giants Jupiter and Saturn both rotate about the Sun in a period of 11.85 years and 29.5 years, respectively. As each of these planets transit through the heliocentric zodiac, they align once about every eleven years.

Solar Maxima

Solar maximum occurs once every eleven years, when the planets Jupiter and Saturn come together to form a 180 degree angle or straight line (**conjunciton** or **opposition**) in relation to the Sun. At this time, this synchronous event of Jupiter and Saturn creates Spring Tide (high tide) conditions on the surface of the Sun when the photosphere expands. As a result, sunspots, solar flares, winds, and storms are more frequent. In heliocentric astrology, the aspect of solar maximum is called a **conjunction** or an **opposition**.

Solar Minima

Solar minimum occurs once every eleven years in the time between periods of high solar activity, when Jupiter and Saturn are no longer aspecting the Sun with synchronicity. If we use the model of the Moon and Sun pulling on the Earth's tides, we can estimate that just like the effect of the Moon's quarter phase, the Sun experiences Neap Tide (low tide) at times of the solar minima, as Jupiter and Saturn form a 90 degree angle, **square** or **trine,** astrological aspect with the Sun.

Just as the Sun and Moon affect the tides, oceans, weather, and atmosphere of the Earth, so too do the great gas giants Jupiter and Saturn pull on the Sun to create Spring Tides. It is the presence of distorted positions in the Sun's natural magnetic field (magnetic reversals) that give rise to sunspots during a time of solar maximum as a result of the acting forces of outer planets Jupiter and Saturn.

Cosmic Lifecycles

How is the **cosmic radiation** that causes evolution born?

When we explore the effects of cosmic radiation, it becomes clear that there may be inevitable biodiversity cycles caused by our proximity to supernova explosions and position about the Milky Way Galaxy. Cosmic rays induce high speed, high energy particles that reach the Earth to cause the very mutations in which give rise to **speciation**, thus evolution.

The sight of a spectacular supernova explosion is amongst the rarest delicacies for the astronomer. In the year 1054 CE, Chinese astronomers recorded the sight of a brilliant source that outshone the light of day. This was the sight of the first supernova to be recorded in history, and its documentation mapped the birth of the Crab Nebula. Half a millennium later, two more supernova explosions were seen emanating in the sky — one first recorded by astronomer Tycho Brahe in 1572, then another again in 1604 by **Johannes Kepler**.

Supernova explosions send out a shockwave of high speed, high energy particles in the form of radiation that ripples a tide of concentrated energy about the corridors of the galaxy. This **cosmic radiation** that reaches us from distant locations is one cause of DNA mutation that refashions our biological code by way of the nucleotides, perhaps giving rise to the very genetic changes that call us human.

As the **Sun** traverses about the **Galactic Center**, it moves in and out of the spiral arms of the Milky Way Galaxy. On average, our solar system moves within one of these spiral arms for a total of 40 million years and spends about 80 million years between each spiral. Since the spirals indicate places where stars and planetary nebula clouds are formed, we can assume that when we pass through a spiral arm, we are exposed to a more frequent collection of extrasolar objects and gases. Perhaps, our solar system is enriched by the absorption of interstellar gases, dust, and comets of the spiral arms. Just 10 million years ago, we left the Orion Spiral Arm — out to explore the depths of space in between.

Last Glacial Cycle

What happened during the maximum of the last glacial cycle?

The last **glacial period** is considered a cold phase within the greater **ice age** that is still present today. The ice age itself lasts for a much greater period of time with global effects of cold temperatures and ice sheets that stretch across entire continents. Ice ages are powerful periods in Earth's climate history when the drop in global temperature had the potential to cause the entire planet to freeze over and form a ball of ice, as it has done so before in the past. When we name the 'last cycle' it can be considered the last glacial period that came to a close around 10,500 BCE.

During the maximum of this **glacial period** about 22,000 years ago, glaciers formed to cover many locations across the globe, including sites in North America, Northern Eurasia, the Himalayas, and select locations in the Southern Hemisphere, though this particular period of glaciation had more of an effect on the Northern Hemisphere. The Laurentide ice sheets covered nearly the entire country of what is now Canada, parts of the northern United States, and glaciers, ice caps, and ice fields formed high in the Rocky Mountains and Sierra Nevadas. In Europe, the Scandinavian ice sheet inched across the mainland and northwestern Asia to reach the British Isles, Poland, and Russia, where ice fields were scattered as far as the eastern side of the Taimyr Peninsula in Siberia.

Glaciation occurred across the globe with ice concentrated in high altitudes of Taiwan and Japan, the Alps-Himalaya range, the Atlas of Morocco, and the mountains of Kenya and Kilimanjaro Massif. The Southern Hemisphere was stacked with the Patagonian Ice Sheet of the Andes, glaciers in Australia's Mount Kosciuszko, ice sheets and glaciation across the Southern Alps of New Zealand, and glaciers atop those of the Pleistocene era in Indonesia that still exist, even today.

This last glacial period did not see such drastic changes in global temperature, rather the effects of glaciation were caused by the distribution of heat due to ocean currents and local wind patterns. However, the **ice ages** have the potential to produce more dramatic effects over the course of a much larger time period. Each **glacial and interglacial period** gives us a clue into temperature patterns that cause the freezing and melting of large ice sheets and glacial features within the greater ice age.

If we take a step back 52 million years ago, the Eocene epoch saw to the warming of Antarctica, so that the scenery would appear almost unrecognizable to that of the South Pole today. We see Antarctica as some 'lost continent' buried beneath the ice and snow, but it was once a lush paradise complete with prehistoric turtles and swaying palm trees. At this time, the Antarctic winters were up to 10 degrees (Celsius) higher than they are today, as presented by the evidence in sediment layers beneath the seabed.

It is thought that these warmer conditions were the product of high carbon-dioxide levels or the release of methane in the atmosphere, when **clathrates** (pockets of crystalized gases) escaped from below the ocean floor. A slight warming of the Earth's global temperature has the ability to release these clathrates. With this information, many have anticipated the thawing of Antarctic ice sheets once again due to the current rapid rising levels of greenhouse gases that, in turn, release clathrates to escalate the strength and speed of this heating effect.

The Ice Ages & Precession

How have the **ice ages** and glaciations come and gone?

With recent evidence it seems that **ice ages** and glacial periods have left and returned in a cyclic pattern over the course of several million years. The causes for such climate patterns are many, though one important factor is named the **Milankovitch cycle**, which influences the amount of solar radiation or insolation received at specific latitudes between the poles. It is theorized that Milankovitch cycles explain such changes through the inching frost that ceases to thaw with the summer season. This crucial turning point causes the gradual formation of ice sheets over a long period of time. These inching events have the potential to trigger the dawn of an ice age.

It is thought that **ice ages** are separated by intervals of about 200 million years with chilling temperature effects that extend across tens of millions of years. Approximately 70 million years ago, the Cenozoic period began, and observations of marine sediment give us a clue into these cooler periods of the past. During this current cycle, deep ocean waters cooled on three separate occasions around 36, 15, and 3 million years ago.

Step back 52 million years once again, and the temperatures between the poles of the Earth were less of a contrast. At this time, trees reached both the Arctic and Antarctic, and tropical conditions stretched northward rising high in the latitudes. This period of warmth is known as the Eocene. It comes as no surprise that this warm period was also followed by a drop in temperature and the formation of ice features. After the chill around 36 million years ago took hold, the ice sheets grew across East Antarctica.

How can precession be a cause for climate change?

Precession is just one factor of the **Milankovitch cycle**, which gives us a pattern to estimate the ice ages, glacial, and interglacial periods. These cycles were named after Milutin Milanković, the geophysicist and astronomer who in the 20th Century uncovered the relation between climate change and variations in the Earth's orbital cycles. The wobble of the Earth is what creates the visual effects of precession here on the ground. Precession is the result of Earth's wobble forced by the torque of the Sun and the Moon.

When we learn the power of precession, it becomes clear why the ancients would track this cycle with such enthusiasm. The progression of the Sun through the zodiac belt becomes an allegory of Earth's wobble — the 26,000 year period it takes **precession** to complete one cycle of the Sun traversing through all twelve astrological epochs of the zodiac. The precession cycle was so important to the ancients that architecture was built and dedicated to the days of **equinox and solstice** for an accurate reading of the astrological age by the degree of precession.

Milankovitch cycles seek to track climate change through insolation in step with precession using periods of 23,000 years. The **ice age** occurs as precession forces an area of the Earth to reflect less sunlight near the poles and **perihelion** between the Sun and Earth shifts slowly back through the seasons; thus depriving Earth the warmth of winds to melt the ice that inches with gradual increase each winter. Over time, the frost never leaves the ground, until it turns from chill to deep freeze as centuries pass. The ice slowly multiplies and condenses with the natural forces of gravity to form a massive ice sheet. Right now **perihelion** (the closest location of the Earth to the Sun along its elliptical orbit) occurs just after the winter solstice of the Northern Hemisphere.

Similarly, frozen continents have the potential to thaw when **precession** and **axial tilt** moves ice sheets into the light. If this process occurs in a crucial area of the Earth, it has the potential to cause great changes for the planet. Not only are the ocean currents and winds affected by the change, but the plant and animal species that once resided in the old habitats must either adapt, lest face the threat of extinction. Such abrupt changes may help to explain the cause for patterns of extinction and evolution.

What other factors influence orbital climate change?

Besides precession, other astronomical factors such as **eccentricity** (variations in the ellipse) and **obliquity** (degree of axial tilt) instigate drastic temperature change across the globe. Changes in the eccentricity of Earth's orbit give rise to global temperature fluctuations by way of the orbital path and positional relationship to the Sun. The effect of **eccentricity** is the result of astronomical perturbation from the planets Jupiter for its great size and Venus for its proximity, and its climate changes are linked to astronomical forcing over an orbital inclination course of about 100,000 years. The source of this 100 thousand year pattern is attributed to interplanetary dust cycles or fluctuations in oxygen isotopes from ice core in Greenland and Antarctica, which can be used to track variations in the ellipse.

Obliquity is defined by the angle between the rotational axis of the Earth and the plane of our solar system. This change in degrees from about 22 to 24.5 degrees is heavily influenced by our path about the Sun and influences of the giant planet Jupiter. The degree of tilt is directly demonstrated by the angle of 23.5 degrees between the equator and each of the tropics, the Tropic of Cancer and Tropic of Capricorn.

This estimation of axial tilt is suggested to shift at a rate of 0.128 degrees every one thousand years. Increasing the degree of tilt would create a more dramatic effect on the shifting seasons by an increase in duration and severity of weather. Each cycle of axial tilt or obliquity is estimated to take approximately 41,000 years to complete.

The last factor in the **Milankovitch cycle** or the cause for orbital climate change is the eccentricity of the Earth's path around the Sun that fluctuates in patterns of approximately 400,000 years. The seasons are proportionately linked to the length of time it takes the Sun to traverse from equinox to solstice in a given year. During extreme periods of eccentricity, seasons gain in days, when they occur on the farthest position from the Sun (**aphelion**). When the Earth is at its closest to the Sun (**perihelion**), the seasonal effects last a shorter amount of time.

Despite the many causes for astronomical climate change, the Milankovitch cycle is dominated by **precession** (every 24, 22, and 19 thousand years) in the northern latitudes due to summer insolation, **obliquity** (every 41 thousand years) in the southern latitudes due to seasonal duration, and **eccentricity** (every 400, 125, and 95 thousand years), although nearly absent from the final figures, can still be traced in the cause for global climate change.

Natural Climate Change

What factors besides orbital changes contribute to natural climate change?

Besides the orbital factors that influence Earth's climate cycles, another important element shown in ice core data from Antarctica displayed changes in the concentration of carbon dioxide present. During warm **interglacial periods**, the amount of carbon dioxide in the atmosphere is much higher, and during the cold **glacial periods**, this level drops. These carbon-dioxide level shifts occur sometimes hundreds of years after a minute temperature variation to an area. However, the effects of climate change become amplified, when carbon-dioxide concentrations fluctuate. Simulations suggest that both the **Milankovitch cycle** and carbon dioxide concentration variations in the Earth's atmosphere must be present in order to complete the ice age cycle.

Without a protective atmosphere, Earth would appear more like the surface of **Mars** — cold, barren, and devoid of life. Here on Earth, we rely on our atmosphere to help keep the planet warm and suitable for living organisms, though a change in living conditions brought on by shifts in temperature and overall climate prove that the wider planet has the potential to feel the effects of atmospheric composition.

Heightened levels of atmospheric gases such as carbon-dioxide and methane induce the **greenhouse effect**; thus prompt an increase in global temperature or global warming. The heating effect is caused by the presence of carbon dioxide, methane, and other gases that trap long wave radiation, so that the warmth from this energy does not escape. Solar energy reaches Earth in the form of short wave radiation (UV light that harms biological systems), but it is the long wave (infrared) radiation that becomes trapped to heat the planet.

For this reason, Earth's radiation balance is the key to global climate change. There are just a few ways this balance can be tipped — variations in solar radiation received on Earth due to the planet's orbit, fluctuations in release from the Sun itself, and changes in **albedo** (the amount of solar radiation reflected because of cloud and small particle cover) — to alter the amount of long wave radiation absorbed either by natural means in an excess of cosmic-created radiation or unnatural means through the excess concentration of greenhouse gases that trap heat in the atmosphere.

Loss of the Kingdoms

> "One specific trigger, which at the limit can be merely a single grain added to the pile, can initiate avalanches of a wide range of magnitudes. The magnitude of the avalanche obeys a power law; that is, there are a few large avalanches and many small ones. The relative magnitude of mass extinctions also appears to approximate to such a power law, as do other natural phenomena such as earthquakes and floods."
>
> —Tony Hallam,
> *Catastrophes and Lesser Calamities of Mass Extinction*

What causes mass extinction and evolution events?

Modern scientific study of species extinction, such as the research contained within *Extinctions and the History of Life on Earth*, demonstrates how extinction plays a greater role than origination in diversity patterns of a species. On average, peaks of taxonomic origination and speciation rise out of the threat of extinction to fill each habitable niche every 10 million years. These extinction events can be traced back to two dominating causes, global climate change and oceanic stagnation.

In the past, there have been five known mass extinction events called **the Big Five**. The first known **extinction event** occurred approximately 440 million years ago at the close of the **Ordovician Period** — a small period within the larger Paleozoic Era of ancient species. During this particular extinction named the End-Ordovician event, the drop in global temperature caused glaciation in the Southern Hemisphere and the loss of marine families to include thousands of species classified under each family. Living species named the trilobites and brachiopods suffered widespread extinction at this time.

Conditions for life were improved in the aftermath of the Ordovician event with a more efficient circulation system of ocean currents and oxygenation in the deepest depths of the sea. The sea level dropped, and continental ice sheets froze to span the gap of the Amazon Basin in South America and the Sahara Desert in Africa.

The second mass extinction named the Late Devonian event took place about 370 million years ago to conclude the **Devonian Period**. Much of the damage can be traced in the loss of diverse coral reef ecosystems, marine invertebrates (ammonoids, brachiopods, and triolobites), and vertebrates (conodonts, agnathan, and armored placoderm fish). In addition to the extinctions of the animal kingdom at this time, plants also suffered a significant drop in live numbers.

The third mass extinction named the End Permian event took place approximately 245 million years ago at the end of the **Permian Period**. This third and largest extinction to date is thought to be caused by a combination of rapidly warming climate conditions and plate tectonics that brought about the loss of marine and terrestrial life to make way for the world-wide speciation and diversification of plants to follow.

This extinction event saw to the disappearance of many species such as corals (rugose and tabulate), echinoderms, blastiods and bryzoans, brachiopods, Paleozoic crinoid groups, and vertebrae species such as the herbivores. At this time, the sea-levels dropped and prolonged **anoxia** (the absence of oxygen) was widespread in the oceans. The most significant losses of the End Permian are traced back to the disappearance of insect species. Plants also faded in time at a regional level — an effect thought to be caused by an increase of fungal spores, thus decay. This was the end of the Paleozoic Era or the close of "ancient life".

The causes of this third mass extinction are suggested to be linked to the eruption of the vast Siberian flood basalts. The End

Permian event of marine and terrestrial extinction is recorded in the geologic records through trace indicators of rising greenhouse gas concentrations, possible meteor impacts, and extreme oceanic anoxia in water depths as shallow as 10 meters deep.

The fourth mass extinction, the End Triassic event, occurred approximately 210 million years ago to conclude the **Triassic Period**. This event led to the loss of sponges (calcareous), ammonite species, and the complete extinction of conodonts, benthic bivalves, and brachiopods. It is speculated whether these same effects were seen in species of vertebrae on land, although it is known that terrestrial plants faced crises of regional extinction at this time. The causes of the fourth mass extinction are unknown but are attributed to warming climate and wide-spread oceanic **anoxia**.

The fifth mass extinction, the End Cretaceous event, is perhaps the most infamous and took place about 65 million years ago to close the **Cretaceous Period**, when the bulk of dinosaur species were wiped off the face of the Earth in a single blow. During this epoch in the History of Life on Earth, entire plankton groups (foraminifera and coccolithophorids), cephlapods, ammonites, and the terrestrial dinosaurs disappeared in a mass extinction that reduced the average duration of such an event from tenths of thousands of years down to a few thousand years. As the event ensued, the global sea-level also dropped.

This extinction event of the dinosaurs is thought to have been caused by a catastrophic impact or an excess of volcanic activity that caused the widespread loss of entire species. The result was thought to have been instantaneous and unfolded over the course of a few months to a few years. Following this extinction event, a boom in biodiversity flourished with a wave of evolution to fill each niche.

Before the cause of the End Cretaceous event was assigned to a doomsday asteroid smashing into the Earth to send a catastrophic super-heated shockwave and leave the Chicxulub crater (located in the Yucatán Peninsula) in its wake, Otto Schindewolf speculated that after examining evidence in a Salt Range in Pakistan, the cause of such an instantaneous extinction event may have be linked to a nearby supernova explosion, which sent an excess of cosmic rays toward Earth. In theory, such an influx in **cosmic radiation** has the potential to destroy the ozone layer that shields all life from harmful ultraviolet radiation; thus the effect would have been a lethal dose of radiation exposure.

Despite Schindewolf's former speculations, it is commonly accepted in modern scientific research that the blast of this catastrophic impact, which killed the dinosaurs, sent superheated debris tens of thousands of kilometers from the site. Flaming bits of matter reentered Earth's atmosphere and lit wildfires across the globe. Dust and gases in the form of carbon-dioxide, sulfur-dioxide, and water vapor escaped into the atmosphere.

Just as the eruption of Mount St. Helens in 1980 sent ash high up into the atmosphere to create a shade of artificial cloud cover seen across the globe, the effect of burning wildfires and molten impact material blotted out the Sun and denied the plants sufficient light to photosynthesize. Massive eruptions and lava flow were seen across the flood basalts of the Deccan Traps in Northwest India and lack of sunlight forced global temperatures to drop in what is known as "impact winter". In the aftermath, mammals were permitted to fill the habitat niche of the dinosaurs and branch out with diversification on land and at sea in the decades that followed the End Triassic event.

There is reason to believe a mass extinction event is underway at this very moment, though it does not take the form of a natural Earthly cycle. It is of the 'human consciousness created' category of cause. Any significant rise in carbon-dioxide and harmful atmospheric gases, in the past, has stressed the potential for change in climate in the form of global warming. Other factors besides the greenhouse effect also play an important role in the current extinction. Local factors include the deliberate destruction of ecosystems in the act of deforestation, pollution, and the over-exploitation of nature and its resources.

Where are we in the evolution cycle?

"Hypnotized by mutual mistrust, almost never

concerned for the species or the planet, the nations prepare for death."

—Carl Sagan, *Cosmos*

Despite where we find ourselves in the cycles of natural rhythm here on Earth, there is evidence that we are experiencing a mass extinction at the present moment, though the source is not a sudden catastrophe that strikes us from some remote location out in the space; it is a product of consciousness.

Human consciousness has the potential to understand the causes for natural cycles of the Earth, yet neglect the idea that consciousness itself has any effect on changes in the atmosphere. This is where science becomes a pile of facts and theory begins to open a window of understanding into the flaw of neglecting consciousness as a source of 'cause' from the 'effects' of scientific speculation.

It is true that much of the climate change in Earth's history occurs alongside patterns of extinction and evolution which are thought to coincide with natural cycles of precession, obliquity, eccentricity, cosmic interference, and fluctuations in atmospheric composition. However, the most recent upset of Earth's greenhouse gases and excess of carbon-dioxide and other harmful pollutants has been largely blamed on human activities and industrial developments of the last century.

If we viewed such cyclic evidence from a scientific perspective, we can begin to draw estimations and conclusions for what the future may hold. But add this element of human consciousness into natural Earthly cycles, and what you will find is not natural. That is, the effects of the presence of consciousness can be quite an enigma — there is no prediction for what consciousness can and will do.

Human consciousness has created the excess of carbon dioxide and local pollution through recent technology and industrial inventions. In this way, the Earth is not at the mercy of the natural cycles alone but also the humans that dwell at its edges, and the more collected human consciousness grows to be, the more powerful it becomes. For all parts of one idea moving in the same direction grant the beast speed to overcome the opposition and triumph over a vast realm of conscious thought as the accepted societal 'norm', which sends the Earth off to build all progression around a single idea, and this is why we continue our daily lives unappalled by the amount of damage we do to our own planet.

We must remind ourselves of the significance of our own monuments created out of humanity's affinity for natural aesthetic beauty and harmony — those in which accentuate a love of Nature and Life itself. The Taj Mahal built in the 17th Century in India is one such wonder of the world that reminds us of the subtle symmetry and architectural magnificence of Nature; for the construction of Taj Mahal is recorded in history to have been built a monument of Love — a tribute to harmony, the affinity, and intense passion the emperor Shah Jahan felt for his late wife, Persian princess Mumtaz Mahal. The constructive elements used in the blueprint of each building and garden within Taj Mahal resound the subtle symbols and motifs of harmony reflected in Nature.

When we look at the monumental architecture of Taj Mahal, we see the white shimmering marble exterior turned yellow by the presence of industry. Yellowing of the marble has become the most recent cause for concern, as pollution tarnishes the exterior surface of the temple. Taj Mahal is built upon a hillock with a wooden post foundation designed to receive water from the River Yamuna. This architectural design requirement provides the posts the moisture needed to avoid dry rot. At the present time, the River Yamuna is receding and cracks can be spotted in the walls. The waters of the River Yamuna continue to recede with the presence of industry and human activities. The loss of the Yamuna River is not only the loss of an architectural masterpiece of the medieval Islamic period, but it also counts as the destruction of an entire ecosystem.

In China, similar consequences of human intervention mature with each passing day to breed a new set of environmental catastrophes. One case of dramatic, local climate change would be the growing deserts of the Gansu Province in China. This edge of China was once the route to the Silk Road — the western end of the Great Wall. Now the western outskirts of the Gobi Desert grow with land each passing day due to the increase of domestic farm animals into the area.

The amount of cattle, sheep, and other domestic animals has quadrupled over the past fifty years, and the lands have been overgrazed to the point that the loosened grasses have completely blown away. These fragile areas have been overturned by the excess of grazing animals as well as drought conditions, which cause grasslands to disintegrate with desertification. These massive changes across the terrain of western China show us the power of human intervention.

This overgrazing in step with slash and burn agriculture and industrial deforestation have caused a lowering of the surface temperatures of the planet by way of sunlight absorption across the **color spectrum**. The darkest green forests absorb more heat and light than the lighter green grasslands, and in turn, the light green grasses absorb more heat than the pale-sanded desserts.

If we take one more step back and look at the globe for signs of mass extinction, the changes begin to appear in the form of statistics. We are currently experiencing a vast deforestation across the wider planet that has stripped us of our rainforests and erased regional habitats — the loss of entire species. The marine equivalent of a rainforest, the coral reefs, have also disappeared and left the oceans looking just as barren as the deserts upon land. Rather the former flourishing habitats in waters such as the Gulf of Mexico continue to turn in tides of fishes belly up, as the once wondrous ocean floors begin to resemble a wasteland.

Pollution seems to spill from human hand each place we go, until local species become threatened merely by our presence. The most serious side effect of our occupation that sees to changes across the globe remains the climbing levels of greenhouse gases, which produce a heating effect in the form of global warming. Humanity has personally seen to the rising concentration of greenhouse gases in Earth's atmosphere through excessive industrial farming, deforestation, and the burning of fossil fuels.

As if the threat of widespread animal extinction is not enough cause for concern, we are pushing the forefront of our own disaster. The rise in global ocean temperatures and circulation of warming water currents to the poles has begun the melting process of thick Arctic and Antarctic ice sheets.

It seems the increase in temperature has taken its toll on Mother Nature as the west side of Antarctica begins the melting process that has the potential to cause it to float. This effect was recently found to be irreversible at its current stage of progression.

The west side of the Transantarctic Mountains is built from systems of glaciers and massive ice sheets, such as those similar to the Ross Shelf frozen atop ocean water. When the waters begin to warm, entire ice sheets float with the current, and eventually fall away. In turn, the ice sheets and glaciers held back by the barrier of floating ice shelves will also fall away in rapid succession.

The melting of such massive amounts of the world's ice has the potential to raise the sea level by the meters and shift the coast lines inland — the location where much of the Earth's population currently resides. Experts in Antarctic climate change have suggested that the disappearance of a large portion of the Antarctic glaciers and ice sheets would take only minor fluctuations in average ocean temperature, such as that of a single degree.

The Interruption of Intelligence

How have humans disrupted the intelligence of Nature?

We need not intervene to bring intelligence back to Nature, since our actions more often than not reflect the conquering instinct of the individual — the disease of egoism born in the mind of man. If we were to extract the bulk of water from the melting ice sheets of Antarctica, we would disrupt the enrichment of terrestrial lands by way of the precious silts contained within the ice and glaciers. Just as our modern dams have destroyed natural circulatory systems and biological networks, this act of exploitation would upset the balance of ancient silt cycles that brings nutrients and minerals back to the land and creatures of the Earth.

The whole of humanity has a tendency to destroy the Earth and all intelligence that ever came about as a product of Nature, and at the same time, look beyond the frontiers of space in the name of 'contact' with consciousness or the thought of interacting with an 'intelligent' species. In doing so, we deny even a glance at the rarest and the wisest living beings that already thrive among us.

A signature of the wise is outlined in a song that echoes in the depths of the world's oceans. If we listen close, the songs of whales can be heard with melodies of harmonization and intricate vocalization. These whale-songs are sounded at low frequencies and repeated beat per beat, per measure, and note. Each song lasts an average of fifteen to thirty minutes, and the composition of a piece evolves from month to month.

Yet, the wisdom of a whale is revealed in its memory — the remembrance of a song. Whales often leave behind a song in a particular location during migration only to revisit this same spot months later. Upon their return to the location of the song, the whales begin to harmonize the melody at the precise note where they once left off.

For the bulk of whale history, there were no humans in vessels to disturb the deep oceans. In these early days, it is thought that whales could communicate from anywhere in the world. Within the past few hundred years, whale songs have been silenced. It is thought that nearly two hundred years ago, the fin-back whale could communicate across distances of 10,000 kilometers or more at a frequency of 20 Hz. Now this distance is reduced to just a few hundred kilometers, as misguided frequencies of human manufacturing pollute the invisible realms.

How can we reverse the destruction of the natural world?

> You have brains in your head.
> You have feet in your shoes

> You can steer yourself
> any direction you choose.
> You're on your own. And you know what you know.
> And YOU are the guy who'll decide where to go.

It is most important to be kind to the delicate systems upon which we rely for our own survival. As the exceedingly dominate species on this planet, we must rule over the kingdoms of the Earth with benevolence; we must balance the masculine and feminine aspects within our conscious perceptions to reach the common ground, recognize affinity, and create harmony by focusing our interest on the highest road above and between the left and the right.

Human empathy is the highest form of our emotion that allows us to exhibit the most valuable quality for all living species and future generations of this Earth — Love. We must use our intuition to guide us with affirmation to focus on empathetic wishes for the future of our species and all that is Life. We must also exhibit a love for both the living and the dead, wander the winding roads of past human history without fear, and learn to live alongside one another to strive toward harmony through the recognition of affinity — that which brings all possibilities and points of view together in perfect harmony to compose a brighter song for the future of the Earth.

We can — by directing our conscious fire that emanates force of will in a constructive, rather than destructive, manner to bring balance back to Nature.

> So be sure when you step.
> Step with care and great tact
> and remember that Life's a Great Balancing Act.
> Just never forget to be dexterous and deft.
> And never mix up your right foot with your left.
>
> —Dr. Seuss, *Oh, the Places You'll Go*

XII. Cosmic Astrology

How has the practice of astrology transformed over the ages?

When we look to the natural history of the Earth for answers, it becomes clear that both cosmic and local 'human consciousness created' elements are factors that affect climate change. The results of Earthly cycles and human intervention have the potential to breathe life or extinguish all trace of it. Therefore, the question of climate change should be one of utmost importance, since climate is also linked to mass extinction events of the past.

It becomes easier to define the phrase 'we are all connected' when we take notice of our own ability to affect the planet and all that is creation on Earth, but to step back and view the wider picture, the sky above holds the key to natural seasonal rhythms and Earthly cycles. Just like the weather, we can use these natural rhythms, the changes in Earth's orbit found in the **Milankovitch cycle** to predict the unraveling of an **ice age**, since astronomical signals for climate change occur with regularity. But also like the weather, we must take into account the 'unexpected' or unforeseen factors that upset the balance of these more predictable natural patterns.

When we trace back the origins of the tropical zodiac to their initiation in the ancient world, we begin to learn that astrology did not always serve the same purpose for early sky-watchers as it does in the present day.

To the farmer, astrology was a necessary tool for successful agrarian life, and to the traveler, a map of directions for navigation by land and sea. To the scribe, astrology was structured as time — those natural orbital cycles that shaped the measure of a minute, a day, and calendar year. The jotting of aspects and nativities added accuracy to the earliest records and flood patterns began to take shape. To the astronomer, astrology was the allegory of precession invented in the 'astrological ages' that take a total of about 26,000 years to complete the equinox sunrise traverse through each of the twelve zodiac signs, but to the mystic, astrology was the future foretold.

For the first time, mathematics and the wandering stars gave rise to the accurate prediction of future events in the sky, such as an eclipse. In the computer age, people spit out probabilities and estimations in the form of statistics (like no one's business). Scientific method has touched everything in the world that we know. It seems natural for us to see no significance in our everyday ability to 'prove' something through science or to 'predict' the outcome of that which has already been observed and otherwise, 'proven'. But to the ancients, this 'proof' of accurately predicting the future sky took on magical qualities, until it was transfigured into the art of divination.

The Harmony of the Universe

In what ways does the fabric of the universe sing in harmony?

Through the use of dimensional models, the universe begins to take the form of a dynamic, interconnected process down to the last atom. We do not often pay much attention to the coincidental subtleties that draw universal patterns and shapes in the larger structure. Yet when we explore deeper into the macrocosm, we discover the ripples of infinite microcosm, and the nature of our reality begins to reveal its secrets. As Jung once said, "In all chaos there is a cosmos, in all disorder a secret order."

The entire solar system works like a machine that if one piece is missing, the others fail to operate in harmony. We know through the use of scientific models that if we removed the planet Mars from the solar system, the orbits of the remaining planets would go haywire. The universe is just the same, every tooth of every gear fits together, just so. The numbers that write the mathematics behind our fundamental understanding of reality in physics could not be modified in any way, or else the universe itself would cease to exist — and these are our constituents.

For this reason, the geometry or the relationship between parts of the structure behind a dimension is the key to how it operates. These geometric ratios create the interlocking relationships of reality that draw outcomes of chance from what is permitted as possible and brought about through the probabilities of circumstance. The divine proportion of material existence outlines a structure of Nature that strives for balance, a golden ratio that harmonizes all parts of the whole.

> "Every living being is an engine geared to the wheelwork of the universe. Though seemingly affected only by its immediate surrounding, the sphere of external influence extends to infinite distance. There is no constellation or nebula, no sun or planet, in all the depths of limitless space, no passing wanderer of the starry heaven, that does not exercise some control over its destiny — not in the vague and delusive sense of astrology, but in the rigid and positive meaning of physical science.
>
> More than this can be said. There is no thing endowed with life — from man, who is enslaving the elements, to the humblest creature — in all this world that does not sway it in turn. Whenever action is born from force, though it be infinitesimal, the cosmic balance is upset and universal motion results."

—Nikola Tesla,
How Cosmic Forces Shape our Destinies

Humanity's Place in the Cosmos

In what ways does our place in the cosmos have an effect on humanity?

The stars seem to ease our obsession with the fourth dimension (time). What becomes so fascinating about the wandering stars is our ability to know where they will be from one day to the next. This ability to track the future movement of planets allows us to master time in the most subtle way, but some have wondered where humanity fits into this prediction of future events through tracking the position of celestial objects on the background of stars.

In the ancient world, it was through nativity that astrologers interpreted individualistic meaning from the planets and stars to paint the scenes of one's own destiny. Sometimes the astrological aspects helped shape conditions for events in the form of retrograde periods, transits, and eclipse omens, though the true purpose of astrology is to reveal to humanity the connection between the future positions of the planets and stars and the unfolding of Time and Life on Earth.

We do certainly trek quite close to this idea, when we combine our current understanding of the causes for global warming, since climate change directly affects the conditions for life on Earth. If we understand that the Sun, Moon, Jupiter, and Venus all influence parts of the Milankovitch cycle and Jupiter and Saturn are pivotal forces behind the sunspot cycle, then it becomes a more tangible realm of thought to explore this connection as a new form of **cosmic astrology**.

It just so happens that our ancient ancestors had been tracking these cycles of obliquity in axial tilt and precession caused by Earth's wobble long before our time. The discovery of the Antikythera mechanism also reveals that ancient peoples knew about another natural rhythm — the orbital cycles of the ellipse — though it was not yet named eccentricity.

In another way, the path of the Sun around the Galactic Center also seems another promising branch of cosmic astrology, since astronomical forcing, radiation balance and meteor impacts are colossal factors for life and extinction, thus evolution. The Sun's orbit about the galaxy should be monitored with close attention.

When we see the patterns of marine mass extinction, it becomes easier to look to the stars for an all-encompassing 'global' answer to explain these vast natural changes on Earth. In the same way, the position of celestial objects in the sky does bring rise to a change in 'circumstance' that has a very real effect on the behavior of life on Earth. If we remember that the basis of human thought takes the form chaos, we can see that thoughts are made from probability and possibility due to perceived circumstance in time. Our thoughts are directly shaped by the world around us.

But more importantly, as human beings, we do not escape the natural rhythms of the Earth. When the planet experiences a change in 'circumstance' due to natural Earthly cycles, we can bet that humanity will also be influenced.

What is the importance behind the way in which we view the cosmos?

> "If you will think of ourselves as coming out of the Earth rather than having been thrown in here from somewhere else... we are the Earth. We are the consciousness of the Earth. These are the eyes of the Earth. And this is the voice of the Earth."
>
> —Joseph Campbell, *The Power of Myth*

Our own cosmic philosophy has an enormous impact on the way in which we view and interact with the world. We use our cosmic philosophy to shape our own perception of the 'reality' around us. Our increasingly popular modern perspective of the Big Bang that prompted the beginning of space-time also predicts its own inevitable demise as some distant process of nature. What was the birth of the visual reality — the initial moment when our paradigm of existence as we perceive it first came into being — also foretells the end of the entire universe as we know it as the original energy slows in time.

In this material perspective there is no room to take into consideration what is human or simply, conscious. With this view of 'the beginning', we become passive in our attempts to 'foresee' and master destiny — not only that of our own lives but the fate of the world around us — by adopting such an objective attitude toward reality. We put nature at a distance this way and take no responsibility for any human part in the wider process.

When we look at the cosmologies of the ancients, the presence of consciousness sometimes preceded the dawn of existence. Thought or consciousness itself was often hinted as the essence of the 'aether' that brought all matter into being. The physical reality was created in the image of a thought. In a way, we give up our 'will' to nature and the unfolding process around us by denying the existence of human conscious intervention.

As suggested by the Big Bang, does the expansion of space-time ever just cease to exist? Or like our own understanding of things in the physical realm, does the collapse of our universe signify it is not destroyed only changed in form? Is there any real basis for cause and effect in this case — for without a 'something' before 'nothing' how can 'something' spontaneously exist? We cut our ties with this question at the edge of the visible universe in space-time.

We base this interpretation of existence on the assumption that the physical reality, that which can be perceived through the senses, through observation, is all there is to this world, though recent advancements in theoretical physics tell us that the universe as we know it is constructed from multiple dimensions — some of which are not so readily perceived.

We can imagine these dimensions with the mathematical

formulas of string theory, and with these equations, we discover a world of ten dimensions of space and one of time. The dimensions that make up this reality interlock in geometric proportions with some dimensions so small, they remain curled up inside the existence of another. We look to string theory to give us a 'universal formula' for the mathematics of the cosmos. If the master equation is ever complete, our interpretation of existence will be wiped clean to once again gain a new name.

Despite our attempts to understand the universe in terms of higher dimensions, we fail to ever experience such alternate realms of reality. But reality echoes through the eyes, ears, and antennae of consciousness — the thing in which perceives a self-constructed illusion of the overlap of dimensions. As it perceives, it also influences this 'reality' by interacting with it from the invisible realm; thus this universe we call reality and all philosophies of its beginnings and orderly ends must also envelope not only the material world but the totality of all streams of conscious existence.

The Power of Conscious Intervention

How is conscious intelligence the force that will save us all?

> "We make our world significant by the courage of our questions and by the depth of our answers."
>
> —Carl Sagan, *Cosmos*

There can be no definition to a process that is continuously written by the **Manifestation** of conscious thought into the material reality, since the very presence of an autonomous paradigm — the Spirit that interacts from outside the initial 'cause' or order established at the Source — proves the universe has not yet and never will be completely defined.

The universe is not entirely predictable, and because of this, the study of cause and effect cannot fully satisfy all possible probabilities hidden within the invisible aether of existence. **The Source** alone lacks the **Spirit** of conscious intervention. We are all just temporary states of matter and energy, the product of thought and the will of an idea, whether planned or unplanned.

We are taught that the objects of the cosmos undergo natural evolution, from birth to death, the energies rise from the dust and patterns of particles grow and shape the complexity of the universe. Our universe must fix and fashion its dimensions to correspond to change with flourishing diversity and ever-weaving codes of interlocking polar complexity, and during this process, Nature exhibits a conscious intelligence and adaptive favoring for affinity. We too, must seek a harmonious paradigm shift.

We must abandon **the Tower**, for truth brings with it the heavy rains, the challenging winds, and lightning from the sky that flashes the fire and weakens the brick, until such a time arrives when the structures that built the very foundation upon which we once stood are swept up in the blaze. Our current framework is beginning to crumble. As we fix our gaze to the floor below our feet, we must see the inevitable — the amendment of time as the floorboards dissolve right before our eyes, and we have no choice but to fall. Had we only listened for the thunder, observed the clouds advancing toward us, and had we foreseen the promise of lightning to ignite the spark, our fate might not lie in a pile on the ground.

Try if we will, the rickety tower cannot be mended; for the weight of former material has become heavy, obsolete — and **the Tower** so high in the sky as it totters in a silent battle with Time. It is our only option to step down from the tower before it collapses upon us — we must abandon the shifty framework, lest the chaos of falling rubble destroys us all.

Cosmic Astrology

XIII. Encyclopedia of Astrology

abyss - primal chaos or undefined space before time; also "bottomless" or limitless.

aether - the "quint" or fifth classical element outlined by Pythagoras in ancient Greece and named the quintessence or quality of the upper air of the abyss; also "ether" and the Sanskrit "akasha". It is the dodecahedron of the Platonic solids. In the modern era, aether is considered to be a medium for the transmission of electromagnetic frequencies. It is the essence of limitless — the weightless, invisible and all-permeating force — contained in all substance; the astral light that encompasses all space.

affinity - a synchronous event of natural harmony that connects perceived acausal possibility in the mind of archetypal thought (the invisible) with causal circumstance (the visible) resulting in the formation of a symbol.

affirmation - a symbol of the mind that invokes the memory of Divinity or the initial affinity.

air - one of the four classical elements outlined by Pythagoras in ancient Greece and named the universal power or the quality of the lower atmosphere of the heavens; also the Latin "aer" or Sanskrit "marut". It is the octahedron of the Platonic solids with qualities of both hot and wet. In the modern era, it is considered the substance of gas or the spirit of intelligence contained within all things. It is limitless — that which fills the form or reacts to pattern.

Akashic Records - in occult teaching, an esoteric concept that refers to the astral memory of all consciousness in time; based on the Sanskrit word for aether or "akasha". It is a library of all thought, dream, will, action and emotion of past consciousness and pensive reflections of the Anima Mundi. In the spiritual world, those who possess the key to astral vision can access the door to these histories.

almanac - a table, book, or pamphlet printed with the calendar months, weeks and days of the annual seasonal cycle; the etymology remains uncertain, though is speculated to have been derived from the ancient Greek "almenikhiaka" meaning "calendar" or the Arabic "al-manākh" meaning "climate". Almanacs made use of the astrological ephimeres in order to map the lunar phases, eclipses, climate changes, seasonal weather, and tide information for planting and navigation. The first almanac was recorded to have been printed in the year 1457 CE, and in 1473 CE, German astronomer Regiomontanus (Johann Müller) published "Ephemerides ab anno". Regiomontanus' almanac exists a significant time-signature artifact of the first printed almanacs to enforce its historic significance.

the ambient - the quality and form of that which is in motion; the underlying current of waves and electromagnetic frequencies that envelope the abyss. In local terms, the magnetic field surrounding the Earth manipulated by Nature — the flux and flow of cosmic rhythm induced by the planetary positions, cycles of the Sun and interactions with probability and circumstance in the event of cosmic phenomena.

anoxia - in geochemistry, the loss of molecular oxygen in sea, fresh and groundwater sources. This deprivation of dissolved oxygen spawns a realm of inhabitable waters for the bulk of marine life. In the records of Earth's geologic past, time periods of widespread oceanic anoxia have been recorded as a significant factor and cause for extinction events.

aphelion - the location in which Earth reaches its farthest position from the Sun on its elliptical orbit. This principle of celestial mechanics was outlined by Johannes Kepler in the 17th Century with Kepler's first law of planetary motion.

Aquarius - the eleventh astrological sign of the tropical zodiac that spans from 300 degrees to 330 degrees on the zodiac belt to hold the fourth fixed sign within the season of winter; from the Latin "water carrier" represented by the symbol (♒). The zodiac sign Aquarius is named the Sun sign for those born between the dates of January 21st to February 19th in tropical astrology and February 15th to March 14th in sidereal astrology. Aquarius is assigned the traditional planetary ruler Saturn, the modern ruler Uranus, and can be found within the Air triplicity.

The Archer - (see Sagittarius)

archetype - a universal pattern of thought or primordial image which takes the form of an object, event, person, or motif contained within the mind of the collective unconsciousness; the Greek "archetypos" or original pattern pronounced through the use of a symbol.

Arabic Parts - in Arabic astrology, invisible transiting aspects of astrological significance; also named "Arabian Points" or "lots". The Arabic Parts are calculated on a given day by measuring the distance between the position of the Sun placed at the ascendant (rising sign on the eastern horizon at sunrise) and the degree of a celestial body such as the Moon, Venus, Mars, or other objects that draw astrological aspects within the plane of the zodiac belt.

Aries - the first astrological sign of the tropical zodiac that spans from 0 degrees at the ascendant (ASC) to 30 degrees on the zodiac belt to initiate the first cardinal sign with the season of spring; from the Latin "ram" represented by the symbol (♈). The zodiac sign Aries is named the Sun sign for those born between the dates of March 21st to April 20th in tropical astrology and April 15th to May 15th in sidereal astrology. Aries is assigned the planetary ruler Mars and can be found within the Fire triplicity.

Aristarchus of Samos - (310 BCE - 230 BCE) the ancient Greek mathematician and astronomer who was among the first to propose a Sun-centered solar system known as heliocentric theory. One record of his ideas is contained within the "The Sand Reckoner" — a scientific criticism documented by inventor Archimedes. Aristarchus borrows his name from his home, the island Samos near Miletus, the ancient heart of Ionian scientific speculation in the Aegean and a product born of the Ionian Enlightenment.

ascendant - in traditional astrology, the invisible aspect or point that initiates the nativity at 0 degrees and reveals the zodiac sign of the first astrological house, as it rises or ascends above the plane of the eastern horizon; the degree of the rising sign.

astrolabe - a time-keeping invention and astronomical device that dates as far back as antiquity and transformed into intricate planetary models and astronomical mechanics in the medieval Arabic world.

astrology - the practice of cosmic observance that seeks to interpret the significance of the relationship between the Earth and the position of the luminaries — the stars, planets, Moon, and Sun. In tradition, the astrologer observes and records the synchronous angles and relationships that connect the position (degree) of aligning celestial bodies to form astrological aspects. These aspects are weighed across a wide range of factors and interpreted in various branches of astrology, such as mundane, electional, medical, horary (natal or horoscopic), or cosmic astrology.

astrological aspects - those transitory positions of the luminaries on the backdrop of the zodiac belt that constitute an interpretable relationship in the degree of separation or orb between two or more interacting celestial bodies that form a significant angle of geometric symmetry; also familiarity.

astrological houses - the twelve "houses" are measurements or 30 degree "lots" of segmented time that correspond to the location of invisible and visible planetary aspects as revealed on the eastern horizon over the course of one day; also decans in ancient Egyptian astrology. The first house is initiated along the zodiac belt at the position of 0 degrees to signify the ascendant. The second to the eleventh houses span from 30 to 330 degrees in 30 degree increments, while the twelfth and final house completes the circle at 360 degrees.

In the casting of nativities, the astrological houses outline the signature life path granted to the querent and interpret the nature of future interactions between the original nativity and transiting astrological aspects to come.

astrological interpretation - the negative or yin expression of the universe in cosmic possibility.

Astronomical Clock - in Prague, the Orloj or medieval astrolabe-style clock can be found built into the tower of City Hall in the Old Town Square. It measures local (European), solar, lunar, sidereal, and Old Bohemian time and remains the oldest surviving gear-clock in operation that tracks the ancient Babylonian time system of "unequal hours". The intricate dials along the outside each define a system of measurement for time — the Sun pointer to indicate the solar year, the moon to track the lunar year and phases, the zodiac signs to map the seasons, and the star pointer to distinguish sidereal time by the date of vernal equinox.

astronomical observation - the positive or yang expression of the universe in cosmic order.

atmosphere - gas, dust, and any "air" with mass that surrounds a celestial body. The atmosphere of Earth is mainly composed of nitrogen, oxygen, argon, and trace amounts of carbon-dioxide in addition to other gases; it is biologically sustained and acts as a radiation shield that protects Life from harmful cosmic and solar rays or ultraviolet radiation.

autumn equinox - the astronomical point that marks the location where the ecliptic (plane of the solar system) crosses the equator to depart the latitudinal position of the observer; the cardinal point that initiates the season of autumn at the third quarter of the zodiac cross. The autumn equinox is observed when the hours of day equal the hours of night.

axial tilt - (see obliquity)

Azure Dragon - in Chinese astrology, one of the four celestial beasts known as "Qing Long" that rules the direction of East and the season of spring; also the Korean "Cheongnyong", Japanese "Seiryū" and Vietnamese "Thanh Long".

the bagua - in Tao, the primordial and fundamental principles of manifested reality represented by eight symbols as extensions of either yin or yang; the eight trigrams. The bagua is octagonal with "ba", eight "guas" or regions.

benefic aspect - an astrological aspect that forms a harmonious angle of three as the base (trine and sextile). Planetary rulers are also considered benefic aspects when placed in a position of rulership or exaltation.

The Balance - (see Libra)

Big Bang theory - in the modern era, a common cosmology of mathematical and theoretical scientific speculation that interprets the universe as an echo of the original primordial force, which erupted reality into being from one single point and brought about the cause of the visible universe and all effects of life contained within. Reflections of the initial explosion of the Big Bang still linger in continuous motion and aid the construction of the dimensional reality in the form of inherent polarities and mass-energy ratios.

bioelectromagnetism - in modern biology, the interaction between micro and macro biological networks and electromagnetic fields or frequencies. Research of this relationship is traced in the electromagnetism produced in living cells, tissues and greater organisms. Bioelectromagnetism is also observed in the response of an organism, as it is introduced to external electromagnetic frequencies.

In human biology, it is the study of the electric currents that power the nervous system and the natural magnetism outlined by the meridians. On a wider scale, bioelectromagnetism is used to connect geomagnetic fields with animal migration patterns and to predict the effects of man-made frequencies.

birth chart - (see natal chart)

black hole - a region of absolute gravity due to such high mass and compact density that it warps the fabric of space-time, so that no matter, not even light, can escape the attraction of its massive pull. A black hole is formed during the death of a colossal star such as a supernova, as it collapses under the weight of gravity; due to the weight of such massive proportions, it freezes in a state of collapse to form the event horizon.

Calculations predicting the presence of black holes were first outlined in Albert Einstein's general theory of relativity and later elaborated upon with the addition of the Schwarzschild radius. Black holes cannot be visually observed, but the presence of such an object can be estimated by the amount of x-rays and other forms of electromagnetic radiation it emits and the interactions between its region of influence and nearby objects.

Black Tortoise - in Chinese astrology, one of the four celestial beasts known as "Xuan Wu" that rules the direction of North and the season of winter; also the Korean "Hyeonmu", Japanese "Genbu" and Vietnamese "Huyền Vũ". The Black Tortoise is sometimes referred to as the "Black Turtle" or "Black Warrior".

blue shift - the observance of an object that appears to emit a blue signature, as it shifts to shorter wavelengths due to its accelerating motion in time toward the relative point of the viewer's perspective.

The Bull - (see Taurus)

caduceus - in ancient mythology, the staff of Hermes or Mercury represented by two snakes intertwined up the rod and surmounted by wings. It is referenced in the mythology of Asclepius the healer with a single snake, and in modern times, it is a widely accepted symbol for healing.

Cancer - the fourth astrological sign of the tropical zodiac that spans from 90 degrees at the Imum Coeli (IC) to 120 degrees on the zodiac belt to initiate the second cardinal sign with the season of summer; from the Latin "crab" represented by the symbol (♋). The zodiac sign Cancer is named the Sun sign for those born between the dates of June 21st to July 20th in tropical astrology and July 16th to August 15th in sidereal astrology. Cancer is assigned the planetary ruler the Moon and can be found within the Water triplicity.

Capricorn - the tenth astrological sign of the tropical zodiac that spans from 270 degrees at the midheaven (MC) to 300 degrees on the zodiac belt to initiate the fourth cardinal sign with the season of winter; from the Latin "horned goat" represented by the symbol (♑). The zodiac sign Capricorn is named the Sun sign for those born between the dates of December 22nd to January 20th in tropical astrology and January 15th to February 14th in sidereal astrology. Capricorn is assigned the planetary ruler Saturn and can be found within the Earth triplicity.

cardinal signs - the four cardinal points on the compass of the zodiac cross, where the ecliptic meets the celestial equator — Aries, Cancer, Libra and Capricorn; the seasonal markers of spring, summer, autumn, and winter, respectively. Cardinal points reflect the location of the equinoxes and solstices. In traditional astrology, cardinal signs are associated with new beginnings, and those who are born under this quadruplicity possess the spirit of enterprise.

celestial beasts - in ancient Chinese astrology, four symbols to depict the celestial rulers of the compass in the sky — the Black Tortoise of the North "Xuan Wu", the Vermilion Bird of the South "Zhu Que", the Azure Dragon of the East "Qing Long", and the White Tiger of the West "Bai Hu". Each celestial beast also represented a season — the dragon of spring, the phoenix of summer, the tiger of autumn, and the turtle of winter.

chaos - the conscious spirit of irregularity and random chance in the Universe; opposite cosmos.

Chinese calendar - in China and various regions in Asia, a lunisolar calendar used to track the solar year in time with the phases of the Moon; also the "Han calendar". This calendar is currently used to measure the civil year in China, and begins upon the rise of the second new moon following the winter solstice. The Chinese calendar tracks a total cycle of 60 years, and each year is given a quality (yin or yang) and assigned a zodiac animal. Every two years an element of Wu Xing — Wood, Fire, Earth, Metal, and Water — replaces the previous element.

Chinese Zodiac - the twelve zodiac signs or animal constellation patterns used to introduce a New Year and outline the 60 year period (12 years x 5 = 60 years) of the Chinese calendar — Rat, Ox, Tiger, Rabbit, Dragon, Snake, Horse, Goat, Monkey, Rooster, Dog, and Pig; also the "Shēngxiào" or "birth likeness".

circadian rhythm - any biological cycle or pattern that can be traced back to a day (about 24 hours); also known as the "biological clock" and derived from the Latin "circa", approximately, and "diem" from "dies" meaning day. Circadian rhythms are endogenous or self-sustained, yet the maintenance of such a twenty-four hour cycle is entrained or synchronized by external cues called "zeitgebers" like sunrise, sunset, pressure, and temperature fluctuations that prompt the activation of the internal biological response.

classical planets - the first seven planets of the geocentric model (Earth-centered solar system) known to ancient astronomers — the Sun, Moon, Mercury, Venus, Mars, Jupiter, and Saturn.

collective unconscious - in analytical psychology, the common ground of mental thought that exists within all humans. The original ideas of the collective unconscious were first introduced by Carl Jung to explain archetypes and motifs that hold a linear significance and act as universal symbols.

conjunction - an astrological aspect that denotes a 0 degree angle relationship between two or more celestial bodies within an 8 degree orb of separation.

Nicholaus Copernicus - (19 February 1473 - 24 May 1543) the astronomer and mathematician who reshaped the solar system model with heliocentric theory in his research contained within "De revolutionibus orbium coelestium". Copernicus lived in Polish Prussia and traveled to Italy (Bologna and Rome) during the age of the Renaissance. He left us with the ground shaking paradigm shift or Copernican Revolution that initiated the entrance of the heliocentric solar system.

corpus callosum - the dense collection of neural fibers that unite the left and right hemispheres of the brain; from the Latin "tough body".

The Crab - (see Cancer)

cosmic astrology - the branch of modern astrology that seeks to interpret the relationship between macro and micro cosmic rhythms of Nature and Life on Earth. Cosmic astrology is based on the "cause" for observable natural cycles and their "effects" on Earth in order to estimate circumstances or future conditions inherent to all Life — tracking the equinox and solstice to map the involuntary ritual of the changing winds and seasons, the sunspot cycle to measure solar activity, the cycles of the Sun and Moon to foresee the changing tides and weather, the Milankovitch cycle of precession, obliquity, and eccentricity to predict climate change, and the galactic year to map the Sun's traverse about the Milky Way through the thick of each spiral arm.

Cosmic Cross - a grand astrological pattern drawn on a natal chart and composed of a completed square — two **squares** precisely aligned to form a square or rectangle shape — crossed in the middle by two **oppositions** or an "X" of diagonal lines.

cosmic egg - within the ancient cosmogony of the earliest creation myths; the seed that contained the whole of existence before all was hatched into reality at the birth of the universe.

cosmic microwave background radiation - the oldest light in the universe traced back to an ancient form of thermal energy or uniform isotropic radiation that can still be measured and observed as an eternal echo of the Big Bang in the fabric of space-time.

cosmogony - a philosophic concept or theoretical study of the cosmos used to explain the origins of existence and the initial forces that brought about the birth of the universe or conscious reality.

cosmology - a philosophic concept or scientific study of the origination, evolution, and eventual completion of the universe. In the modern era, one leading cosmology in science, the Big Bang theory, is made possible through the patterns of dimensional framework outlined by the mathematics and physics of the universe, while conceptual implications of the meaning of "cosmos" and conscious reality are recorded as symbols through the histories in the myth and esoteric traditions of the ancient philosophies and religions.

cosmos - in classical philosophy, the ancient Greek concept of the predictable and harmonious order of the Universe; opposite chaos.

cosmic radiation - high speed, high energy and mass particles that originate in the extreme temperature cauldrons of extrasolar objects. Cosmic radiation reaches the Earth in the form of cosmic rays that interact with particles in the atmosphere to produce lower energy states.

creative cycle - in the Taoist philosophy of Wu Xing, "shēng" or the generative and nourishing order of the elements — Wood, Fire, Earth, Metal, and Water, respectively. This cycle forms a pentagon shape, as each of the elements supports the force of the next.

creative principle - the inherent intelligence and force of Nature in balance. The harmonization of the initial forces of chaos united with cosmos.

cubit - an ancient unit of measurement (45.72 centimeters) derived from the length between the elbow and middle fingertip; in the Old Kingdom of Egypt (2,700 BCE), the "royal cubit". According to Marcus Virtruvius, the cubit measured six "palms" or one and a half Roman "pedes" or feet.

Leonardo da Vinci - (15 April 1452 - 2 May 1519; Julian) the artist, inventor and scientist who is famed to represent the archetype of the true "Renaissance Man" in his numerous curiosities and discoveries of cosmic proportion. Da Vinci outlines the existence of the golden ratio in his illustrative model of the human form "the Virtuvian Man". Leonardo is from the town of "Vinci" in the former Republic of Florence in modern-day Tuscany, Italy. He is remembered for the encoded blueprints of his inventions and countless works of art that reflect ratios of divine proportion.

Deity - an archetypal emotion or concept held in the mind of the collective unconscious and pronounced through the use of a universal symbol.

decanate - a third of a zodiac sign or one of three 10 degree subsections of each zodiac sign used to denote planetary rulership by elemental triplicity.

decanic astrology - an ancient branch of astrology in which the decans of 30 degrees outlined the ruling planets by the elemental quality of each triplicity — Fire, Earth, Air and Water — in the subsequent and corresponding order the decanate signs were introduced within each zodiac sign.

Rene Descartes - (31 March 1596 - 11 February 1650) the philosopher, mathematician, and writer who questioned the connection between the natural world and conscious reality in such a reasonable way that he is considered to be the "father of modern philosophy". Descartes spent time traveling between the Kingdom of France and the Dutch republic. His focus of philosophical debate was reasoning for and against the existence of a soul outlined in "The Passions of the Soul". He left his signature in history with the phrase "Cogito ergo sum" — "I think, therefore I am".

descendant - in traditional astrology, the invisible aspect or point that initiates the nativity at 180 degrees and reveals the zodiac sign of the seventh astrological house, as it descends below the plane of the western horizon; the degree of the descending sign.

Divinity - a symbol of synchronous observance or significance that relates one's Deity in the mind to the harmonization of exterior causal and interior acausal psychological events; the revelation of "the Absolute" or One Principle that guides this Reality.

Dog - in Chinese astrology, the eleventh sign of the zodiac used to signify the eleventh year in a calendar of twelve lunisolar cycles. The dog is a yang sign of the fixed element metal in the fourth trine.

Dog Days - the hottest days of summer named after the ascent of the "Dog Star" — Sothis' rising or the modern day Sirius tracked by the Egyptians to initiate the Nile flood season; in the Northern Hemisphere the height of midsummer's Sun in the months of July and August and in the Southern Hemisphere January and February.

Dragon - in Chinese astrology, the fifth sign of the zodiac used to signify the fifth year in a calendar of twelve lunisolar cycles. The dragon is a yang sign of the fixed element wood in the first trine.

earth - one of the four classical elements outlined by Pythagoras in ancient Greece and named a derivative of matter or the quality of heaviness of the terrestrial world; also the Latin "terra" or Sanskrit "bhūmi". It is the cube of the Plationic solids with qualities of both cold and dry. In the modern era, it is considered the solid or dense state of matter that attracts objects through gravity. It is limiting — that which forms pattern or takes shape.

eccentricity - in astronomy, the eccentric variation in the perfect sphere of a planetary orbit due to the size and distance ratio of the object in which it orbits.

eighth house - the eighth of the twelve astrological houses at 210 degrees from the point of the ascendant on the zodiac belt. It is the house of passions and transformations ruled by the planet Pluto and the zodiac sign Scorpio.

Albert Einstein - (14 March 1879 - 18 April 1955) the cosmic philosopher and theoretical physicist who is named the "father of modern physics" as tribute to his contributions to the mathematical formulas of the universe and thoughts on the cosmos with his general theory of relativity. Einstein was a great thinker of cosmic order at a time of triumphing chaos between world wars. He was born in the Kingdom of Württemberg and obtained American citizenship in the year 1940. Einstein left us with a scientific trinity of interlocking universal constituents with the formula $E=mc^2$ (energy = mass x constant^2).

electional astrology - a branch of traditional astrology that seeks to interpret the conditions of future events against the weight of configurations or astrological aspects between the celestial bodies. This particular form of divination made use of "omens" as a product of fortunate and unfortunate aspects and events such as the sight of an eclipse. Electional astrology dates back to the time of ancient Babylon where it was originally developed for state affairs to be cast in courts and for use on the battle field.

electromagnetic radiation - in physics, electromagnetic (EM) waves, light, or photons that carry energy which can be measured and categorized by the duration of the wavelength. In modern science, all electromagnetic radiation carries a signature wavelength in the measure of its sine curve and possesses a frequency or duration — determined in the visible spectrum by its color.

electromagnetic spectrum - the range of all possible wavelengths of electromagnetic radiation. The electromagnetic spectrum is divided into categories of frequencies from low frequency radio waves (the longest wavelengths) to infrared, microwaves, visible light, ultraviolet radiation, x-rays, and gamma rays (the shortest wavelength).

elemental triplicity - the four sets of three zodiac signs that correspond to each of the four classical elements — the Fire, Earth, Air and Water signs. In ancient astrology, triplicities were separated by 120 degrees or trine.

eleventh house - the eleventh of the twelve astrological houses at 300 degrees from the point of the ascendant on the zodiac belt. It is the house of collective wishes and united efforts ruled by the planet Uranus and the zodiac sign Aquarius.

elliptical orbit - the eccentric, ovoid deviation of the perfect spherical orbit due to the pull of gravity from the object about which it orbits.

emission spectrum - the range of electromagnetic radiation emitted by chemical elements or compounds and measured across an emission spectrum of color to denote a frequency or radiation wavelength. In modern chemistry, the emission spectrum is used to identify the chemical composition of an unknown substance.

ephemeris - a calendar table of future transits and astrological aspects of the celestial bodies. The first ephemeris tables known in existence were records of star locations from the 17th Century BCE forward written in cuneiform inside the greater collection of tablets named the "Enuma Anu Enlil" of ancient Babylon.

ephemeris of Venus - a calendar table of future transits and astrological aspects of the planet Venus. The first Venus ephimeris tables can be found in both the ancient Babylonian and Mesoamerican records. The "Venus Tablet of King Ammiziaduga" or "Tablet 63" was the earliest Babylonian cunieform tablet of Venus ever recorded and can be found in the wider collection of "Enuma Anu Enlil". The Maya also recorded a calendar to outline the ephemeris of Venus as early as the 11th Century BCE in the collections of the "Dresden Codex".

equinox - the cardinal astronomical point at which the ecliptic (plane of the solar system) crosses the degree of the equator (0 degrees latitude); occurs twice a year at the initiation of spring and autumn during the months of March and September.

evening star - the planet Mercury or Venus as it appears at sunset in the west. Venus as the evening star has the potential to glow up to 15 times brighter than Sirius or the brightest star in the sky; also the Greek "Hesperus" or Latin "Vesper".

Encyclopedia of Astrology

exaltation - in traditional astrology, an astrological transit that denotes the planetary ruler occupies a sign of a similar nature; also promotion to "dignity". Exhalation refers to the zodiac sign of the specified luminary's most fortunate, powerful or "exalted" position.

extrasolar - in astronomy, of or existing outside the immediate solar system.

fall - in traditional astrology, an astrological transit that denotes the planetary ruler occupies its opposing place of exaltation; also "detriment" or when opposite its ruler, "debility". Fall is the zodiac sign of the specified luminary's most unfortunate, restricted, or disadvantageous position.

female - in geometry or cosmic philosophy, that which is bent or curved; the divine feminine principle.

Fibonacci sequence - in mathematics, the numeric sequence of integers in which the sum of the first two numbers equals the third number, and the sum of the second and third numbers equal the fourth and so on in sequential order (0, 1, 1, 2, 3, 5, 8, 13, 21, 34, 55, 89, 144 …). This sequence of numbers was recorded by ancient Indian mathematicians, though it is named for Leonarda da Pisa — also known as Fibonacci. The Fibonacci sequence is derived from the formula $[F(n) = F(n - 1) + F(n - 2)]$; also the "Liber Abaci".

fifth house - the fifth of the twelve astrological houses at 120 degrees from the point of the ascendant on the zodiac belt. It is the house of individual expression and creativity ruled by the Sun and the zodiac sign Leo.

fire - one of the four classical elements outlined by Pythagoras in ancient Greece and named a derivative of power or the reactionary substance of the terrestrial world; also the Latin "ignis" or Sanskrit "agni". It is the tetrahedron of the Platonic solids with qualities of both hot and dry. In the modern era, it is the substance of plasma or the conscious fire or creative force — the will of life. It is limiting — that which takes form or shapes the pattern.

first house - the first of the twelve astrological houses at 0 degrees from the point of the ascendant on the zodiac belt. It is the house of initial individualist endeavors and self-identity of the ego ruled by the planet Mars and the zodiac sign Aries.

fixed signs - the four fixed points on the compass of the zodiac cross — Taurus, Leo, Scorpio and Aquarius; In traditional astrology, fixed signs are associated with maintaining the status quo, and those who are born under this quadruplicity possess the spirit of steadfast determination.

Flower of Life - in sacred geometry and ancient spiritual tradition, the symbol that starts with a single circle in the center. At the center of this first circle is the point at which the line that draws six even spaced duplicates about the original circle all overlap. The addition of the first circle creates the vesica piscis, the third circle creates the "Tripod of Life" or Holy Trinity, and the addition of the remaining circles create seven in total — this is the "Egg of Life". With this shape of seven circles, the pattern repeats from the center of these six additional circles to create the Flower of Life.

In esoteric tradition, the Flower of Life corresponds to a geometric representation of the possibility of Nature and fundamental mathematical forms of existence in space-time.

Fortuna - (see Part of Fortune)

fourth dimension - the mathematical plane of three geometric values in space and one of motion, duration or time described as velocity in the dimension of space-time; units of time or "t" in relation to variables of distance, x, y and z on a graph.

fourth house - the fourth of the twelve astrological houses at 90 degrees from the point of the ascendant on the zodiac belt; the location of the "nadir" meaning "opposite" or "Imum Coeli" (IC) named "the bottom of the sky" or the point opposite midheaven where the ecliptic crosses the Northern meridian to denote the native's 'roots'. It is the house of instinct and environment ruled by the Moon and the zodiac sign Cancer.

fractal - in mathematics, geometry, and nature, a repeating sequence, shape or pattern that cultivates a continuous measure of the original scale with replicating self-similarity.

frequency - in physics, the measure of oscillation, rotation, or wave by the frequency or duration of occurrence in time; f in mathematics and the unit Hertz (Hz).

full moon - a phase of the moon that occurs once a lunar month, when the Sun and Moon form an opposition aspect or 180 degree angle in relation to the Earth.

Galactic Center - the location at the center of the Milky Way Galaxy, which contains the globular cluster that in theory orbits the point of a supermassive black hole; object Sagittarius A (Sgr A). The Galactic Center exists between Sagittarius and Scorpio at the bottom of the constellation Ophiuchus.

galactic year - in astronomy, the duration of time it takes the Sun to traverse about the Galactic Center of the Milky Way Galaxy or about 225 to 250 million years on Earth; also the cosmic year.

Gemini - the third astrological sign of the tropical zodiac that spans from 60 degrees to 90 degrees on the zodiac belt to introduce the first mutable sign within the season of spring; from the Latin "twins" represented by the symbol (♊). The zodiac sign Gemini is named the Sun sign for those born between the dates of May 21st to June 20th in tropical astrology and June 16th to July 15th in sidereal astrology. Gemini is assigned the planetary ruler Mercury and can be found within the Air triplicity.

geocentric theory - in pre-Copernican astronomy, the model of the Earth-centered solar system orbited by the spheres of the "wandering stars" or seven classic planets — the Sun, Moon, Mercury, Venus, Mars, Jupiter and Saturn.

glacial period - in geology and climatology, a time interval of cold temperatures and glacial advance within the greater ice age. The last glacial period ended about 15,000 years ago.

Goat - in Chinese astrology, the eighth sign of the zodiac used to signify the eighth year in a calendar of twelve lunisolar cycles. The goat is a yin sign of the fixed element fire in the fourth trine.

The Goat - (see Capricorn)

golden ratio - in geometry and mathematics, the number value of phi (1.618) or the ratio of the Latin "sectio aurea" or golden section defined further by the Fibonacci sequence (0, 1, 1, 2, 3, 5, 8, …); also the "golden mean", the "golden number", or "divine proportion".

Grand Trine - the astrological aspect pattern in which three or more celestial bodies form precise trines at 120 degrees to complete an equilateral triangle shape.

Great Conjunction - an astrological conjunction between the Jupiter and Saturn in 18 to 20 year cycles due to the duration of each planet's orbit. The "Greatest Conjunction" also occurs when Jupiter and Saturn are conjunct in complete opposition to the Sun.

greenhouse effect - the elevation of surface temperatures on Earth due to the effects of thermal radiation absorption by way of atmospheric gases or an excess of long-wave radiation.

Gregorian calendar - based on the Julian calendar system, the calendar that reformed the occurrence of leap year and the date of the vernal equinox under Pope Gregory XIII in 1582; the current civil calendar of about 365.2425 days per year.

heliacal rise - the point on the eastern horizon at which a celestial body ascends over the visible sky or plane of observation.

heliocentricism - in astronomy, the model of the solar system with the Sun placed as the center axis of orbit suggested as early as the 3rd Century BCE by Aristarchus of Samos and implemented in the 16th Century CE after the introduction of heliocentric theory in Nicholaus Copernicus' "De revolutionibus orbium coelestium".

heliopause - the boundary or barrier at which the solar winds reach the stellar winds at the edge of the Empire of the Sun and surrounding interstellar medium. Just outside the heliopause, solar charged particles disappear, temperatures drop, magnetic fields shift, and cosmic rays are more abundant.

Hindu Trimurti - the Hindu concept of "three forms" or cosmic forces — Brahma the creator, Vishnu the preserver or maintainer, and Shiva the destroyer or transformer; also the "Great Trinity".

Horse - in Chinese astrology, the seventh sign of the zodiac used to signify the seventh year in a calendar of twelve lunisolar cycles. The horse is a yang sign of the fixed element fire in the third trine.

horoscope - in ancient astrology, the nativity constructed from the point of the ascendant at 0 degrees.

Hypatia of Alexandria - (350 CE - 415 CE) the philosopher, mathematician, and astronomer who taught at the Library of Alexandria just before the city's intellectual demise brought about by her death and initiating the turn of the Dark Ages which concluded the era of Hellenistic thought. Hypatia traveled to Athens and Rome to enrich her education before becoming one of the most renowned teachers in her home city of Alexandria. She was head of the Platonist school, made use of the astrolabe, and edited Euclid's *Elements* and Ptolemy's *Almagest*. Hypatia would be remembered as, "both skillful and eloquent in words and prudent and civil in deeds." A woman, "who made such attainments in literature and science, as to far surpass all philosophers of her own time."

hypothalamus - the chamber in the brain that connects the endocrine system to the nervous system of the body by way of the pituitary gland. The hypothalamus contains a concentration of small nuclei and secretes neurohormones that effect the production of pituitary hormones. Many body functions such as hunger, thirst, circadian rhythm, and body temperature are controlled by the hypothalamus.

ice age - in geology and climatology, an extended time period of cooling surface and atmospheric temperatures, glacial advance in alpine regions, and polar ice sheets that increase albedo (the measure of reflected sunlight). Ice ages are characterized by cold glacial and warm interglacial periods.

infinity - in physics, mathematics and philosophy, the value of an unlimited number or an innumerable measurement represented by the symbol (∞).

interglacial period - in geology and climatology, a time interval of warm temperatures and glacial retreat within the greater ice age. The current Holocene interglacial period began about 11,700 years ago.

invisible aspects - those invisible transitory positions or invisible astrological aspects of the luminaries drawn from the point of the ascendant at 0 degrees; the ascendant, descendant, imum coeli, midheaven, parts of fortune, the nodes, and the astrological houses or lunar mansions.

Julian calendar - based on the Roman calendar system, the calendar that reformed the number of days in each of the twelve months and added a leap day in February every four years under Julius Caesar in 45 BCE; the former civil calendar of about 365.25 days.

Carl Jung - (26 July 1875 – 6 June 1961) the psychiatrist and psychotherapist who founded Jungian or analytical psychology with emphasis on various elements of archetypal thought, the individual psyche, and the 'collective unconsiousness'. Carl Jung dedicated much of his research to the study of the psychology and the applied understanding of perceived spiritual phenomena. He was born in Switzerland and served as a military physician during World War I. Jung left us with the theory of the collective unconscious and its thought symbols, the archetypes.

Jupiter - in traditional astrology, the fifth planet of the solar system that rules over the zodiac signs Sagittarius and Pisces, finds detriment in Gemini and Virgo, exaltation in Cancer and fall in Capricorn; depicted by the symbol (♃). The orbit of Jupiter equals about 11.86 years and the synodic period 399 days. Jupiter retrograde cycles last for about 121 days.

Johannes Kepler - (27 December 1571 – 15 November 1630) the mathematician and astronomer who defined the mathematical formula for an ellipse based on the mass, distance and speed ratio of an orbiting sphere. Johannes Kepler was a German resident of the Holy Roman Empire and supported the heliocentric model of the Earth outlined by Nicholaus Copernicus. His research wrote the equations that define the variation in the sphere of an ellipse with Kepler's laws of planetary motion.

Kepler–Poinsot polyhedra - in geometry, the polyhedra that add four basic shapes to the Platonic solids. The Kepler-Poinsot polyhedra are stellations of the dodecahedron and icosahedron that form a five pointed face, star, or pentagram shape.

Kite - the astrological aspect pattern in which three or more celestial bodies form a precise Grand Trine that is also sextile (on two sides) and in opposition (on the third side) with another planetary figure to display a kite shape.

left brain - in psychology, the theory or allegory of left hemisphere dominant brain functions as a product of the physical location of these thought processes. Brain functions contained within the left hemisphere include critical thinking, deductive reasoning, recognition of abstracting symbols, and the articulation of language. The left brain is associated with logic, communication, and organization.

Leo - the fifth astrological sign of the tropical zodiac that spans from 120 degrees to 150 degrees on the zodiac belt to hold the second fixed sign within the season of summer; from the Latin "lion" represented by the symbol (♌). The zodiac sign Leo is named the Sun sign for those born between the dates of July 23rd to August 22nd in tropical astrology and August 16th to September 15th in sidereal astrology. Leo is assigned the planetary ruler the Sun and can be found within the Fire triplicity.

Libra - the seventh astrological sign of the tropical zodiac that spans from 180 degrees at the descendant (DSC) to 210 degrees on the zodiac belt to initiate the third cardinal sign with the season of autumn; from the Latin "balance" represented by the symbol (♎). The zodiac sign Libra is named the Sun sign for those born between the dates of September 23rd to October 22nd in tropical astrology and October 16th to November 15th in sidereal astrology. Libra is assigned the planetary ruler Venus and can be found within the Air triplicity.

The Lion - (see Leo)

the luminaries - in traditional astrology, the celestial bodies that give light and influence other celestial bodies with astrological aspects.

lunisolar calendar - a calendar that measures time in solar years and lunar months based on the cycles of the Sun and Moon.

the Magi - in the ancient religion of Zoroastrianism, the priests or sages who were practiced in various forms of magic and mysticism such as astrology, alchemy, divination, and other esoteric traditions.

The Maiden - (see Virgo)

male - in geometry or cosmic philosophy, that which is straight; the divine masculine principle.

malefic aspect - an astrological aspect that forms a discordant angle with two as the base (squares and sometimes oppositions). Planetary rulers are also considered malefic aspects when placed in a position of debility or fall.

Maya - in ancient philosophy, the unreality of subjective existence or the apparent perception of that which is the visual reality from the Sanskrit "illusion" or "delusion".

Benoit Mandelbrot - (20 November 1924 - 14 October 2010) the mathematician and cosmic philosopher who contributed his research to mathematical sequences and symmetries of "self-similarity" and fractal geometry, philosophies of chaos theory, and inherent mathematical cosmologies. Benoit Mandelbrot moved to France from his birthplace in Warsaw in 1936 and taught at universities in both France and the United States. He is best known for the fractal sequence of geometric order named the Mandelbrot set.

Manifestation - in cosmic philosophy, the formation of a paradigm or the creative principle born of the interlocking polarities between the Source of order and the Spirit of consciousness; the product of harmony or affinity.

Mars - in traditional astrology, the fourth planet of the solar system that rules over the zodiac signs Aries and Scorpio, finds detriment in Libra and Taurus, exaltation in Capricorn and fall in Cancer; depicted by the symbol (♂). The orbit of Mars equals about 687 days and the synodic period 780 days. Mars retrograde cycles last for about 72 days.

Mayan calendar - the collection of ancient calendar systems recorded by various Mesoamerican peoples dating back to the

5th Century BCE; based on the interlocking 260 day "tzolkin" and 365 day "haab" cycles.

medical astrology - in ancient astrology, the system of iatromathematics derived from personal aspects of natal astrology, and planetary transits of mundane astrology and used in medicine by early physicians.

Mercury - in traditional astrology, the first planet of the solar system that rules over the zodiac signs Gemini and Virgo, finds detriment in Sagittarius and Pisces, exaltation in Virgo, and fall in Pisces; depicted by the symbol (☿). The orbit of Mercury equals 88 days and the synodic period 116 days. Mercury retrograde cycles last for about 22 days.

metabolism - the chemical transformations or processes in living organisms that regulate and control enzymes to maintain cellular homeostasis within the body.

metaphysics - in philosophy, the psychological study of the fundamental nature of being, the essence of existence and manifestation of properties that prompt the apparent visual reality — 'the World'. Metaphysicians explain and define the meaning of cause and effect, space and time, dimensional existence, and conscious perception.

Metonic Cycle - the astronomical measure or calendar of 19 years closest to the nearest common multiple of the Moon and Sun or lunar and solar cycles (about 19 solar years to 235 synodic lunar months); also the Greek "Enneadecaeteris" or "nineteen years".

midheaven - in traditional astrology, the invisible aspect or point found within the tenth house that marks the location where a transiting planet reaches the median between the points of the ascendant and descendant; also "Medium Coeli" (MC) or "middle of the sky".

Milankovitch cycle - the cycle of astronomical patterns

(eccentricity, obliquity and precession) used to track and predict variations in climate conditions, global temperature, glacial, and interglacial periods as well as the ice ages. The Milankovitch cycle is named for Serbian astronomer and geophysicist Milutin Milanković who contributed research to the study of planetary climatology.

Monkey - in Chinese astrology, the ninth sign of the zodiac used to signify the ninth year in a calendar of twelve lunisolar cycles. The monkey is a yang sign of the fixed element metal in the first trine.

Monster - in the mathematics of group theory, a member of the Monster group of finite order predicted by Bernd Fischer and recorded by Robert Griess in 1982; also the Fischer-Griess monster or the "Friendly Giant" represented by M or $F(1)$. It is the highest order of the sporadic group in which the divisors consist of the 15 supersingular primes.

Moon - in traditional astrology, the satellite of the Earth that rules over the zodiac sign Cancer, finds detriment in Capricorn, exaltation in Taurus and fall in Scorpio; depicted by the symbol (☽). The Moon also carries two invisible aspects named the lunar nodes — the points in which the Moon's orbit crosses the ecliptic (plane of the solar system); the symbol (☊) signifies the north or ascending node and (☋) the south or descending node.

morning star - the planet Mercury or Venus as it appears at sunrise in the east. Venus as the evening star has the potential to glow up to 15 times brighter than Sirius or the brightest star in the sky; also the Greek "Eosphorus" or "Phosphorus" and Latin "Lucifer", the 'light-bringer'.

mundane astrology - the traditional branch of astrology that derives planetary configurations and astrological aspects in order to forecast future conditions and transits for people, places, and events or political affairs.

mutable signs- the four mutable points on the compass of the zodiac cross — Gemini, Virgo, Sagittarius and Pisces; in traditional astrology, mutable signs are associated with continuous flexibility and change, and those who are born under this quadruplicity possess the spirit of versatility.

natal astrology - the traditional branch of astrology that derives planetary configurations, astrological aspects, and houses from one's natal chart in order to forecast future conditions and transits for the querent; also horary or horoscopic astrology.

natal chart - in traditional astrology, the record of all astrological aspects and house locations at the time, place, and date of one's birth. also the natal wheel or birth chart. The astrological aspects of a natal chart are drawn by planetary configurations and houses initiated at the degree of the ascendant (0 degrees).

nativity - (see natal chart)

negative - in mathematics, the subtraction or minus factor, and in cosmic philosophy, the feminine principle of all that is considered inaction, irregularity, and dark; that which is associated with "chaos".

Neptune - in modern astrology, the eighth planet of the solar system that rules over the zodiac sign Pisces, finds detriment in Virgo, exaltation in Leo, and fall in Aquarius; depicted by the symbol (Ψ). The orbit of Neptune equals about 165 years and the synodic period 367 days. Neptune retrograde cycles last for about 158 days.

new moon - a phase of the moon that occurs once a lunar month when the Sun and Moon form a conjunct aspect or 0 degree angle in relation to the Earth.

Sir Isaac Newton - (25 December 1642 - 20 March 1726; Julian) the mathematician, physicist, and cosmic philosopher who is named the "father of classical physics" for his contributions to the natural laws of motion and universal gravitation. Isaac Newton also delved in the curiosities of astrology and reorganized the histories using ancient records of astrological aspects and ephemeris tables within "The Chronology of Ancient Kingdoms Amended". He was born in a hamlet in Lincolnshire, England and attended college to research mathematics and eventually construct, "Philosophiæ Naturalis Principia Mathematica". Newton left us with the theory of gravity and his achievements of great scientific measure described in his epitaph, "Nature and nature's laws lay hid in night; God said "Let Newton be" and all was light."

ninth house - the ninth of the twelve astrological houses at 240 degrees from the point of the ascendant on the zodiac belt. It is the house of personal philosophy and exploration ruled by the planet Jupiter and the zodiac sign Sagittarius.

obliquity - in astronomy, the oblique variation in axial tilt or the shift in degree of separation between the orbital plane and rotational axis of a planet.

Ogdoad of Hermopolis - in ancient Egyptian myth, the "paut" of eight gods in the ancient city of Hermopolis in the Old Kingdom (about 2686 BCE to 2134 BCE); from the Greek "eight-fold". The Ogdoad of Hermopolis are four pairs of male and female gods represented in hieroglyphs as snakes or frogs. Together these eight gods — Nu and Nut, Hehu and Hehut, Kekui and Kekuit, and Kerh and Kerhet (Amen and Ament) — take the shape of the infinite eight depicted as the infinity symbol (∞).

Oort Cloud - the spherical cloud that envelopes the boundaries of the solar system's gravitational influence and comprised of comets, icy planetoids, and planetesimals; also Öpik. The Oort Cloud was named after Dutch astronomer Jan Oort.

opposition - an astrological aspect that denotes a 180 degree angle relationship between two or more celestial bodies within an 8 degree orb of separation.

Ophiuchus - the "thirteenth" astrological sign of the zodiac that spans from 248 to 265 degrees on the zodiac belt to signify the point in which the ecliptic crosses the galactic equator; from the Greek "water-bearer". The zodiac sign Ophiuchus is named the Sun sign for those born between the dates of November 29th to December 17th. Ophiuchus is assigned the fixed ruler the Galactic Center and can be classified as a sign of the fifth element aether.

orb - in traditional astrology, the degree of separation between luminaries that form astrological aspects.

Orion - the hidden astrological sign of the zodiac opposite Ophiuchus that spans about 5 degrees between Taurus and Gemini on the zodiac belt to signify the point in which the ecliptic crosses the galactic equator; from the Akkadian "Uru-anna" or "light of the heavens". The zodiac Orion is a Moon sign. Orion is assigned the fixed ruler the Galactic Center and can be classified as a sign of the fifth element aether.

Ox - in Chinese astrology, the second sign of the zodiac used to signify the second year in a calendar of twelve lunisolar cycles. The ox is a yin sign of the fixed element water in the second trine.

Pantheistic - of the cosmic interpretation Pantheism from the Greek "pan" meaning all and "theos", god. Pantheists recognize the one absolute, all-encompassing reality that is Deity or the eternal acting force of Nature.

Part of Fortune - in Arabic astrology, the invisible transiting aspect "lot" or "Part of the Moon"; also "Fortuna". The Part of the Moon is calculated on a given day by rolling back the natal chart so that the location of the Sun is placed at the ascendant (0 degrees at the rising sign or sunrise) and with this new chart the modified degree of the Moon (minus the difference in degree of the Sun for day charts and plus the difference in degree of the Sun for night charts) indicates Fortuna.

Pascal's triangle - the ancient sequence or triangle arrangement of binomial coefficients recorded in 1653 within "Traité du triangle arithmétique" by French mathematician Blaise Pascal. The series starts with number 1 and branches off from the bottom to form a triangle by adding the original numeric value (1) to the value of the numbers on the left and right in the row above. If no numbers are present, add zero.

perihelion - the location in which Earth reaches its closest position to the Sun on its elliptical orbit. This principle of celestial mechanics was outlined by Johannes Kepler in the 17th Century with Kepler's first law of planetary motion.

phi - in mathematics, art and architecture, the number value of the golden ratio 1.618 [(1 + √5) / 2 ≈ 1.618] depicted by the letter (Φ) of the Greek alphabet.

Philolaus of Croton - (470 BCE - 385 BCE) the Pythagorean philosopher of classical antiquity who is credited as one of the earliest minds that sought to correct geocentricism with a model in which the planets revolve about the "Central Fire". Philolaus was likely from the island Croton of the greater Magna Graecia and lived at a time of great philosophic discovery and thinkers Socrates and Plato. His legacy is the cosmology of the "harmony" that intervenes the course of the eternal limiting and unlimited elements of the universe.

Pig - in Chinese astrology, the last sign of the zodiac used to signify the twelfth year in a calendar of twelve lunisolar cycles. The pig is a yin sign of the fixed element water in the fourth trine.

pineal gland - in biology, the endocrine gland located at the center of the brain between the two cerebral hemispheres in the epithalamus of vertebrae species. The pineal gland is the source of melatonin production (a derivation of the hormone serotonin) that prompts functions of the biological clock in seasonal patterns and sleep and wake cycles known as circadian rhythm; it is named for the resemblance of its shape to that of a pine cone.

The pineal gland exists as the only unpaired organ within the brain and is also speculated to be the only source of DMT secretion in the body. For this reason, its function has been granted a wide range of philosophical and spiritual implications in the past as the "seat of the soul" or the center of creativity, mysticism, and higher states of conscious perception.

Pisces - the twelfth astrological sign of the tropical zodiac that spans from 330 degrees to 360 degrees on the zodiac belt to introduce the fourth mutable sign within the season of winter; from the Latin "fishes" represented by the symbol (♓). The zodiac sign Pisces is named the Sun sign for those born between the dates of February 19th to March 20th in tropical astrology and March 15th to April 14th in sidereal astrology. Pisces is assigned the traditional planetary ruler Jupiter, the modern ruler Neptune and can be found within the Water triplicity.

Platonic solids - in Euclidean geometry, the five regular solids or convex polyhedra named for the number of faces in each shape. Plato theorized that the five regular solids — the tetrahedron, cube, octahedron, dodecahedron and icosahedron — were geometric representations of the elements — Fire, Earth, Air, Aether, and Water, respectively.

Platonic Year - the measure of time as the sum of the twelve astrological ages depicted by the 30 degree segments of each zodiac sign at a measure of 2,160 years or a total of about 26,000 years (2,160 years x 12 ≈ 26,000 years) to complete the "Great Year".

Pluto - in modern astrology, the ninth planet of the solar system that rules over the zodiac sign Scorpio, finds detriment in Taurus, exaltation in Aries, and fall in Libra; depicted by the symbol (♇). The orbit of Pluto equals about 248 years and the synodic period 367 days. Pluto retrograde cycles last for about 162 days.

positive - in mathematics, the addition or plus factor, and in cosmic philosophy, the masculine principle of all that is considered action, order, and light; that which is associated with "cosmos".

Prana - in ancient Hindu wisdom, the Sanskrit "life force" or "breath of life" that originated with the Sun and acts as a universal energy to connect the elements of Nature. Prana is associated with the element air.

precession - the orientational variation between a celestial body's axis of rotation and the plane of its orbital path or ellipse.

precession of the equinox - in astronomy, the precession of the celestial sphere in the shifting of pole stars caused by the wobble of the Earth. In astrology, the precession of the equinox is tracked by the motion of the Sun's retrograde movement backward through each of the zodiac signs to introduce the astronomical ages once about every 2,160 years for a total of about 26,000 years to complete the zodiac circle traverse with the Platonic Year. The precession of the equinox occurs at a rate of 1 degree about every 72 years.

primeval forces - in cosmic theory, the two basic eternal forces of nature — the infinite, undefined, or limitless expanse of space and time. Primeval forces can be categorized as male and female, positive and negative, light and dark, or electricity and magnetism.

primeval states - in cosmic theory, the basic eight eternal states of the universe — the infinite that takes the shape of eight, the states that formed as a result of the separation of "earth" and "sky", or the states of the early universe in the form of plasma and radiation interacting in space-time; the infinite eight can be categorized as male and female or the opposing positive and negative polarities of the four basic eternal states and two primeval forces that shape the elements.

primordial matter - in cosmic theory, the force that existed within the "cosmic egg" or the photon energy that resulted from the explosion of the Big Bang at the birth of the visual universe.

primordial nucleosynthesis - the process that prompted the formation of the first chemical elements — in hydrogen (H), helium (He) and lithium (Li) isotopes — caused by the initial explosion of the Big Bang. Primordial nucleosynthesis took place as an immediate product of the Big Bang within the first 10 seconds to 20 minutes of this dimensional universe.

Pythagorean Theorem - in mathematics, the formula for the geometric ratio or dimensional symmetry of a right triangle ($a^2 + b^2 = c^2$) where "c" represents the hypotenuse (the longest side opposite the 90 degree right angle), while "a" and "b" represent the value of the two remaining sides. Pythagoras introduced this theorem to Greece, yet record of its origins date as far back as the age of ancient Babylon.

qi - in ancient East Asian wisdom, the "life force" or inherent energy contained within all living things; also "chi" or "ki". Qi is associated with the element air.

quadruplicity - the three sets of four zodiac signs that correspond to the quality or polarity — the cardinal, fixed, and mutable signs. In ancient astrology, quadruplicities are separated by 90 degrees or square.

quarter phase - a phase of the moon that occurs twice a lunar month when the Sun and Moon form a square or 90 degree angle in relation to the Earth.

Rabbit - in Chinese astrology, the fourth sign of the zodiac used to signify the fourth year in a calendar of twelve lunisolar cycles. The rabbit is a yin sign of the fixed element wood in the fourth trine.

Rat - in Chinese astrology, the first sign of the zodiac used to signify the first year in a calendar of twelve lunisolar cycles. The rat is a yang sign of the fixed element water in the first trine.

Encyclopedia of Astrology

red shift - the observance of an object that appears to emit a red signature, as it shifts to longer wavelengths due to its decelerating motion in time away from the relative point of the viewer's perspective.

restrictive cycle - in the Taoist philosophy of Wu Xing, "kè" or the destructing and controlling order of the elements — Wood, Earth, Water, Fire, and Metal, respectively. This cycle forms a pentagram shape, as each of the elements weakens the force of the next.

retrograde - in astronomy, the apparent observation of a planet, as it slows to reverse its orbital path backwards through the zodiac belt to complete the retrograde cycle. The illusion of retrograde on the ground is due to the Earth or position of observation overtaking the orbital position of a planet — Mercury, Venus, Mars, Jupiter, Saturn, Uranus, and Neptune — by way of proximity to the Sun.

Just before a planet turns retrograde, it appears to slow as the Earth's shorter orbital distance catches up to meet it. At the moment the Earth and the retrograding planet become conjunct, the observed planet reaches a standstill, and the two have come to the closest possible distance in the solar system. As the aspect transits in time, the Earth overtakes the position of the planet, and the retrograde runs the planet in reverse. The illusion of distance allows the reverse motion to be corrected, after the planetary positions separate by degrees of space in time.

right brain - in psychology, the theory or allegory of right hemisphere dominant brain functions as a product of the physical location of these thought processes. Brain functions contained within the right hemisphere are the ability to recognize patterns, perceive images, and communicate emotions. The right brain is associated with intuition, sensitivity, imagination, and creative expression.

rising sign - (see ascendant)

The Ram - (see Aries)

Rod of Asclepius - in ancient Greek mythology, the staff of Asclepius the physician represented by a single snake intertwined with a rod; a symbol for "the healer".

Rooster - in Chinese astrology, the tenth sign of the zodiac used to signify the tenth year in a calendar of twelve lunisolar cycles. The rooster is a yin sign of the fixed element metal in the second trine.

ROYGBIV - (see visible spectrum)

rulership - in traditional astrology, the system of zodiac signs assigned to planets that aspect at their most powerful position — a dwelling place or "home" of the planetary ruler; also 'domicile'.

sacred geometry - according to the structural formulas of Euclidean mathematics and Pythagorean geometry, the collection of geometric shapes, ratios, sequences, proportions, and numeric patterns that define the order or stability of "cosmos" and fashion the universe or visible reality with dimensions. Sacred geometric shapes are displayed as spiritual symbols to explain the broader implications and esoteric wisdom of synchronous universal law.

Carl Sagan - (9 November 1934 - 20 December 1996) the cosmic philosopher, astronomer, and astrophysicist who authored and presented a world of facts, history, and research that introduced a modern explanation of "cosmos" inspired by scientific method, the application of technology, and skeptical inquiry. Sagan lived in the United States at a time of avid space exploration and manned lunar missions. He inspired the world with a historic public series of cosmic wonderment and a dream of intelligent life beyond the stars.

Sagittarius - the ninth astrological sign of the tropical zodiac that spans from 240 degrees to 270 degrees on the zodiac belt to introduce the third mutable sign within the season of autumn;

from the Latin "archer" represented by the symbol (♐). The zodiac sign Sagittarius is named the Sun sign for those born between the dates of November 22nd to December 21st in tropical astrology and December 16th to January 14th in sidereal astrology. Sagittarius is assigned the planetary ruler Jupiter and can be found within the Fire triplicity.

Saturn - in traditional astrology, the sixth planet of the solar system that rules over the zodiac signs Capricorn and Aquarius, finds detriment in Cancer and Leo, exaltation in Libra, and fall in Aries; depicted by the symbol (♄). The orbit of Saturn equals about 29.45 years and the synodic period 378 days. Saturn retrograde cycles last for about 138 days.

Scorpio - the eighth astrological sign of the tropical zodiac that spans from 210 degrees to 240 degrees on the zodiac belt to hold the third fixed sign within the season of autumn; from the Latin "scorpion" represented by the symbol (♏). The zodiac sign Scorpio is named the Sun sign for those born between the dates of October 23rd to November 21st in tropical astrology and November 16th to December 15th in sidereal astrology. Scorpio is assigned the planetary ruler Mars and can be found within the Water triplicity.

The Scorpion - (see Scorpio)

Seal of Solomon - the astrological aspect pattern in which six or more celestial bodies form two precise Grand Trines to display a Grand Sextile separated by increments of 30 degrees to complete the six pointed star; also the Star of David.

second house - the second of the twelve astrological houses at 30 degrees from the point of the ascendant on the zodiac belt. It is the house of personal will and value of worth ruled by the planet Venus and the zodiac sign Taurus.

self-similarity - in mathematics, the fractal of a sequence that is "similar" or proportionate to the ratio and scale of the pattern repeated in the whole.

seventh house - the seventh of the twelve astrological houses at 180 degrees from the point of the ascendant on the zodiac belt; the location of the descendant (DSC). It is the house of companionship and the shadow self ruled by the planet Venus and the zodiac sign Libra.

sextile - an astrological aspect that denotes a 60 degree angle relationship between two or more celestial bodies within an 8 degree orb of separation.

Shintō - the ancient, indigenous myths and religion of the islands of Japan that become an organized tradition around 660 BCE; also "kami no michi". Shintoism is a tradition at balance with Nature and the "essence" or "spirit" of life contained within all things is described as "kami" — a category of sacred power, deity, or divinity.

sidereal astrology - the traditional astrological system that divides the orbit of the Earth or plane of the ecliptic into twelve zodiac signs of 30 degrees each (12 x 30 degrees = 360 degrees) in order to track the annual transit cycles by the fixed star positions and true zodiac constellations that hold the celestial sphere. The tropical and sidereal systems of astrology separate at a rate of about 1.4 degrees each century.

sidereal time - the measure of time based on the apparent motion of the fixed stars as a point of reference or the duration of a sidereal day and sidereal year (also stellar year) in step with the background of stars. The sidereal day is about 23 hours, 56 minutes, and 4.0916 seconds.

singularity - in physics and Einstein's general theory of relativity, a single position in the fabric of space-time that denotes the location of absolute gravity due to the collapse of such a colossal object that its mass and density exceeds the Schwarzschild radius.

Encyclopedia of Astrology

sixth house - the sixth of the twelve astrological houses at 150 degrees from the point of the ascendant on the zodiac belt. It is the house of personal dexterity and attitudes toward work and life ruled by the planet Mercury and the zodiac sign Virgo.

Snake - in Chinese astrology, the sixth sign of the zodiac used to signify the sixth year in a calendar of twelve lunisolar cycles. The snake is a yin sign of the fixed element fire in the second trine.

solar alignment - in architectural design, the element of alignment between the fundamental construction of a structure and an exterior solar event, such as the equinox or solstice, commonly found in the blueprint of traditional temples and passage tombs.

solar maximum - the zenith of the sunspot cycle in which solar activity — solar flares, winds, and ejections — is much more prevalent due to a high number of sunspots. Solar maximum peaks once about every 11.8 years on average.

solar minimum - the retreat of the sunspot cycle in which solar activity is much less prevalent due to a low number of sunspots. Solar minimum sets in once about every 11.8 years on average.

solar time - the measure of time based on the apparent motion of the Sun as a point of reference or the duration of a solar day and solar year (also tropical year) in step with the seasons; the solar day is about 24 hours.

solstice - the cardinal astronomical point where the ecliptic (plane of the solar system) crosses the degree of the tropics (currently 23.5 degrees north and south of the equator); occurs twice a year at the initiation of summer and winter during the months of June and December.

the Source - in cosmic philosophy, the source of mathematics or geometric symmetry of the visible reality that constructs the dimensions of circumstance under the weight of all possible probabilities contained in the invisible realm; also the manner of cosmos, the positive, limiting, or determinate force — opposite the Spirit.

sphinx - in ancient Egyptian myth, a creature with the head of a human, the body of a lion, the legs of a bull, and the wings of an eagle; also the Assyrian "lamassu". The sphinx is a symbol of the zodiac cross or the wheel of four cardinal points that moves through the zodiac belt across the ages to match the precession of the equinoxes and solstices.

the Spirit - in cosmic philosophy, the spirit of consciousness, possibility or random chance that reflects on the probabilities of perceived visible circumstance from the realm of the invisible reality; also the manner of chaos, the negative, limitless, or undefined force — opposite the Source.

spring equinox - the astronomical point that marks the location where the ecliptic (plane of the solar system) crosses the equator to near the latitudinal position of the observer; the cardinal point that initiates the season of spring at the first quarter of the zodiac cross. The spring equinox is observed when the hours of night equal the hours of day.

square - an astrological aspect that denotes a 90 degree angle relationship between two or more celestial bodies within an 8 degree orb of separation.

stellar nucleosythesis - the formation of new chemical elements by way of nuclear fusion between the pure hydrogen (H) and helium (He) to produce the "primary elements" that make up life. Stellar nucleosynthesis of large mass stars permits the s-process or slow capture of neutrons that span the periodic table of elements up to bismuth (Bi).

Star of David - (see Seal of Solomon)

summer solstice - the astronomical point that marks the location where the ecliptic (plane of the solar system) reaches its closest incline position to the Earth at the latitude of the Northern or Southern Tropic line opposite the position of the observer; the cardinal point that initiates the season of summer at the second quarter of the zodiac cross. The summer solstice is observed when the hours of day surpass the hours of night.

supernova nucleosynthesis - the formation of heavier chemical elements by way of nuclear fusion between the primary chemical elements from silicon (Si) to iron (Fe). The colossal mass of a supernova permits more intricate processes of nuclear fusion that form the heavier elements to include iron peak vanadium, chromium, cobalt, manganese, and nickel. Heavier elements result from the r-process or rapid capture of neutrons, while most remaining elements up to uranium (U) are produced in the blast of a supernova explosion.

Sun - in traditional astrology, the star of the solar system that rules over the zodiac sign Leo, finds detriment in Aquarius, exaltation in Aries, and fall in Libra; depicted by the symbol (☉).

sunspot cycles - the periods of solar maxima and solar minima that make up the total solar magnetic radiation and ejection activity cycle of the Sun by the measure of visible sunspots. The sunspot cycle spans an average duration of 11.8 years between each solar maximum and minimum. In cosmic astrology, the sunspot cycle is the result of the aspecting transits of giant outer planets Jupiter and Saturn.

symbol - any concrete object, glyph, or shape used to invoke an archetype or abstract concept of the conscious mind.

synastry - the branch of natal (horoscopic or horary) astrology that interprets the effects of synastry aspects between one or more natal charts in order to forecast relationship conditions.

synastry aspects - in traditional astrology, any astrological aspect drawn between one or more natal charts in order to signify the nature of the energy exchange or quality of conditions for interaction between each person involved.

Taiji - the "Supreme Polarity" and highest principles of ultimate and eternal differentiation — the limiting principle of polarity — that was instilled in Wuji; also the "Supreme Ultimate" or "Great Absolute". The polarities outlined in Taiji (yin and yang) interact to produce the five elements of Wu Xing.

Tao - an ancient Chinese philosophy of the "way" or path; also "Dao". Taoist philosophies originated with the great thinker Laozi, and some main concepts are outlined in the underlying universal principles of yin and yang (Taiji), the elements (Wu Xing), and the eight trigrams of the bagua.

T-square - the astrological aspect pattern in which two or more celestial bodies form a precise opposition at 180 degrees that is also square another planetary figure at 90 degrees to display a "T" shape.

Taurus - the second astrological sign of the tropical zodiac that spans from 30 degrees to 60 degrees on the zodiac belt to hold the first fixed sign within the season of spring; from the Latin "bull" represented by the symbol (♉). The zodiac sign Taurus is named the Sun sign for those born between the dates of April 21st to May 20th in tropical astrology and May 16th to June 15th in sidereal astrology. Taurus is assigned the planetary ruler Venus and can be found within the Earth triplicity.

tenth house - the tenth of the twelve astrological houses at 270 degrees from the point of the ascendant on the zodiac belt; the location of the midheaven (MC). It is the house of responsibility, contribution, and achievement ruled by the planet Saturn and the zodiac sign Capricorn.

Nikola Tesla - (10 July 1856 - 7 January 1943) the electrical engineer, inventor and cosmic philosopher who brought the power of electricity and wireless technologies to the world. Nikola Tesla was born a citizen of the Austrian Empire named the "father of robotics", as he is the first to invent a radio controlled device, a small mechanized boat. After Tesla became an American citizen, he worked to harness the power of the earth by experimenting with lightning, generating electricity with the waters of Niagara Falls, and discovering the importance of frequency. Tesla left us with the system of alternating current and the dream that a technology may one day free the world from war.

third eye - the spiritual or esoteric concept of the invisible eye that exists within the mind — situated in the brain behind the middle of the brow line — to allow access to higher dimensions or conscious perceptions; also the "inner eye" or the Sanskrit "ajna" or "brow chakra".

third dimension - the mathematical plane of three geometric values described as a dimensional plane of length, width, and height granting thickness, depth, or volume to an object; units represented by the cubed (x^3) superscript or the variables x, y, and z on a graph.

third house - the third of the twelve astrological houses at 60 degrees from the point of the ascendant on the zodiac belt. It is the house of lower thought and communication ruled by the planet Mercury and the zodiac sign Gemini.

Tiger - in Chinese astrology, the third sign of the zodiac used to signify the third year in a calendar of twelve lunisolar cycles. The tiger is a yang sign of the fixed element wood in the third trine.

the Tower - in traditional tarot, card XVI of the Major Arcana used to represent Enlightenment, sudden dissolution, and the crisis of chaos in the aftermath of awakening; also "the Lightning".

transit - in traditional astrology, the event that occurs when a celestial body occupies the location of a previously established visible or invisible astrological aspect.

trine - an astrological aspect that denotes a 120 degree angle relationship between two or more celestial bodies within an 8 degree orb of separation.

Tropic of Cancer - the location of the Northern Tropic (currently 23.5 degrees) used to mark the point at which the ecliptic reaches its northern-most latitude to initiate the June solstice; the summer solstice of the Northern Hemisphere and the winter solstice of the Southern Hemisphere.

Tropic of Capricorn - the location of the Southern Tropic (currently 23.5 degrees) used to mark the point at which the ecliptic reaches its southern-most latitude to initiate the December solstice; the winter solstice of the Northern Hemisphere and the summer solstice of the Southern Hemisphere.

tropical astrology - the traditional astrological system which divides the orbit of the Earth or plane of the ecliptic into twelve zodiac signs of 30 degrees each (12 x 30 degrees = 360 degrees) in order to track the annual seasonal cycles by the four cardinal points of the zodiac cross (equinoxes and solstices) initiated at the vernal equinox.

twelfth house - the last of the twelve astrological houses at 330 degrees from the point of the ascendant on the zodiac belt. It is the house of hidden dreams of the soul and karmic ends ruled by the planet Neptune and the zodiac sign Pisces.

The Twins - (see Gemini)

The Two Shads - (see Pisces)

ultraviolet radiation - a wavelength of electromagnetic radiation shorter than visible light but longer than X radiation (X-rays); also ultraviolet rays or (UV) light. Ultraviolet radiation is emitted by the Sun and other man-made sources such as specialized lamps and light bulbs. Some solar ultraviolet rays fall under the non-ionizing category, while those that fall under the ionizing category have the ability to cause chemical reactions and damage biological systems.

Underworld - the invisible realm beneath the surface of the Earth. In traditional astrology, the portion of the natal chart (luminaries and zodiac) that lies below the horizon of visible sky from the point of the descendant to the ascendant.

Uranus - in modern astrology, the seventh planet of the solar system that rules over the zodiac sign Aquarius, finds detriment in Leo, exaltation in Scorpio, and fall in Taurus; depicted by the symbol (⛢). The orbit of Uranus equals about 84 years and the synodic period 370 days. Uranus retrograde cycles last for about 151 days.

Venus - in traditional astrology, the second planet of the solar system that rules over the zodiac signs Taurus and Libra, finds detriment in Scorpio and Aries, exaltation in Pisces, and fall in Virgo; depicted by the symbol (♀). The orbit of Venus equals about 225 days and the synodic period 584 days. Venus retrograde cycles last for about 41 days.

Vermilion Bird - in Chinese astrology, one of the four celestial beasts known as "Zhu Que" that rules the direction of South and the season of summer; also the Korean "Jujak", Japanese "Suzaku" and Vietnamese "Chu Tước". The Vermilion Bird is sometimes referred to as the "Red Bird" or "Red Phoenix".

vernal equinox - the date in which the ecliptic crosses the vernal point of the celestial equator (a projection of Earth's equator) to allow the Sun to rise over 0 degrees latitude to initiate the season of spring; From the Latin "ver" for "spring". Occurs at a date during the month of March in the Northern Hemisphere and September in the Southern Hemisphere.

Vesica Piscis - the geometric shape of two intersecting circles forming an almond or "mandorla" (*it.*) in the overlap. The first circle represents a single dimension, while the addition of the second circle, a second dimension. In the modern era, the shape of a vesica piscis is used in a "venn diagram" to outline the overlap of common qualities between two variables in the overlay of a pair of circles — and with each extra variable, a circle is added.

Virgo - the sixth astrological sign of the tropical zodiac that spans from 150 degrees at the ascendant to 180 degrees on the zodiac belt to introduce the second mutable sign within the season of summer; from the Latin "virgin", using "vir" for "man" and the Greek "gyne" for "woman" to characterize an androgynous maiden represented by the symbol (♍). The zodiac sign Virgo is named the Sun sign for those born between the dates of August 23rd to September 22nd in tropical astrology and September 16th to October 15th in sidereal astrology. Virgo is assigned the planetary ruler Mercury and can be found within the Earth triplicity.

Virgo Cluster - the colossal collection of 1300-2000 spiral, elliptical and dwarf galaxies located about 5×10^7 light years away in the constellation Virgo, of which the Milky Way Galaxy and Local Group are regionalized as part of the greater Virgo or Local Supercluster. Its sheer magnitude is best captured in its size of 8 degrees across in the night sky, where it can be observed in the constellation Virgo. The Virgo Cluster exists a massive collection of planets, stars, galaxies, and most importantly black holes which interact and emanate sound in the form of shockwaves.

visible spectrum - a range of light or electromagnetic radiation wavelengths observable to the human eye in the form of color; from the Latin "spectrum" or "appearance". The visible spectrum is a portion of the wider electromagnetic spectrum. It is projected through the use of the three primary colors — Red, Blue, and Yellow — to blend all other colors — Orange, Green, Indigo, and Violet.

Marcus Vitruvius - (80-70 BCE - 15 BCE) the master architect and engineer who recorded and applied ancient architectural techniques, and styles, mechanical systems and machinery, modes of astrolabes and clocks, and ancient philosophies of acoustics and aesthetic proportion outlined in "De architectura".

He served as a Roman ballista during the reign of Julius Caesar. Vitruvius is well known for his contributions to the golden ratio of human proportion that were later revived during the Renaissance as "Homo Vitruvianus" — the Vitruvian Man by Leonardo da Vinci.

water - one of the four classical elements outlined by Pythagoras in ancient Greece and named the attractive force in motion or the quality of cohesion of the terrestrial world; also the Latin "aqua" or the Sanskrit "áp". It is the icosahedron of the Platonic solids with qualities of both cold and wet. In the modern era, it is considered to be the substance of liquid or the spirit of conscious intuition contained within living things. It is limitless — that which shapes form or attracts pattern.

The Water-Bearer - (see Aquarius)

White Tiger - in Chinese astrology, one of the four celestial beasts known as "Bai Hu" that rules the direction of West and the season of autumn; also the Korean "Baekho", Japanese "Byakko" and Vietnamese "Bạch Hổ".

winter solstice - the astronomical point that marks the location where the ecliptic (plane of the solar system) reaches its furthest incline position from the Earth at the latitude of the Northern or Southern Tropic line opposite the position of the observer; the cardinal point that initiates the season of winter at the fourth quarter of the zodiac cross. The winter solstice is observed when the hours of night surpass the hours of day.

the World - in traditional tarot, card XXI of the Major Arcana used to represent "the Absolute", the totality of all-encompassing aspects and completion.

Wuji - the "Supreme Ultimate" one, non-polar yet supreme acting polar force — the limitless or unlimited principle — that existed before the instillation of Taiji; also the abyss of the ultimate or boundless primordial universe.

Wu Xing - in Tao, the ancient Chinese philosophy of the five phases or elements — Wood, Fire, Earth, Metal, and Water — used to outline the creative and restrictive cycles of Nature.

yang - in Taoist tradition, one of the dual interlocking polar principles of existence; the active, aggressive, masculine quality of Nature. It is the essence of light, heat, and dry that reacts to yin.

yin - in Taoist tradition, one of the dual interlocking polar principles of existence; the non-active, passive, feminine quality of Nature. It is the essence of dark, cold, and wet that attracts yang.

zenith - the highest point a celestial object ascends on a given day at true 'noon'. In traditional astrology, the zenith is the position at which the astrological aspect is exalted or most powerful.

zeroth dimension - the absence of dimension or non-dimension; the singularity, neutrality, or equality between opposing forces of positive and negative.

zodiac belt - the twelve zodiac signs of 30 degrees or the 360 degree projected circle of the ellipse against the backdrop of seasonal constellations led by the point of the vernal equinox.

Zoroastrianism - the ancient Persian religion of the philosopher Zoroaster that became an organized tradition as far back as the 6th Century BCE; also Magianism, Mazdaism or Zathustrianism. Zoroastrianism fused together the pantheon of early Iranian deities into one Ahura Mazda, "Ahura" meaning light and "Mazda" wisdom, and the two forces of Spenta Mainyu "progressive thought" and Angra Mainyu "destructive thought".

The addition of Zurvanism brought with it the concept of "Zurvan" or limitless space and time that existed as one before the creation of Ahura Mazda. Other sects used Ahura Mazda to represent "good" or Spenta Mainyu and Ahriman to depict "evil" or Angra Mainyu.

Encyclopedia of Astrology

TheCosmicJoker.com

References

I. Introduction to Astrology

Manly P. Hall, *Astrological Keywords*, (Lanham: Littlefield, Adams & Co., The Philosophical Research Society, 1975).
Joanne Wickenburg, *A Journey through the Birth Chart*, (Reno: CRCS Publications, 1985).

II. Natal Chart Basics

C. G. Jung, *Modern Man in Search of a Soul*, trans. W. S. Dell and Cary F. Baynes, (San Diego: Harcourt Brace Jonanovich, 1933).
William Lilly, *An Introduction to Astrology*, (London: G. Bell & Sons, 1852).

III. The Significance of Angles & Aspects

Anthony Aveni, *Empires of Time: Calendars, Clocks and Cultures*, (New York: Basic Books, 1989).
Assignment Discovery: The Golden Ratio,
http://videos.howstuffworks.com/discovery/30014-assignment-discovery-the-golden-ratio-video.htm.

Descartes and the Pineal Gland, (Stanford Encyclopedia of Philosophy), http://plato.stanford.edu/entries/pineal-gland/ revised 18 September 2013.

Rene Descartes, *Passions of the Soul*, 1649 CE, trans. Johathan Bennett, 2010-2015.

Hunting the Hidden Dimension, television broadcast, (PBS: Nova), 24 August 2011.

Genchi Kato, *A Study of Shinto: The Religion of the Japanese Nation*, (New York: Barnes & Noble, 1971), Urabe-no-Kanekuni, (Shinto poet), ca. 720 CE.

Johannes Kepler, *Harmonices Mundi [The harmony of the world]*, 1619 CE, trans. E.J. Aiton, A.M. Duncan, and J.V. Field, (Philadelphia: The American Philosophical Society, 1997).

Johannes Kepler, *Mysterium Cosmographicum [The Secret of the Universe]*, 1596 CE, trans. A. M. Duncan, (New York: Abaris Books, 1981).

Benoit Mandelbrot, *The Fractal Geometry of Nature*, (San Francisco: W. H. Freeman, 1982).

Sir Isaac Newton, *The Mathematical Principles of Natural Philosophy*, trans. Andrew Motte, (New York: Daniel Adee, 1846), https://ia600300.us.archive.org/8/items/newtonspmathema00newtrich.pdf.

Plato, *Timeaus*, 360 BCE, trans. Benjamin Jowett (The Internet Classics Archive), text version, http://classics.mit.edu/Plato/timaeus.html, 1994-2009.

Vijay Tankha, *Ancient Greek Philosophy: Thales to Gorgias*, (New Delhi: Dorling Kindersley Pvt Ltd, 2006), Aristotle, De caelo [On the Heavens], 350 BCE.

Vettius Valens, *Anthology*, ca. 150 to 175 BCE, trans. Mark T. Riley, http://www.csus.edu/indiv/r/rileymt/VettiusValens entire.pdf, 10 December 2013.

Marcus Vitruvius, *Marcus Vitruvius Pollio: de Architectura*, ca. 15 BCE, trans. Bill Thayer, http://penelope.uchicago.edu/Thayer/E/Roman/Texts/Vitruvius/1*.html, updated 7 December 2009.

IV. The History of Astrology

Asger Aaboe, *Episodes From the Early History of Astronomy*, (New York: Springer-Verlag, 2001).

Anthony Aveni, *Stairways to the Stars: Skywatching in Three Great Ancient*

Cultures, (New York: John Wiley & Sons, 1997).

Archimedes, *The Sand-Reckoner*, ca. 3rd Century BCE, trans. Thomas Heath, (Cambridge University Press, 1897), http://www.sacred-texts.com/cla/archim/sand/index.htm.

Nicholaus Copernicus, *De revolutionibus orbium coelestium [On the revolutions of the spheres]*, 1543, (The University of Texas), http://www.geo.utexas.edu/courses/302d/Fall_2011/Full text - Nicholas Copernicus,_De Revolutionibus (On the Revolutions),_1.pdf, 2011.

Mihai Eminescu, *Evening Star*, 1883 CE, (Radu Narcis Velicescu, 1994-2014), http://www.romanianvoice.com/poezii/poezii_tr/eveningstar.php.

James Evans, *The History and Practice of Ancient Astronomy*, (New York: Oxford University Press, 1998).

William J. Fielding, *Strange Superstitions & Magical Practices*, (Philadelphia: Circle Books, The Blakiston Company, 1945).

David H. Kelley & Eugene F. Milone, *Exploring Ancient Skies: An Encyclopedic Survey of Archeoastronomy*, (New York: Springer Science + Business Media, 2005).

V. Celestial Folklore

Aaron J. Atsma, *ASKLEPIOS*, (New Zealand: Theoi Project), http://www.theoi.com/Ouranios/Asklepios.html, 2000-2011.

Carl Jung, *Psychological Reflections:An Anthology*. (New York: Princeton University Press, 1953).

VI. Astrological Symbols in Ancient Civilization

Albert Einstein and George Bernard Shaw, *On Cosmic Religion and Other Opinions and Aphorisms*, (Dover Publications, 2009).

Abolqasem Ferdowsi, *Shahnameh: The Persian Book of Kings*, trans. Dick Davis, (New York: Penguin Books, 2007).

Holy Bible with the Apocryphal/Deuterocanonical Books, New Revised Standard Version Bible, (HarperCollins Publishers, Division of Christian Education, 2007).

Laozi, trans. by D.C. Lau, (Chinese University Press, 1989), Book 10, (47).

R. G. H. Siu, *The Tao of Science: An Essay on Western Knowledge and Eastern*

Wisdom, (Cambridge: The MIT Press, The Massachusetts Institute of Technology, 1964).

VII. The Stars — Nature's Calendar

Ancient Computer, television broadcast, (PBS: Nova), http://video.pbs.org/video/2364988981/, 3 April 2013.

Hesiod, *Works and Days*, ca. 700 BCE, trans. Hugh G. Evelyn-White, 1914, (Theoi E-Texts Library), http://www.theoi.com/Text/HesiodWorksDays.html, 2000-2011.

How to read time [Astronomical Clock, Prague], (Pražská informační služba: PragueWelcome.com), http://www.staromestskaradnicepraha.cz/en/astronomical-clock/how-to-read-time/, 2013.

Johannes Kepler, *Somnium [The Dream, or posthumous work on lunar astronomy]*, 1608 CE, (Madison, Milwakee, London: University of Wisconson Press, 1967).

Poor Richard Improved, 1754, (Founders Online: National Archives), http://founders.archives.gov/documents/Franklin/01-05-02-0051, ver. 2014-05-09. The Papers of Benjamin Franklin, vol. 5, July 1, 1753, through March 31, 1755, ed. Leonard W. Labaree, (New Haven: Yale University Press, 1962) p. 181–185.

William Shakespeare and David Daniell, *Julius Caeasar* [The Life and Death of Julius Caesar, ca. 1599], 3rd ed., (Bloomsbury Arden Shakespeare, 1998), http://shakespeare.mit.edu/julius_caesar/full.html.

VIII. Equinox & Solstice

Mark Adams, *Machu Picchu Secrets*, (National Geographic Society Online), http://travel.nationalgeographic.com/travel/top-10/peru/machu-picchu/secrets/, 1996-2014.

Rob Bryanton, *Imagining the Tenth Dimension*, video, http://www.youtube.com/watch?v=JkxieS-6WuA, 2012.

Charles Freeman, *Egypt, Greece and Rome: Civilizations of the Ancient Mediterranean*, 2nd ed., (Oxford: Oxford University Press, 2004).

Lisa Krause, *Sun to Illuminate Inner Sanctuary of Pharaoh's Temple*, (National Geographic News: NationalGeographic.com), http://news.nationalgeographic.com/news/2001/02/0221_abusimbel.html, 21 February 2001.

Laghada, *Vedanga Jyotisha*, ed. & trans. K.V. Sarma, T. S. Kuppanna Sastry (New Delhi: Indian National Science Academy, 1984).

Newgrange, http://www.newgrange.com/.

Sten Odenwald. *Technology Through Time, Issue #72: Ancient Astronomical Alignments*,
http://sunearthday.nasa.gov/2011/articles/ttt_72.php.

Philolaus of Croton, *Pythagorean and Presocratic: A Commentary on the Fragments and Testimonia with Interpretive Essays*, ed. Carl A. Huffman, (New York: Cambridge University Press, 1993), Philolaus fragment, 6.

Surya Siddhanta, trans. Pundit Bapu Deva Sastri, (Calcutta:, The Baptist Mission Press by C. B. Lewis 1861).

IX. Zodiac Archetypes

William George Aston., *Shinto: The Ancient Religion of Japan*, (London: Constable & Company Ltd, 1921),
https://archive.org/details/shintoancientrel00astorich.

E. A. Wallis Budge, *The Gods of the Ancient Egyptians or Studies in Egyptian Mythology*, (London:Methuen & Co., 1904).

Baron D'Holbach, *The System of Nature or laws of the moral and physical world*, 1868 (New York: Burt Franklin, 1970), p 170.

Carl Jung, *Collected Works of C.G. Jung, Volume 11: Psychology and Religion: West and East*, (New York: Pantheon Books, 1958).

Plato, *The Republic*, VII, 360 BCE, trans. Benjamin Jowett, (The Internet Classics Archive), text version,
http://classics.mit.edu/Plato/republic.8.vii.html, 1994-2009.

Religions | Zoroastrianism, (BBC Online),
http://www.bbc.co.uk/religion/religions/zoroastrian/, 2014.

X. The Limiting & the Limitless

S. N. Balagangadhara, *The Heathen in His Blindness"--: Asia, the West, and the Dynamic of Religion*, (New York: E. J. Brill, 1994), Acharya Jinasena, Mahapurana, 898 CE.

Philolaus, (Stanford Encyclopedia of Philosophy),
http://plato.stanford.edu/entries/philolaus/, revised 18 July

2012.

Carl Sagan, *Cosmos*, (New York: Ballantine Books, Carl Sagan Productions, 1980).

XI. Evolution & Extinction Cycles

Joshua E. Brown, *Science: There's Something Ancient in the Icebox: Researchers find three-million-year-old landscape beneath Greenland Ice Sheet*, (The University of Vermont Online), http://www.uvm.edu/~uvmpr/?Page=news&storyID=18309, 17 April 2014.

Sing C. Chew, *Ecological Futures: What History Can Teach Us*, (Plymouth: AltaMira Press, 2008).

Sing C. Chew, *The Recurring Dark Ages: Ecological stress, climate changes, and system transformation*, (Plymouth: AltaMira Press, 2007).

Extinctions in the History of Life, edited by Paul D. Taylor, (Cambridge: Cambridge University Press, 2004).

M. Fritz and B. Loewly, *On the Connexion of Sunspots with Planetary Configuration*, (London: The London, Edinburgh and Dublin Philosophical Magazine & Journal of Science, Volume XLI., Fourth Series), January to June 1871.

J. D. Haigh, M. Lockwood, M. S. Giampapa, *The Sun, Solar Analogs, and the Climate*, (New York: Springer-Verlag, 2005).

Tony Hallam, *Catastrophes and lesser calamaties: The causes of mass extinctions*, (Oxford: Oxford University Press, 2004).

Eric Lambin, *The Middle Path*, trans. M. B. DeBevoise, (Chicago: The Univeristy of Chicago Press, 2007).

Chris Landau, *Planetary-Spin heat, Jupiter-Saturn-Solar Tidal-Sunspot coupling and Planetary-Solar alternating magnetic field rings*. (The American Institute of Professional Geologists), 4 October 2010, http://www.aipg.org/Events/mtg_proceedings/2010annmtg/Landau, 20Chris.pdf.

Richard A. Muller & Gordon MacDonald, *Ice Ages and Astronomical Causes: Data, spectral analysis and mechanisms*, (Chichster: Springer-Verlag, 2000).

Michael R. Rampino, *The Galactic Theory of Mass Extinctions: An Update*, (New York: NASA Goddard Institute of Space Studies, 1998).

Dr. Seuss, *Oh the Places You'll Go!*, (New York: Random House, 1990).

XII. Cosmic Astrology

Joseph Campbell with Bill D. Moyers, *The Power of Myth*, television broadcast, (PBS, 1988).

George Musser, *What Would Happen If Earth and Mars Switched Places?*, (The Scientific American, http://blogs.scientificamerican.com/observations/2011/06/09/what-would-happen-if-earth-and-mars-switched-places/, 9 June 2011).

Nikola Tesla, *How Cosmic Forces Shape Our Destinies: Did the War Cause the Italian Earthquake*, (New York: New York American, 7 Feb 1915).

XIII. Encyclopedia of Astrology

Nicholas deVore, *Encyclopedia of Astrology*, (New York: Philosophical Library, 1947).

Illustrations

Anastasiya Drake. *Cover Art & Lady Vitruvia.*
The Cosmic Joker. *Platonic Space & The Encirclopedia.*
Sam Gorrin. *The Budding Flower of Life.*
Amir Mansour. *Fontana della Pigna, Osiris the Singularity & Key to the Milky Way.*
Steen. *The Orloj, Faces of the Equinox, Ecliptic Transits of the Tropics, The Harmony of Three & The Great Cosmic Traverse.*

Links

The Bioelectromagnetic Society, https://www.bems.org/journal.
Calendars through the Ages, http://www.webexhibits.org/calendars/calendar.html.
Click on the symbol of an element to see its atomic emission spectrum, http://chemistry.bd.psu.edu/jircitano/periodic4.html.
The Hellenistic Astrology Website, http://www.hellenisticastrology.com/
Simulator of the astronomical dial of the clock [Astronomical Clock Prague], http://www.orloj.eu/en/orloj_simulator1.php.

Thank You!

Thank you for reading and supporting independent publishing! Please leave a review and follow along on Instagram, Facebook, or Twitter, and find out more about upcoming books and events at publisher website and blog theoracleslibrary.com.

Love,

-The Oracle

Follow The Oracle's Library:

Instagram: @theoracleslibrary

Facebook: @oracleslibrary

Twitter: @oracleslibrary

theoracleslibrary.com

www.ingramcontent.com/pod-product-compliance
Lightning Source LLC
Chambersburg PA
CBHW022108150426
43195CB00008B/316